Power to Change

POWER
TO CHANGE

FAMILY CASE STUDIES IN THE
TREATMENT OF ALCOHOLISM

Edited by

Edward Kaufman, M.D.

GARDNER PRESS, INC.
NEW YORK   LONDON

GARDNER PRESS, INC.
19 Union Square West
New York 10003

All foreign orders except Canada and South America to:
Afterhurst Limited
Chancery House
319 City Road
London N1, United Kingdom

Library of Congress Cataloging in Publication Data
Kaufman, Edward.
        Power to change.

    Bibliography: p.
    Includes index.
    1. Alcoholics—Family relationships—Case studies.
2. Family psychotherapy—Case studies. I. Title.
[DNLM: 1. Alcoholism—Therapy—Case studies. 2. Family
therapy—Case studies. WM 274 P887]
RC565.K364   1983   616.87'106   83-5594
ISBN 0-89876-091-7

PRINTED IN THE UNITED STATES OF AMERICA

Book design by Raymond Solomon

Contents

CONTRIBUTORS

Joan Ablon, Ph.D., Professor
Medical Anthropology Program
Departments of Epidemiology and International Health
and Psychiatry
University of California, San Francisco

Genevieve Ames, Ph.D., Fellow
Prevention Research Center
Family Practice Division
Berkeley, California

Donald A. Cadogan, Ph.D.
550 North Rosemead Boulevard
Pasadena, California

William Cunningham, L.C.S.W.
Deputy Director for Community Health Programs
Department of Public Health
City and County of San Francisco

Donald I. Davis, M.D.
Director, Family Therapy Institute of Alexandria
Clinical Associate Professor of Psychiatry
George Washington University Medical School
Alexandria, Virginia

Catherine E. Huberty, M.S.W.
Alfred Adler Institute of Minnesota
Community Intervention
Minneapolis, Minnesota

David J. Huberty, M.S.W.
Coordinator of Alcohol Detoxification Services
Chemical Dependency Family Therapist
Central Minnesota Mental Health Center
St. Cloud, Minnesota

Edward Kaufman, M.D.
Associate Professor in Residence
Director of Psychiatric Education
Director of Family Therapy Programs
University of California, Irvine, Medical Center

Pauline Kaufmann, M.S.W., C.S.W.
Director of Family Therapy
Phoenix Foundation
100 West 78th Street
New York, New York

Eleanor Killorin
Family Social Science
University of Minnesota
St. Paul, Minnesota

Barbara S. McCrady, Ph.D.
Director, Alcohol Services
Associate Professor, Brown University
Providence, Rhode Island

Nora E. Noel, Ph.D.
Psychology Department
Brown University
Butler Hospital
345 Blackstone Blvd.
Providence, Rhode Island

David H. Olson, Ph.D.
  Family Social Science
  University of Minnesota
  St. Paul, Minnesota

Jane Roschmann, M.A., M.F.C.C.
  Private Practice
  Irvine, California

M. Duncan Stanton, Ph.D.
  Family & Marriage Clinic
  Dept. of Psychiatry
  University of Rochester
  Rochester, New York

Stanley A. Terman, Ph.D., M.D.
  Director, Institute for Strategic Change, Surfside, California
  Clinical Assistant Professor of Psychiatry
  University of California, Irvine
  Staff Psychiatrist, Special Treatment Unit
  Veterans Administration Medical Center
  Long Beach, California

Bob Woods, B.A.
  Mental Health Worker
  County of Orange
  Human Services Alcoholic Program
  Westminster, California

Preface

Family therapists have turned recently to the field of alcoholism with great enthusiasm, after years of neglect. This is in part because the family patterns of alcoholics are so fascinating and have begun to attract family therapists, who have in turn developed several workable systems for the family treatment of alcoholics. These treatment approaches vary greatly and include structural, strategic, behavioral, multiple family, and systems techniques. One common factor in the approach of each of these therapeutic schools is a system to get the identified patient off alcohol, which is implemented early in treatment. Although most therapists can be associated with one system or another, they generally espouse an integrated approach which borrows from different types of therapies. This integration of therapies is, of course, superimposed on and blended with each therapist's unique personality and style. With so many excellent family therapists turning to the field of alcoholism, a book that develops and presents these systems as they are used in the treatment of individual families is definitely indicated. Hence this present volume.

No book on alcoholism would be complete without a chapter from the group of family therapists at the George Washington University Medical School. This group includes Murray Bowen, Peter Steinglass, Dave Berenson, and Steve Wolin, in addition to Don Davis, the author of Chapter One. The George Washington group has been well known for its view of the adaptive and homeostatic aspects of alcoholism behavior and systematic techniques for cooling down the family in crisis. Davis has developed an integrated approach which incorporates structural, strategic, communication training, behavioral and neurolinguistic programming techniques.

My personal psychoanalytic training left me with typical analytic biases against behavioral therapies. However, this bias disappeared immediately when I read Noel and McCrady's chapter, which is so filled with valuable techniques and interventions that can be a part of any family treatment system that it is by far the longest chapter in this book. Its length is also justified in that it includes two different case histories—which permits a broader application and understanding of their methods. Their dramatic results with a case as difficult as Mrs. N. demonstrates the powerful change potential of their form of therapy.

No book of mine would be complete without a chapter from my mentor, colleague and "illegitimate mother," Pauline Kaufmann. Pauline's power as a therapist is significantly related to her intense charisma. It is this charisma which permits her paradoxical, space-giving interventions to be so successful with this chaotic and difficult family.

David Olson is best known for his outstanding quantitative instrument development and assessments of families in general, as well as specifically with families with a chemically dependent member. He has joined with Ellie Killorin to write an article about the treatment of the "Chaotic Flippers" a family which had been described frequently by Olson in prior articles on the circumflex model of family evaluation. Their chapter demonstrates how basic family research techniques can be integrated into a comprehensive family treatment approach.

The Hubertys are an example of a husband and wife co-therapy team who have integrated their individual styles as well as their dyadic relationship into their therapeutic work. They have also blended Adlerian concepts, family of origin work, homework tasks, and the use of early recollections into an Alcoholics Anonymous centered program.

Donald Cadogan one of the first family therapists to work in the field of alcoholism, published an important article on the success of this modality back in 1973. He has continued his work with multiple couple groups since that time. In the case discussed, he demonstrates the utility of treating an alcoholic couple in a group where other couples are not alcoholics.

The chapter by Joan Ablon, Genevieve Ames, and William Cunningham does not deal with the family therapy of an alcoholic family but presents a 22-month in-depth study of such a family. Through their intensive study of the family as a system as well as an in-depth analysis of each individual family member, they are able to present an unusually comprehensive view of an alcoholic family. Their study of the family in the home offers a unique opportunity to understand the family as it really exists. This family is also typical of the many families with an alcoholic member who are touched by treatment only briefly and ineffectively. The reader may be challenged to prescribe a treatment plan which would work with this "ideally appearing" family.

Stan Terman's chapter is another example of the use of a couples group, in this case exclusively for alcoholic couples. That multiple family groups of various types are more common in the treatment of alcoholism than any other disease is further evidence of the national thrust towards family approaches to alcoholism. Terman also espouses an integrated family therapy approach which incorporates Gestalt and psychodrama into strategic therapy, with emphasis on the use of paradox.

Duke Stanton has conducted the most systematic study to date of the families of heroin addicts. He has also described a sophisticated and workable system for treating these families, that utilizes strategic and structural techniques. Stanton here addresses an important problem with alcoholic families: treating the child of an alcoholic when the family is not available. Thus, he combines Bowenian family of origin work with a strategic approach to perform family-oriented therapy without the family being present. This is an important contribution to any therapist who treats a client with a family history of alcoholism.

I have included two chapters of my own work because they focus on two relatively different approaches which I utilize. The chapter written with Jane Roschmann and Bob Woods is an example of the use of interwoven multiple family groups (MFG) in the treatment of alcoholism. As these groups require one or more co-therapists and several families in treatment at the same time, it is often not possible for solo practitioners to use this modality. The multiple family group model is one that I would strongly espouse for any group practice or clinic which treats the problem of alcoholism. When the MFG terminated, this model was no longer available to me and so I utilized the solo family therapy approach in the treatment of alcoholism for the "family who wouldn't 'give up'." Although I label my approach "structural dynamic," because my two primary influences are the structural therapy of Minuchin and an active psychodynamic orientation, my system of family therapy is quite eclectic. Thus, when an individual family's needs call for a shift in technique, I may use any of the approaches described in this book, although the treatment strategies are always adapted to each family and grafted onto my own personality and style.

After fifteen years of struggling with the problems of substance abuse, I discovered the power of family therapy in the mid 1970's. I have found family therapy the needed ingredient to provide "the power to change" these families. I hope that the reader will be able to identify with and incorporate the techniques described in this book so that he/she can develop this powerful influence for changing families with an alcoholic member.

Edward Kaufman, M.D.
ORANGE, CALIFORNIA

Power to Change

1

I need help to stop drinking:

An integrative family therapy approach to the
management of a family in early recovery.

Donald I. Davis, M.D.

INTRODUCTION

I pull out all the stops in the treatment of alcoholism. My natural
propensity for integrating diverse schools of therapy, which is a
challenging luxury in many cases, seems a necessity when I work
with families with one or more actively drinking alcoholic members.
Maybe that is why I have chosen to write about a case that stands
out for being both relatively easy and clearly successful. I hope
that by doing so I will not get mired down in a description of a
series of crises and, instead, will be able to show and stay in touch
with the essential issues and interventions in this family therapy
case that are archetypical of my experience with the treatment of
alcoholism.

Before I describe the case, a little background is in order. After
some eight years of rather intensive experience with alcoholism
clinical research and treatment, I approached this case with some
very definite assumptions. One is that, regardless of how it started,
the heavy use of alcohol comes to serve certain important functions
in the family of the alcoholic. These are unique to each family, and
will need to be substituted for or eliminated (1). A second is that,
while one person was coming in asking for help, I could be more
effective and indeed more ethical by working with at least the
whole family currently living at home together (2). A third is that

Alcoholics Anonymous (AA), AlAnon, and AlAteen can be compatible with and supportive to family therapy (3). A fourth assumption is that the use of alcohol by the alcoholic must be very well controlled or preferably stopped before even a very skillful family therapist can be effective, and therefore, that family therapy skills must be applied directly to eliminating the drinking problem as early as possible, even if many other problems that usually respond well to therapy are identified (4). I have written about the bases for these assumptions at length in references 1 through 4, and therefore will not expand on them here.

I view alcoholism as a final common pathway disorder. By this I mean that one can develop it through multiple pathways, both environmental and physiological. From my reading of the research literature, I have also concluded that the single most important etiologic factor is exposure to heavy use of alcohol. In short, I suspect anyone can become alcoholic, and it really is not useful to pursue how one got started. We must deal in the present with the physiological aspects of alcoholism tolerance and withdrawal, the conditioned stimuli to drink, the functions alcohol has come to serve for the drinker and his or her family in their interactions, and any maturational impairment that is a consequence of chronic heavy drinking.

THERAPY BACKGROUND

My own approach to family therapy is an integrative one. By integrative I mean that in my training and practice, and teaching, I have attempted to learn, in some depth, utilize, and transmit diverse theories and techniques. My training has included intensive work with first-generation teachers Jay Haley, John Grinder, and Richard Bandler, and their colleagues. Earlier, there were also prominent psychoanalytic teachers whose influence is surely extant in my thinking, but rarely is consciously activated in my practice. My training has included lesser but nonetheless serious exposure to first- or second-generation teachers of Bowen cross-generational approaches, individual and marital behavioral schools of therapy, and a smattering of an infinity of other concepts of change of both Eastern and Western origins that I plagiarize rapaciously out of the conviction that the more we add to our treatment repertoire, the more we can address usefully in our clients. In his exhaustive reviews, Gurman surmised that there is no one school of therapy, individual or family, that had demonstrated itself to be clearly better than all others for all conditions (5). At the same time some approaches do appear better for certain conditions, for example, structural family therapy for the treatment of certain psychosomatic disorders (6). I believe it would be a shame for a modern family therapist not to be able to call upon existing effective techniques for a given condition because he or she is only skilled in one, necessarily limited school of therapy. Multiple schools exist because different seminal thinkers primarily addressed different dimensions of human experience.

My version of integration involves adding together the theories and techniques from diverse schools that together begin to deal adequately with all of the dimensions of experience along which we may want to intervene in therapy. Nowhere has this effort to integrate proven more valuable to me than in the comprehensive treatment of alcoholism. I believe this is so precisely because alcoholism, even though its consequences look so familiar time after time, can occur in so many different preexisting contexts.

THE J. FAMILY AND THE FIRST INTERVIEW

This is the story of a relatively brief intervention with the J. family, a nuclear family of six. Mr. and Mrs. J., Ann and Bob, were each forty-seven years old. For more than six years, both had been daily very heavy drinkers. Then one winter day, Bob had stopped drinking. He had not gone for help, he had just stopped altogether. One month later Ann started to go to AA meetings. Over several months, she continued to go to AA, and she managed to cut down her drinking greatly, but at times she still drank to oblivion. In the early fall, Ann went to her family doctor and asked for Antabuse (a drug whose sole purpose is to make people sick when they ingest ethyl alcohol). Her doctor was one of several family practitioners with whom we work closely at the Family Therapy Institute of Alexandria. Ann arrived at his office intoxicated. Because of her intoxication, he declined to prescribe Antabuse. Instead he told her to see me. In making his referral, her doctor also may have been influenced by the frequent visits to his office from Ann's children. He had seen thirteen-year-old Freddie often for headaches and seventeen-year-old Carrie just as often for stomach aches.

When Ann first called me, she said she had been going to AA for about nine months and she couldn't stop drinking entirely. She could go two to three weeks without a drink, then would drink again for two months or more. She wanted to come in herself to get help stopping drinking. I told her I can usually be most helpful if I have a chance to meet other family members as early as possible. We agreed that she and Bob would come in together at first and that their children also might be invited in if we were to continue to work together.

As is my custom in most first interviews, I asked Bob and Ann each to tell me briefly in their own words what they would like to accomplish from talking with me. They were way ahead of most alcoholics in family therapy in that they didn't deny, skirt, or minimize alcohol as a problem, nor did they even debate the merits of achieving abstinence. Ann simply said she was seeking a way to stop drinking. And Bob blandly confessed that he only came because Ann had asked him to. He too only wanted Ann to be able to stop drinking.

Here I confess that this family is not typical. In dealing with alcoholism, usually I spend much of my energy and exercise most of my wiles and craft just to reach the point at which this family began. But I have written about that elsewhere (4). Now I want to focus on and grapple with the (often simultaneous) phase of therapy that deals with making other changes, changes within a family system that had had plenty of time to make its adaptations to alcoholic parents.

The initial request for Ann's and Bob's desired outcomes had taken only several minutes. I spent the rest of the first session looking for issues in the family that were in need of attention. In particular, I went after drug problems in the children and interactional deficiencies between Ann and Bob. The likelihood of the former I knew was high; the latter were a certainty. I also thought that Bob would only return and the children would only come in if I could establish a good reason for their involvement before the end of the first session. Otherwise they as a family, like many families, would be happier to deposit the identified problem person in the family, Ann, for help with her drinking and leave well enough alone.

What I found in my brief but highly tailored search was the epitome of the catalog of complications one finds in a family with alcoholic parents. In this family there were no immediate crises to obscure the more subtle, wide-ranging issues that are always present. Bob had a decent government job. The children were not in trouble with the law, and there was no talk of divorce. Money was tight but there were no imminent foreclosures or debt crunches. Yet everyone as individuals in their relationships with one another was functioning below their own previous best levels.

Ann's main complaint was that, "I can't sit and talk with my husband like everybody else does" (referring to other couples). She felt that she had been able to talk with him until about seven years earlier, when she had started drinking daily before Bob came home from work. Bob had begun drinking heavily about the same time. Neither really knew if one had increased before the other. Ann also noted that their sexual activity had decreased over the heavy drinking years. They typically had intercourse now less than once a week. The exception was that the past summer, when Bob was dry and Ann had temporarily stopped drinking, they had had intercourse twice a week, as they had in the past.

Regarding their four children, Ann reported that the extent of her yelling at them, and they at her, varied directly with the level of her alcohol intake. This had become most apparent when Bob had stopped drinking. The yelling between Ann and the kids had persisted at its customary high frequency until Ann too cut down on alcohol. Since she was still drinking at the time of the first session, the yelling was still present, but to an extent commensurate with her reduced alcohol intake.

This much of their story I believed because it fit with my experience with families and with my reading of studies in the literature. That is, when one or both spouse(s)/parent(s) drink(s) heavily, talking and sexual intimacy become impaired, and there is increasing yelling and disrespectful behavior between children and parents. And when drinking stops or even diminishes, there is some improvement. In fact, there may be a return, at least on the part of the parents, to the previous most mature level of relating, a level which a therapist may not be able to predict well

while drinking persists. Stopping drinking itself does readily produce some lasting improvements in family relationships. Unfortunately, there is no accurate converse. Attempting to produce
lasting gains in family interactions while leaving the drinking of
an alcoholic in the family unchanged tends toward being futile and
is a long and arduous task at best.

Other impressions they attempted to leave with me I brushed
aside. Chief among these was the notion that it was evident everything would be fine if Ann just stopped drinking. A corollary to
this seemed to be their assertion that, while the kids had some
problems, we really didn't need to discuss them in therapy. The
former impression required the assumption that Ann's and Bob's
previous most mature interactional behavior was all they needed
even at this stage in their lives. Couples with an alcoholic spouse
fail to resolve or even to develop the mechanisms necessary to
resolve the inevitable differences all couples will have, so my guess
was that their first notion was false. As for the kids' problems
either being nonexistent or not needing direct attention, it is not
unheard of, but I require proof.

By doggedly probing about the children, I rapidly exposed the
children's needs for intervention and at the same time easily observed Ann's and Bob's interactional barrier to dealing effectively
with certain issues.

I learned that thirteen-year-old Freddie, entering his freshman
year of high school, had frequent headaches for which he had
made many visits to the family doctor. His headaches had become
less common over the previous year but still occurred. Seventeen-
year-old Carrie, now starting her senior year, had used marijuana
in unknown amounts, but frequently, for years and had suffered
stomach aches necessitating many trips to the family doctor. Like
Freddie, she had also shown some improvement in symptoms and
in school work over the preceding year. Bob Jr., at eighteen and
a half, had managed to graduate from high school the year before
but remained a regular heavy user of marijuana and beer. He lived
at home. His few friends were substance abusers. While he did
have a job from 3:00 P.M. to 9:00 P.M., it had no future. In addition,
Ann got him out of bed at 2:00 P.M. and drove him to work each
day. She resented doing it but felt guilty if she didn't. Ann found
herself being very defensive with Bob Jr. when she preferred not
to go along with his wishes. So she did what he wanted. Besides,

it was unsafe for him to drive their car, and he could not afford one of his own. There had been a recent decrease in yelling and swearing between Bob Jr. and each of his parents. As for the oldest child, Annie, aged twenty, I was told she was "okay," had a job, and was living in her own apartment. It was not until I could talk with the other children in person that I learned that the younger siblings worried about their oldest sister's drinking and driving habits.

Through asking Ann and Bob to talk to one another in my presence about what behavior they expected of Bob Jr., I learned also in the first session the limits of their ability to problem-solve and communicate effectively. I noticed that Bob gave terse responses in a tone of voice that Ann took as angry (sometimes mistakenly) whenever they explored dealing with Bob Jr. on anything. There was much guessing or mind reading about what the other one meant and little or no feedback offered or clarification sought or provided without my instigation. There was, however, little animosity. The problem as Ann and Bob saw it was in Bob Jr. I was witness to their best level of communication. It was a relief to them again to be talking that well with one another after years of yelling alternating with long silences. I suspected they had managed adequately until one or two children had entered teenage years. Then the children's challenges to their togetherness had exceeded the capacity of their communication skills to resolve family issues jointly, and their drinking had increased sufficiently to prevent them from making the time and energy commitment needed to stretch their coping skills (enough to accommodate to their normal developmental transition). I made no attempt to explore the historical evolution of their problems. For me, it is enough that I see, hear, and sense what behavior is occurring that enables the problems to persist in the present and that I have some concept to guide me as a working hypothesis. Then I intentionally intervene. The consequences of my intervention will either confirm my hypothesis or rapidly allow me to refine and improve upon it. Successful change will often, though not necessarily, be accompanied by considerable understanding on the part of individuals or the entire family. I welcome the understanding as a confirmation of progress that is also apparent in behavior. I pursue, though, relevant change in behavior by the most efficient means available. As in their case, I usually intervene in the first session, even when

I state that the first two sessions are just an evaluation, at the end of which I will make my recommendations. By the time I make a recommendation, I want the family to have some idea how I will work with them and to have already experienced some positive outcome from therapy.

With Ann and Bob, the interventions in the first session were twofold. One was that I saw to it, through coaxing them into giving feedback and clarifications, that they carried their discussion of how to deal with Bob Jr. a little further toward mutual understanding and resolution. The second was that I went on record confirming for them that they were in fact dealing with alcoholism/substance abuse in themselves and in at least one child.

PHASE ONE[1]*: ANN ALONE

I chose to meet with Ann alone the next two sessions on purely pragmatic grounds. While I had planted the seeds of concern over couples issues and child substance abuse, I had no illusions. Bob and Ann were still wedded to the notion that if Ann stopped drinking they would have all that they wanted from therapy, or perhaps better stated, all that they could hope for. I had been consciously engaged in raising their expectations. As part of that, I withheld Antabuse. I had surmised in the first session that Ann wanted to take Antabuse and probably would have used it safely and effectively. Family life would then have become more tolerable before Bob or Ann had sufficient motivation to continue therapy, even to get help with their substance-abusing son. And Ann would not have learned how to talk over a difference with Bob without the urge to drink. Hence, I suspected that she would remain, unnecessarily, dependent on Antabuse.

So I respected the presenting problem, which I do not always do, but I recommend that one have an awfully good reason if one does not. In each of the two sessions with Ann, I relied largely on Neuro-Linguistic Programming (NLP™) skills. The second session (first with Ann) focused on giving Ann a new thought strategy for

*This is Phase One[1] because the true Phase One, of course, was the initial interview already described.

delaying action when she has the desire to take a drink. In the third session, I took on the task of installing an "I can stay to talk (with Bob) o.k." state in place of her previous "uptight, knot in stomach" state in response to hearing Bob sound angry.

In that first session with Ann alone, then, I dealt exclusively with her drinking habits. More specifically, I learned how her thinking perpetuates her alcohol abuse and then taught her an alternative sequence of thoughts which she was sent home to practice. I learned that she could go for hours or even days at times without interest in alcohol, then all of a sudden (with sufficient cues or conditioned stimuli) she would become aware of a feeling that she would like to have a drink which she called a "desire." Next, she would say to herself, "Don't think about it," which predictably led to a doubling of the intensity of the desire. This cycle would inevitably lead to the desire becoming strong enough that she would act on it. Having done so, she usually drank until she fell asleep. I offered her another set of thoughts as soon as she got the "desire." The sequence I gave her was taken directly from a conversation I had with Robert Dilts, first author of *Neuro-Linguistic Programming, Vol. I*, which I recommend as the best background resource on thought strategies and strategy changes (7). This strategy was, first, to have her say to herself as soon as she felt the desire for alcohol, "What are my choices?" She was then taught, in sequence, to say to herself, "I have two choices," and to picture each choice in another sequence. First she pictured taking a drink and thought how she would feel immediately (good, relieved, etc.) and how she would feel a little while or sometime later (regretful, etc.). Next she pictured leaving the drink, not taking it, and how that would leave her feeling immediately (disappointed, craving) and a while later (relieved, self-confident, etc.). Next she compared only the while-later feelings of taking or leaving the drink and was instructed to tell herself on the basis of that comparison either, "I'll take it," or "I'll leave it" and act on whichever she said.

At the next session, Ann reported having used alcohol on only one occasion, but that she consumed a whole bottle of wine at that time. Fortunately, this one drinking incident was precipitated by an interaction with her husband so I could move swiftly and naturally into changing certain of her responses to her husband, in preparation for a couple-oriented phase of therapy. The precipitant in this episode had been Ann's hearing Bob sound angry at her, followed by his walking out overnight. In response to perceiving his tone as angry, she reported that she (typically) got "uptight," had a "knot in stomach," and didn't know how to talk to him. When alcohol was around she would then drink "so I can talk to him o.k." In the present incident, she feared that if she had used her new strategy and not taken a drink, she would not have known how to talk to him and would have prolonged his anger at her; whereas the current sequence of hearing anger, drinking, saying something to Bob, and having him walk out could be relied upon to cool things off by the next day. Knowing this sequence, I went looking for something to replace (and improve upon) the function of alcohol when Ann hears Bob sounding angry. What I sought and found within Ann were her own internal resources for knowing how to talk to someone without knots in her stomach. Drawing upon NLP™ techniques for rapidly associating new internal states with conditioned stimuli that previously elicited dysfunctional responses (8,7), I elicited certain positive states from Ann's own past in which she was confident she could talk over issues effectively. Having established an "anchor" for these states, I could then quickly reelicit these positive states in association with her recollections of recent times with her husband when he sounded angry. When she was able to reexperience these times and imagine how she could have handled them differently, more effectively, and to her complete satisfaction, I then had her anticipate future confrontations with Bob. When she could imagine handling those well in the future she was sent home to test it out and with instructions to bring Bob with her next session.

PHASE TWO: THE COUPLE

Sessions four, five, and six were conjoint couples sessions spanning four weeks because I was away one week between sessions five and six. Improving communication skills, or more specifically learning to stay with a discussion over differences to the point of feeling understood and reaching a resolution without regret, was the main focus of these sessions. At first I emphasized their working out strictly couples issues. That progressed so rapidly that I quickly guided them to parenting issues in preparation for subsequent family sessions. So often, in my experience, this type of family would have come in around a child-focused problem, such as an oldest son's substance abuse and underachievement in school or one of the other children's psychosomatic problems. And then I would have been moving from parenting issues to couples issues. In this case I was very consciously reversing that order. I think there is now a literature on the importance of moving toward couples' therapy with child-focused initial complaints but not enough yet on the need to move toward parenting interventions when the initial client/patient is an adult. This is particularly important with chemically dependent parents.

Couples work moved rapidly because, according to both Bob and Ann as well as my observation, Ann had changed her behavior dramatically following the anchoring in, in session three, of certain new responses to an angry tone. "I didn't even hear him get angry this week!" said Ann at the start of session four. This was said in spite of Bob's impression that he had not been different that week. In fact, Bob recalled at least one incident at a family dinner when he positively was annoyed and reported that Ann had not given her usual angry look or response. Both had been pleased with their handling of that situation.

I'm getting used to such heretofore fantastic accounts. When a new state has been effectively installed where previously a negative conditioned response had always occurred, the typical report is like Ann's; i.e., "He/she didn't even do it this week!" I don't know whether the changed response is so sensed by the spouse that the spouse's behavior is immediately altered or if it is just that one's internal state is so changed that the old behavior is no longer experienced as having the same intent. Perhaps it is both. In any case, Ann was now more flexible in her response to either inferred or actual anger from Bob. This, of course, made it much easier to teach them the basics of giving feedback and seeking clarification. Having had them practice in session four, I sent them home with the assignment to use every issue as an opportunity to practice more feedback and clarification. This assignment was given with the proviso that they only practice when neither had had anything to drink. I also warned them that if Ann stopped drinking she was likely to demand more of an equal say in family matters, for example, how money was spent. This was said to make the inevitable prove palatable by associating it with health. As I do in nearly every session, I inquired in this one too about drinking the past week. Ann had drunk earlier the day of the session. She no longer drank in response to anger from Bob or any other family member. But there were still some other cues that were sufficiently potent to override her (increasingly utilized) new strategy for delaying drinking.

Ann's changed response to anger from Bob had quickly generalized to her children. She reported that for the first time she was now firm without overreacting with Freddie. For example, she had successfully insisted that he stop watching a football game on television one evening and clean up his room instead, and to her amazement, he had kissed her before bed even so. Pursuing these changes further, in session five I had Ann and Bob apply their growing communications skills to resolving certain differences over limits to be set with seventeen-year-old Carrie regarding use of the family car. At this point, I also introduced some structural intervention. Bob had been the only one effectively to present limits, and the kids had treated Ann with a lack of respect characteristic of many children with their alcoholic parents. Hence, I assigned Ann to tell Carrie the new rules "that she and her father had agreed upon."

Two weeks later, in session six, Ann reported that she was pleased that she and Bob were not fighting, and that they were talking more and their sex life was fine. She had taken a drink one day the previous week for no known reason, and as typically happened, that led to finishing a whole bottle of wine. There had been no other drinking incidents. I spent some time on couples issues and then moved toward the children. For the couple, I assigned going out at least one night per week, without the children, for six weeks. At least one of these times was to be with "new" people. By that they knew I meant that they were expected to reach out, to begin to make some social ties with non-problem-drinking acquaintances. Like most long-time heavy drinkers, their social lives had dwindled away or become limited to a circle of others who were also problem drinkers. I wanted to increase intimacy, but also to establish a non-problem-drinking social circle. Ann still attended AA, but it was not serving that purpose for them.

During this same session, I spent a part of the time raising the parents' expectations of Bob Jr. We confirmed that, in fact, he drank and smoke pot excessively every day, had had several minor skirmishes with the law, occasionally tyrannized younger brother, Freddie, and was going nowhere in a career. I got the beginning of an agreement that they really did expect more of him. Then it was agreed that the family, minus Annie who was living out of their home, would all come in together starting the next week.

PHASE THREE: THE FAMILY

The remaining sessions were all family sessions. They included both parents and between one and all four of the children. There were four weekly sessions before a four-week hiatus, for theirs and my vacation over Christmas and New Year's, and five weekly sessions after the break.

For session seven, the first family session, the three children living at home had been invited by me, and were told by their parents that they were expected to attend. Carrie and Freddie came. Bob Jr. lied about having some work to do and stayed away. His absence received belabored attention from me, with the end result being an assignment for each of the other family members to tell Bob Jr. how he or she had wanted him at the family session for their own sakes. The rest of my efforts were spent in educating Carrie and Freddie about dealing with alcoholism in parents. First, I told them that kids don't cause alcoholism in their parents. And, like so many kids of alcoholics, they admitted they each truly suspected it was their fault. Next, I told them about AlAteen and how going there would teach them more than I could about how to take responsibility for their own reactions to a parent's drinking, and not for the drinking itself.

Bob Jr. did join the others for the next session. Much of the session was spent assessing and then confirming his substance-abuse problem. The whole family had been playing down and thereby colluding in his alcohol and pot abuse. I saw to it that I documented and explicated my opinion as a professional that Bob Jr. was chemically dependent and that I got all the other family members to commit themselves that Bob Jr. was in their own opinion an alcoholic and a pot abuser as well. My main device in accomplishing this objective was a plodding, ponderous set of inquiries into his daily drug-use habits. In the end I could summarize that he currently drank a six-pack or more of beer a day plus smoking at least a joint of pot a day. He had used much more of each until the month before. In addition, he had had one traffic accident while drinking and had frequently missed morning work at various jobs because of hangovers. Again, I described and strongly promoted AlAnon and AlAteen for family members of alcoholics. I had already given information on when and where meetings were held. Finally, I gave Ann and Bob the assignment to come up with explicit expectations of Bob Jr. while he continues to live in their home.

Bob Jr. did not come to session nine. But some of his behavior at home was different. For a change, he had kept his room straightened up and had come home by 11:00 P.M., and there had been no known incidents of drinking and driving the past week. Also, Carrie and Ann had gone to an AlAnon meeting and liked it. Bob had planned on going to an AlAnon meeting with Ann, but had not because "she drank that evening." I instructed him to go by himself, for himself, in the future, regardless of who drank when.

I found myself able to attend now to some more subtle communication problems and to a hierarchical reversal. Here was Carrie raising an issue her mother had brought up to her that was directed at changing her father's behavior. Not only was she acting as a go-between, but she was doing so by pointing a finger at her father in a scolding fashion. I promptly interrupted Carrie and asked Ann to speak for herself to Bob. I persisted in keeping Ann and Bob talking over issues between them while Carrie only listened. One issue emerged through this process that particularly interested me. It turned out that Ann had known that Bob Jr. had no intention of coming to this session, and she had neither told Bob nor let Bob Jr. know she was disappointed in him. They mutually agreed by the end of the session that she would speak up to her son and would keep her husband informed in the future. How she would do this was rehearsed and then assigned for the ensuing week.

Ann did her assignment so well that Bob Jr. showed up at session ten even with a bona fide case of flu. Also, Bob had picked up on his own on my interactions with Carrie and had asserted himself twice with Carrie over the past week. He had disciplined Carrie effectively, including a useful discussion that led to acceptance of his wish by Carrie both times. I was told these were first-time-ever experiences. I kept up the pressure on Carrie in this session and the next. I was determined to see her in a child role, with her parents sharing full parental responsibility. So when, in session ten, she told her brother Freddie what to do, I interrupted. And when she tried to lead her mother through questioning into opting for alcohol in the house over the holidays just to be "festive," I made her rephrase what she had said in the form of a request. Then I supported and encouraged Ann telling her daughter that she wanted no alcohol around, and there would be none. This was stated even though Ann and I had just agreed that she would now start taking Antabuse, and neither she nor I was afraid she would drink over the holidays.

Why Antabuse, and why now? Like most alcoholics, with Ann, a little drinking inevitably leads to more frequent and heavier drinking. Ann's new strategies for delaying drinking had helped but had simply not reduced her drinking to zero. The occasional drinking was creeping up and Ann, and I, feared it would soon snowball. That in turn would set back their structural family changes immensely, especially with four weeks coming up over vacations between sessions ten and eleven. Interestingly, Freddie and Carrie did not want their mother to take Antabuse, ostensibly out of fear she would either take an accidental overdose or drink while on it. My response to that was simply to ask Ann if she had either of these concerns for herself. She said no, and I promptly gave her a prescription for one 250 mg. tablet of Antabuse to be taken daily.

Four weeks later, Ann and Carrie and Freddie returned all smiles. Bob and Bob Jr. failed to come, for work and unspecified reasons respectively. Ann had taken Antabuse daily and had had no alcohol for one month. The kids were very pleased with their relationship with their mother, and each reported that their grades in school were all of a sudden improving. Their only issues now were that they felt guilty or angry when their father "looks" and "sounds" critical of them to a greater extent than seems warranted at a given moment. I told them that, especially since father wasn't present, I couldn't really change his look or tone of voice, but that we could alter their own reactions when they truly had nothing to feel guilty or angry about except his look or tone. With Carrie watching intently, I then went to work in NLP™ fashion with Freddie. Using anchoring plus a visual-kinesthetic dissociation technique which is useful with phobic-type reactions, I installed what Freddie termed his "happy with myself" state in the context of hearing and seeing in father what seemed to Freddie to represent unwarranted criticism. He could then in his imagination think of alternative ways he could have in the past and could in the future respond to father appearing and sounding that way. For example, he could imagine asking, "You sound angry at me, are you?" and feeling okay as he did so. What works in a session may not carry over to home without adequate anticipation of actual challenges the client must face outside the office. The best preparation is to test out the persistence of new behavior *in vivo* immediately. In the absence of father, I had Ann act as father, using the kids to prompt her until she got the look and tone of voice just right. Carrie had been instructed to do all the same things I was helping Freddie do "for herself," so I was testing both of them. By the end of the session each was able to handle Ann's well-simulated presumed critical look and tone with aplomb.

Ann, Bob, and Carrie came for session twelve. During the week, Freddie had said he had gotten what he wanted from therapy, and Ann had excused him from this session to accept an invitation with a friend. Bob Jr. had relayed through Carrie that he wouldn't come to the sessions because he "doesn't like how his father talks to him." Oldest sister Annie had said during the week that she would come to a session now but then failed to show. In the session itself, Carrie clearly was more comfortable talking with her father. Ann said life at home was sufficiently improved that she wondered about reducing the number of sessions to twice a month. While I agreed that much was improved, I chose to emphasize the failure to come in on the part of Bob Jr. and now Annie too. I was curious, I said, how they could reconcile proposing less frequent sessions on the same day both their oldest children had failed to come in as promised. The rest of the session was spent helping Ann and Bob collaborate further on limit setting with Bob Jr. The understanding at the end was that all of the family would come in next, and sometime after that we might be able to discuss less frequent sessions.

Annie came in for the first and only time to session thirteen. That proved to be enough to reintegrate her into the family and foster her catching up with the changes that others in her family had made. Bob Jr. still refused to come in, and he never did return. The time of session thirteen was evenly divided between a focus on Annie herself and further practice among family members at carrying on a discussion over differences long enough to achieve mutual understanding and resolution. I wanted Annie to see and become a part of this process. First, though, and even more important, I wanted family members to express to Annie whatever concerns they had about her behavior. What came out was that each person had their own private worry over Annie's use of alcohol. Bob admitted he worried that Annie drank and then drove. He gave more than one example. Freddie and Ann told Annie of their secret concerns over the many bottles of liquor in her apartment. Each went on record that they feared Annie was developing an early problem with alcohol. I found from Annie that she routinely had four or more drinks a day and six to eight or more socially with her similarly heavy-drinking friends. I told her that I was concerned about her drinking and then promptly moved on to facilitating others working out their differences. I felt the point about alcohol had been made, and now it would be good for her to hear and see how others could and had made changes. The discussion moved along easily and well. I was particularly pleased to see Carrie and Freddie jointly take on their parents. Carrie was clearly no longer in a quasi-parental role, and father was no longer reacted to as an ogre just because he expressed his most earnest thoughts in a deep voice.

Session fourteen included mother, father, Freddie, and Carrie. They talked well and didn't need me much. Freddie and Carrie reported they had stopped fighting with one another. Bob noted that he and Bob Jr. were talking more and cooperating more with one another. In the session Bob got Ann to agree more explicitly to bring issues to him directly rather than telling them first to one of the kids who then served as a go-between. To foster this, I assigned Freddie to say "Tell Dad," should Ann come to him with an issue meant for Bob. Similarly, I assigned Ann to say "Tell Dad," if one of the kids came to her with a gripe meant for their father. I finished with a proposal that we assess whether or not to continue therapy at the next session.

The same four returned for session fifteen. All said they felt "closer" to one another. Even Annie was calling her sibs and parents more and inviting some of them over at times. They noted how each was now able to talk one to one with any other family member well, with only one exception. Freddie described what I summarized as a recurring "war dance" with his older brother. For example, he would ask Bob Jr. to play ball with him and get a disparaging or sarcastic response. He would then get furious or upset, and they would start yelling at one another, and of course not play ball. Bob Jr. was not available, but I knew from experience that Freddie was receptive to my anchoring in him his more positive resources under circumstances where previously he lost his cool. I knew also that Freddie had been very impressed with the change in himself in response to his father and that he attributed it to my intervention. So I moved over next to Freddie and took a few minutes with him while the others watched and listened. I elicited in him what he called the "in control" state that he wanted to have when his brother taunted him. I established an anchor for it so that I could quickly reelicit it in him, and had him imagine how he would handle his brother's taunts differently with that "in control" resource of his. When he could imagine himself doing that well, I had his father play Bob Jr. saying "Go away, or I'll break your legs" to Freddie. And Freddie kept his cool.

Then I asked if there was anything more they wanted to work on that they felt they couldn't handle themselves. They agreed there might be, but they wanted to try things on their own. I proposed scheduling a follow-up session sometime hence, and they picked a date nine weeks from then. Ann and I agreed that she would continue to take the Antabuse at least until the follow-up session.

FOLLOW-UP

I have follow-up information from two contacts. One was the scheduled session, which actually took place six months after the initial interview. The second was from my phone call to Ann six months later, or one year after they first came to see me.

Ann, Bob, Carrie, and Freddie came in for the scheduled follow-up. All reported they were each and collectively "doing well." Neither Ann nor Bob had had any alcohol. Ann had reduced her Antabuse to alternate days. She felt that was sufficient to give her a little extra time to delay the occasional impulse to drink. She wanted to continue using Antabuse that way at least another three months, and I completely supported that. Carrie had brought her grades up to include several As. Freddie had improved his grades to all As and Bs and was now on the honor roll. Neither child had had any trips to their medical doctor, except that Carrie discovered prescription glasses would relieve occasional headaches following reading. Annie seemed to them to be drinking less and visiting them more.

Bob Jr. had been given specific limits at home and consequences if he failed to adhere to them. He had broken the rules regarding no pot or alcohol use in the home and as a result had been living out of their home for the preceding month. He lived with a friend, had a job, and was totally supporting himself. His friend had been arrested during that month on a DWI (Driving While Intoxicated) charge.

We all agreed that, while the family still had issues to work on, they were now capable of taking them on without help. No future sessions were scheduled. I made clear that any one or all of them were free to contact me at any time in the future and that I would be interested in hearing about them from time to time.

About six months later, I called their home out of curiosity. I think of doing that often with families I've seen, and actually do it occasionally. Ann answered. Bob was out. Ann and I talked about twenty minutes. I began by telling her I was simply curious how they were doing and decided to call and find out, adding that I do that with people I've seen in therapy from time to time. She opened with, "We're way ahead of a year ago." Then she followed with a few supporting examples. Next we got into what remained to be worked on. Personally, she had stopped using Antabuse several months earlier and remained abstinent. She was also pleased that she lost twelve pounds, and wanted to lose only twenty more to reach her ideal weight. Interestingly, it was Bob who had had one slip with alcohol. One day on a business trip out of town, he had volunteered to her, he had taken a drink and ended up having a few more. The next day he stopped drinking again. That had happened two months prior to my call and had not recurred. Between Bob and Ann the only remaining issues were occasional actions with the kids by one parent before both had really agreed. The example given was that Bob had gotten Freddie a moped while Ann was still reluctant about it. Freddie then had an accident on his moped, which didn't hurt him too much but resulted in several hundred dollars' expenses. Since they had not really jointly shared responsibility for the moped, the impulse for Ann to tell Bob, "I told you so," was great. Aside from the accident, however, Freddie was doing quite well in his life. In school he had gotten all As in the last report, except language where he had requested and gotten some tutoring. Carrie had graduated high school and gone to summer school to make up for some deficiencies earlier in high school. She was now enrolled full-time and doing well in a local community college with the realistic goal of transferring the next year to the state university. To my moderate surprise, both Bob Jr. and Annie had moved back into their parents' home. Annie was working as a waitress and had a good chance soon to move up to being the bookkeeper for the restaurant. Drinking was no longer seen as a problem for her. Bob Jr. was not using pot or alcohol in the home. There were at times beer cans seen in his car. On the bright side, he had been promoted to assistant manager of a clothing store and was taking an evening business class at the same community college Carrie attended. I congratulated Ann on their success and agreed with her on the nature of the issues still to be addressed. I thanked her for the follow-up. That was the extent of my phone conversation with Ann.

SUMMARY

In the treatment of this case, I moved from couple to individual, and again to couple and then to family, and back to individual and again to family. Each member of the family became my patient no less than the referred patient. I drew upon structural and strategic family therapy techniques, communication skills training, behavioral assignments, Neuro-Linguistic Programming and no doubt more—the choice of approach depending on which would allow me most efficiently to achieve my intermediate or enabling objective at a particular phase of therapy. Had I continued with Ann and Bob as a couple, I had already considered that I might pursue work with each on their relationships with their families of origin. But I elected to support their interest in working together independent of a therapist, confident that they would return if they got stuck. All of the above is characteristic of what I think of as my "Integrative

Family Therapy'' approach, not just to alcoholism but to any case. What is unique to my treatment of alcoholism is the dogged return to issues around drinking. I do not assume the drinking will go away if I just do some nifty, even if arduous, family intervention. And if it doesn't go away (or in rare cases, become at least genuinely controlled), I do assume that my most elegant interactional accomplishments will not hold up. So I ponderously establish the extent of use of alcohol and other drugs by each family member and the personal and interpersonal consequences of that use to date. Then I bug people during each session about AA, AlAnon, AlAteen, about setting and meeting goals for drug use, and about current limits on drug use in the home. The only other point I would make about what is special to my family therapy for alcoholics is that it almost always requires that I draw upon multiple schools of theory and techniques. That is often but not as consistently true when I treat people dealing with issues other than substance abuse. The present case was easy as cases of alcoholism treatment go. Still, their treatment needs justified multiple modes of intervention and at family, couple, and individual levels. The main difference between the present case and most of my other cases of alcoholism treatment is that the various phases of therapy in most cases take longer to traverse.

REFERENCES

1. Davis, D.I.; Berenson, D.; Steinglass, P.; & Davis, S. The adaptive consequences of drinking. *Psychiatry*, 1974, **37,** 209–215.
2. Davis, D.I. The family in alcoholism. In W.E. Fann; I. Karacan; A.D. Pokorny; & R.L. Williams (Eds.), *Phenomenology and treatment of alcoholism.* New York: SP Medical & Scientific Books, 1980.
3. Davis, D.I. Alcoholics Anonymous and family therapy: Or why family therapy should be seen as complementary and not as a threat to AA and AlAnon. *Journal of Marital and Family Therapy*, 1980, **1,** 65–73.
4. Davis, D.I. Special problems in family therapy posed by alcohol abuse. In M.R. Lansky (Ed.), *Family Therapy and Major Psychopathology.* New York: Grune and Stratton, 1981.
5. Gurman, A.S. Dimensions of marital therapy: A comparative analysis. *Journal of Marital and Family Therapy*, 1979, **5,** 5–18.
6. Gurman, A.S. & Kniskern, D.P. Research on marital and family therapy: Progress, perspective and prospect. In S.L. Garfield & A.E. Bergin (Eds.), *Handbook of psychotherapy and behavior change: An empirical analysis*, 2nd ed. New York: Wiley, 1979.

7. Dilts, R., et al. *Neuro-linguistic programming,* Vol. I. Cupertino, Calif.:
     Meta Publications, 1980.
8. Cameran-Bandler, L. *They lived happily ever after.* Cupertino, Calif.: Meta
     Publications, 1978.

2

Behavioral Treatment of An Alcohol Abuser With the Spouse Present:

Two Case Studies

Nora E. Noel, Ph.D
Barbara S. McCrady, Ph.D.

Clinicians have accorded a high level of importance to the role of the spouse in both the development and treatment of alcohol problems. In addition, a number of treatment outcome studies (reviewed in Paolino & McCrady, 1977) have found that involving the spouse in treatment consistently leads to a slightly more successful treatment outcome than treatment with the spouse involved. However, in these studies, the mode of involvement of the spouse has varied widely, and the literature says little about what type of spouse involvement is the most effective and most economical, and for whom. Because of these questions about couples treatment, a 3½-year, NIAAA-funded research program was begun to study components of spouse involvement in the treatment of problem drinking. In this study, three modes of spouse involvement are being compared: (1) minimal spouse involvement; (2) teaching the spouse how to respond effectively to drinking behavior and how to reinforce nondrinking effectively; and (3) marital therapy. All couples receive individualized behavior therapy for the drinking behavior, and all are treated as couples. Each subject is being followed for eighteen months after the termination of treatment.

A recent chapter (McCrady, 1981) described the case of a couple seen in the marital therapy experimental group. In contrast, the present chapter details two cases in which the spouse was present, but was minimally involved in the treatment. In both cases, the spouse attended all sessions, but no marital or spouse behavior issues were directly addressed. Instead, the focus was on individualized behavior therapy for the problem drinker. The role of the spouse in each case was to observe the treatment and to provide supplementary information.

These two cases were chosen for discussion because of the contrasts they presented. Although both received the same standardized treatment protocol and were treated by the same therapist during the same time period, the differences between the two cases were striking. In one case, the client, Mr. J., was abstinent and cooperative throughout treatment. He and his wife participated well in treatment from the first session through to the end. In contrast, the other client, Mrs. N., continued to report drinking incidents through the first ten of her fifteen sessions of treatment. She was often ambivalent and angry, sometimes not completing her homework assignments, and verbally wrestling with the therapist for control of the treatment sessions. In addition, at least initially, her husband appeared to be sabotaging her efforts to attain sobriety. Our goal in presenting these cases together is to highlight the shaping of a standardized behavior therapy program to fit the needs of particular alcoholic couples, and to consider the role of the spouse in treatment.

DESCRIPTION OF THE PROGRAM

Before detailing the progress of each case, a general description of the overall treatment program will be provided. After screening for appropriateness for the study and obtaining informed consent, data were collected from each couple in two pretreatment assessment sessions, fifteen treatment sessions, and one immediate posttreatment session. At the time of writing, both couples were involved in their eighteen months of follow-up data collection (monthly telephone contacts and in-person interviews at six, twelve, and eighteen months posttreatment).

To be included in the study, clients had to be twenty-one to sixty years old and married to a spouse who was willing to participate in treatment. In addition, they had to report a drinking problem of at least two years' duration, with drinking during the last sixty days, and a minimum of four negative consequences of drinking in the last twelve months. Finally, they had to obtain a score of five or more on the Michigan Alcoholism Screening Test (MAST) (Selzer, 1971). Subjects could be hospitalized for detoxification if necessary.

Grounds for exclusion from the study included drug abuse, schizophrenia, organic brain syndrome, a major affective disorder, or evidence that the spouse was abusing alcohol or drugs. Finally, neither the client nor the spouse could be engaged in any other treatment (including Alcoholics Anonymous or AlAnon) while receiving treatment through the study.

Baseline data were collected to measure drinking, marital functioning, psychological functioning, social/interpersonal skills, and occupational functioning took place. The methods of assessment and results of these measures are detailed for each client within the text.

After assessment, couples were randomly assigned to one of the three experimental conditions and each couple participated in fifteen ninety-minute conjoint treatment sessions, held about one week apart. The research protocol specified certain goals, methods, and between-session homework assignments for each meeting with the therapist, depending upon the experimental condition, but there was enough flexibility in the actual content of the session to be able to tailor the interventions to the client's unique problems. The flexibility of the protocol will be seen in the differences between the two cases detailed below.

In the "minimal spouse involvement" experimental group, the goals of the first three treatment sessions were: (1) teaching the couple to conceptualize drinking as a habit or overlearned behavior, and (2) helping the problem drinker to do a functional analysis of his or her drinking behavior. Following the functional analysis, specific interventions were taught and applied. Problem drinkers were taught stimulus-control procedures (Sessions 4 and 5); rearranging consequences for drinking and sobriety (Sessions 6, 7, and 8); congnitive restructuring techniques (Session 9); planning alternatives to drinking (Session 10); general problem-solving and assertion skills (Sessions 11 and 12); and deep muscle relaxation (Sessions 13 and 14).

The overall goal of treatment was to help the problem drinker achieve and maintain abstinence from alcohol. To this end abstinence was emphasized throughout therapy, and the last session was spent planning maintenance techniques. Handouts given to clients throughout treatment were also viewed as aids to long-term maintenance of sobriety.

Following treatment, couples were again seen by a research assistant for a follow-up data-collection session, and plans were made for monthly telephone contacts.

The other two groups to which the couples could be assigned were the "Spouse Involved" and the "Marital Therapy" groups. These two experimental groups added techniques to teach spouses ways to deal with their partners' problem drinking, and conjoint behavioral marital therapy. Thus, the couples described here were assigned to the experimental group that put the most emphasis on the problem drinker and the least emphasis of the three groups on the spouses or the relationship.

DESCRIPTION OF THE CLIENTS

Mr. and Mrs. J.

Identifying Information

Mr. J., a 49-year-old middle-management executive and college graduate, was referred to the Project for Alcoholic Couples Treatment in July 1981 by a psychiatric social worker at a local hospital. Mr. J. had just been released from the hospital following ten days of treatment for alcohol withdrawal.

At the time of referral, the J.s had been married for sixteen years. This was the first marriage for both. Mrs. J., 45, was a college graduate who did not work outside the home. Both the J.s said that they preferred that Mrs. J. stay home, although they had no children. The J.s were Rhode Island natives of Irish descent who described themselves as traditional, conservative Catholics.

Drinking History and Current Status

Mr. J. reported prior to his hospitalization (his first alcohol treatment) he had done most of his drinking with customers and sales representatives from other companies in restaurants, taverns, and clubs. He also drank at parties and occasionally with Mrs. J. He dated the beginning of his alcohol problems to about eight years before when he had had stomach surgery (not related to alcohol problems). As a result of the operation, Mr. J.'s tolerance for alcohol decreased, and he felt intoxicated after only a few drinks. As a result, even moderate drinking was risky for him.

For the most part, Mr. J. reported that he was able to keep some control of his drinking, but during the year prior to evaluation he had increased his drinking in response to an unusual series of stressful events. First, his mother-in-law, to whom he was close, suffered a stroke that left her paralyzed. Two months later while she was still recuperating, her husband, Mr. J.'s father-in-law, had a severe heart attack. During this period, the J.s were running back and forth between two hospitals, with Mr. J. feeling pressure at work since he had so little time. He gradually began to drink more heavily and, to add to his troubles, he had an automobile accident one night while intoxicated. At the time of evaluation, drivers of both the other cars were suing Mr. J.

Finally, one month prior to treatment, Mrs. J.'s mother had another stroke and died. Mr. J. stopped drinking on the day of her death. Two days later on the morning of her funeral he had a seizure, and briefly lost consciousness. He was taken by ambulance to a hospital, where he spent several days shaking and hallucinating. (Mrs. J. reported that he apparently "saw" several drinking friends, though Mr. J. did not remember hallucinating.) Mr. J.'s physical condition was also assessed at the time of evaluation. Reports from the hospital showed that Mr. J. was fully detoxified, and that his attending physician had recommended multivitamins but no other medication. Liver function tests were all within normal limits except for a high level of GGTP (139 u/1; normal range 0–45 u/1).

Other alcohol problems reported by Mr. J. included "obnoxious" behavior when intoxicated and many arguments with his wife over drinking. He said that at a party or gathering where he felt ill at ease, he would often drink too much and, though normally taciturn and soft spoken, get loud and boisterous. He would discourse at great length about subjects with which he was unfamiliar and loudly insist that his opinion was correct. The arguments with Mrs. J. were usually about this behavior. She said she often felt embarassed by him, and that they generally argued after they got home while he was still intoxicated.

Mr. J., an only child, reported a family history of alcoholism. His father, who had died several years ago, had drinking problems, as did a paternal uncle. Mr. J.'s mother (also deceased) was reported to be a teetotaller.

Interestingly, Mrs. J. described her father as an alcoholic and said that Mr. J. and her father often drank together while watching sports on television on Sunday afternoon. Mrs. J. drank "occasionally," usually limiting herself to one or two glasses of wine with a meal. She reported no problems with alcohol.

Measurement of Drinking Behavior

Prior to beginning treatment, the J.s completed a 365-day drinking history for Mr. J. (Sobell et al., 1980). The J.s were asked to categorize his drinking for each day of the year as abstinent, light (1–2 drinks), moderate (3–6 drinks), or heavy (more than 6 drinks). The couple was asked to recall significant events such as birthdays, holidays, illnesses, and vacations. These were marked on a calendar prior to obtaining the daily drinking history. Recalling these significant events assisted them in recalling Mr. J.'s daily level of drinking.

The 365-day history revealed that Mr. J.'s usual beverage was beer, with occasional vodka tonics. He almost never drank at home. Most drinking was with customers on lunches or dinners (1–2 beers) during the week, or at his father-in-law's house Sunday afternoons (up to 4 or 5 drinks). He also occasionally drank up to four or five beers after playing golf with friends.

During the 365 days prior to treatment, the J.s reported a total of 101 light-drinking days and 18 moderate-drinking days. It was surprising, considering the severity of his withdrawal symptoms, that neither Mr. nor Mrs. J. could find a day in the past year in which Mr. J.'s drinking could be classified as "heavy." There is no reason to doubt the veracity of their reports, so it seems that this level of drinking was enough, in Mr. J.'s case, to induce serious physical and interpersonal consequences.

Two other procedures were used to obtain more details about the factors associated with Mr. J.'s drinking: self-recording cards and a functional analysis questionnaire developed for the present study. The self-recording cards were introduced to the J.s during the first treatment session and used throughout the fifteen weeks of treatment. On Mr. J.'s cards, used daily, he was to record the exact time and situation for each drink consumed. In addition, he was to record any thoughts he had about wanting a drink even though he did not drink in response to the urge. Finally, Mr. J. was to record his marital satisfaction daily, using a 1–7 scale (1 = "very low"; 7 = "greatest ever").

As a validity check, Mrs. J. was asked to record a daily estimate of her husband's drinking as either abstinent, light, moderate, or heavy. She also made a single daily entry on a 1–7 scale of how strong she believed his drinking urges were that day. Finally, on a similar 1–7 scale, she rated her own daily marital satisfaction. Data obtained from these cards will be presented later.

The functional analysis questionnaire or Drinking Patterns Questionnaire (DPQ) (Zitter & McCrady, 1979) presents over two hundred situations, feelings, and thoughts often associated with drinking. The J.s were each asked to complete a DPQ independently between treatment sessions one and two. On the DPQ, the J.s were to endorse all items they thought were associated with Mr. J.'s drinking. These items had been divided a priori into ten major areas: environmental factors associated with drinking; work factors; financial factors; physiological states; interpersonal situations; marital problems; relationships with parents; problems with children; emotional factors; and recent major life stresses. In addition, Mr. and Mrs. J. were asked to endorse items that Mr. J. had experienced from a list describing positive consequences of drinking (e.g., "more able to express good feelings"). Finally, they endorsed items from a similar list of common negative consequences of excessive drinking (e.g., "not liking self").

Based on these assessments, five major areas were identified as related to Mr. J.'s drinking: work factors, environmental factors, interpersonal relationships, emotional antecedents, and major life stresses. Work and factors related to work seemed especially pertinent triggers for Mr. J.'s drinking. He had high prestige but also high pressure in his job as a sales executive for a jewelry company. Furthermore, entertaining clients or prospective clients was an integral part of his work. Thus, he often took parties or group of associates out to lunch or dinner or to play golf, followed by drinks at the country club. In addition, he often stopped on the way home at a particular tavern that was frequented by other sales personnel. Although he often intended just to have a soft drink and see his friends, he would usually drink alcoholic beverages and stay until nine or ten o'clock.

Thus, both Mr. and Mrs. J. felt that work and environmental cues associated with work were the most salient antecedents to Mr. J.'s drinking. Restaurants, the tavern, the country club, and golf were all reminders for him to drink.

Interpersonal situations were also important to Mr. J.'s drinking. He often felt awkward, insecure, inferior, and "different" in social situations, and felt that refusing to have an alcoholic drink would only add to that uneasiness. When others were drinking he felt a pressure to go with the crowd and to "maybe only have one or two." As noted above, even that small amount of alcohol was risky for him. When he did have a drink he would begin to feel more comfortable socially and more competent. Even though he still felt somewhat inferior to others, once he drank he didn't seem to care as much. Thus, drinking alcohol was immediately reinforced.

Mr. J.'s image of himself as incompetent was difficult for Mrs. J. to understand. In fact, he had acquired such a good reputation among the area companies that a rival organization had recently attempted to recruit him. Mr. J. agreed that the company had tried to win him away and that he had even used that to negotiate a salary increase, but he still could not shake the image of himself as inferior and inadequate. Indeed, the higher salary produced more pressure because he felt he had to live up to it.

The emotional antecedents to drinking identified by both the J.s included Mr. J.'s feeling anxious, insecure, inferior, and frustrated. In addition, he identified depression as an important antecedent. Because of the stressful events in the past year, Mr. J. felt depressed fairly often. Interestingly, he was able to recognize that drinking actually made him feel more depressed in the long run, though this awareness did not effectively control his drinking when he was depressed.

Most of the aversive consequences that Mr. J. had suffered as a result of his drinking were described above. Responses on the

Michigan Alcoholism Screening Test (MAST) (Selzer, 1971) and the negative consequences section of the DPQ supplemented the knowledge gained from the interviews. His score on the MAST was 11. The list of negative consequences included: hospitalization for withdrawal, arguments with his wife, driving while intoxicated (and the resultant accident), missing work as a result of both hospitalization and hangovers, not functioning well at work, making a bad impression on others when he drank too much, and depression and guilt.

Psychological/Psychiatric History and Current Status

Mr. J. reported no earlier psychiatric treatment and no previous treatment for drug or alcohol abuse. His perfect score on the Mini Mental Status Examination (Folstein, Folstein, & McHugh, 1975) indicated no organic impairment. In addition, his responses to the Present State Examination (Wing, Cooper, & Sartorius, 1974) did not show any evidence of thought disorder or psychosis.

Mr. J. did, however, appear to be moderately depressed at the time of his initial interview. He reported frequent depressed moods, sometimes related to drinking but most often related to the death of his mother-in-law, the disability of his father-in-law, and the tense legal situation that followed as a result of his automobile accident. In addition, he reported some loss of interest in his job, some decrease in appetite and weight loss (twelve pounds in three months), lowered energy level, and some restlessness and anxiety. This disturbance in mood did not appear severe and seemed directly related to specific precipitants. However, although the decision in treatment was to focus on drinking behavior, occasional monitoring of these depressive symptoms was also planned as part of treatment.

Marital Relationship: Status and Measurement

Although emphasis in this particular experimental group was on minimal spouse participation, the marriage was assessed before and after treatment. In addition, daily self-monitoring of marital satisfaction was obtained during treatment (see description of self-monitoring cards, above), but was never addressed or discussed during treatment.

Two major marital assessment measures were given: the Locke-Wallace Marital Adjustment Test (Locke & Wallace, 1959) and the

Areas of Change Questionnaire (Birchler & Webb, 1977). The J.s scores on the Locke-Wallace Test were similar (his = 115; hers = 122), and their responses suggested that they both felt generally good about their marriage. Both agreed that if they had their lives to live over, they would marry the same person.

The Areas of Change Questionnaire also suggests a minimal level of conflict between the J.s. Their disagreements centered on drinking: Mrs. J. wanted her husband to drink less. Finally, although both reported current satisfaction with their sexual relationship, they alluded to some sexual problems about six months before treatment. Unfortunately, because of the nature of the research project, the therapist was unable to explore this problem area further.

Next, we will turn to a description of the second couple, also in the same treatment protocol at the same time as Mr. and Mrs. J.

Mr. and Mrs. N.

Identifying Information

At the time of her evaluation, also in July 1981, Mrs. N., a high school graduate, was a 49-year-old homemaker. She had been married thirty years to Mr. N., age 52, a disabled assembly-line worker. They had two adopted children, a daughter, age 22, and a son, age 18. Mrs. N. was referred by an intake worker at a local mental health clinic. She had gone to the clinic for help with drinking and depression.

Mrs. N. arrived for her initial interview with a blood alcohol level (BAL) of 0.029 percent. She claimed she had not had a drink since the evening before at 6 P.M. (four beers). The BAL was low enough to allow interviewing to take place, but Mrs. N. was instructed that if she appeared for any session with a BAL greater than 0.05 percent, the session would be rescheduled.

Mr. and Mrs. N. described their situation as a "financial nightmare." Mr. N. had a chronic relapsing debilitative disease and, as a result, was forced into early retirement. His medical bills were generally covered by insurance, but his disability income was only $8,000 per year. Their children lived with them but did not contribute to the household income. The daughter worked full-time as a secretary; the son was unemployed. Mrs. N. had few job skills and had never worked outside the home. She supplemented their income with occasional temporary nonskilled jobs.

Because of his disability, Mr. N., needed to walk with a cane. Occasionally, when "excited" or "angered," he lost all control of his muscles and was unable to walk at all. Thus, Mrs. N. said, she felt the burden of responsibility for keeping things calm in the family. This seemed to be a full-time job, since both the son and the daughter argued frequently and the son was often in trouble with the police.

The N.s said they received some support from Mrs. N.'s mother, who lived next door, and from her married sister, who lived across the street. The N.s described themselves as middle-class New England natives of mostly German descent, who were religious Lutherans.

Drinking History and Current Status

Mrs. N. reported a six-year history of alcohol problems and had received treatment about three years before. Following her treatment (a month in an inpatient facility), she sought no follow-up outpatient care. Nevertheless, both the N.s reported that she had remained abstinent for about eighteen months. She had started drinking again at a low level, but quickly resumed a high intake of alcohol. She attributed the resumption in drinking to stress resulting from her husband's illness and subsequent changes in the family life and financial status.

At the time of referral, Mrs. N. was drinking mostly beer, and an occasional brandy or whiskey. Generally, she would drink about four to six bottles of beer a day, although this was interspersed with occasional heavier days and a few abstinent days. She hardly ever bought her own beer; mostly she drank with her sister, who did not consume as much as she did.

Although her BAL was 0.029 percent when she was evaluated, inpatient detoxification was deemed unnecessary at the time. Both the N.s reported that she had detoxified at home at least twice before with no apparent symptoms. Mrs. N.'s blood pressure was, in fact, low normal (120/70) and she displayed no withdrawal symptoms at the time of her initial interview. Before they left the therapist's office, however, they were given a detailed description of withdrawal symptoms, and were told to contact the therapist or the admissions office at the hospital if any such problems occurred.

None did, and she reported for both sessions with the research assistant with a BAL of 0.0 percent.

Mrs. N. reported several negative consequences of her alcohol consumption, including occasional blackouts, depression, low energy level, and neglect of household responsibilities. Also, when she drank and then tried to stop the arguing between her son and daughter, she usually ended up with an even more intensified situation. Often, she said, she would drink and then "get nasty" with her children and husband. When sober, she would feel guilty about these arguments, and attempt to be conciliatory toward her family. As a result, she did not ask her children for support or help with the housework.

Physical problems also seemed closely associated with Mrs. N.'s drinking. She reported that her physician had told her a few years ago that she had a liver problem (unspecified) and needed to stop drinking. That is when she went into inpatient therapy. A physical examination by her doctor two months before evaluation indicated that Mrs. N.'s liver problems had cleared; the results of the project liver function test supported this. All liver enzymes were within normal range except GGTP (at 168, normal range = 0–35 u/1).

Mrs. N.'s physician also reported that she had had some pain, irregularity, and occasional heavy bleeding associated with her menstrual periods over the past six months. These problems, as well as some of Mrs. N.'s depression, were thought to be due to menopause. However, the physician had not recommended that Mrs. N. be seen by a gynecologist. The therapist suggested this but Mrs. N. did not go. However, she recognized the pain and depression associated with her period as specific and strong antecedents for her drinking.

Mrs. N.'s physician had also prescribed medications to alleviate sleep-onset insomnia and anxiety during the day. To this end, Mrs. N. was taking 15 mg of Dalmane two to three times per week for sleep, and 2.5 mg of Limbitrol about once per day. Since these were prescribed drugs and neither of the N.s reported any evidence of abuse, the project staff agreed that they met the qualifications for inclusion in the study. Mrs. N. was asked, however, to report any changes in the frequency of her medication intake.

Mrs. N. also reported a family history of alcohol abuse. Her father, her three paternal uncles, and her paternal grandfather were all reported to be alcohol abusers. In fact, her father had died about ten years before of alcoholic cirrhosis. Mrs. N. also reported that a maternal aunt and uncle were alcoholics, although her mother, brother, and another maternal aunt were abstinent.

Mr. N. reported that he had, until recently, been a moderate drinker, but currently drank very lightly for fear of aggravating his medical condition. His MAST score was zero.

Measurement of Drinking Behavior

Prior to beginning treatment, the N.s also completed a 365-day history of Mrs. N.'s drinking, which revealed that Mrs. N. drank most often either at her sister's house, at home, or at the bowling alley. Especially during the summer, her drinking was associated with sitting outside at cookouts or by her sister's pool.

Most often, Mrs. N. would go to her sister's house, have two to four beers, and come home. She would sometimes bring beer home with her and hide it behind things in the refrigerator. If she then had an argument with or about her son, she would lock herself in the bedroom and drink some more (maybe another two to four beers).

About once per week, Mrs. N. would go bowling with friends. On those evenings she would usually drink four to six beers. She would often plan not to drink, but if someone was buying a round, she found it difficult to refuse.

In all, Mrs. N. drank 130 days in the year prior to treatment. This was broken down into thirty-six light-drinking days, eighty days of moderate drinking, and fourteen days of heavy drinking. Her usual drinking pattern was at a "moderate" level (3–6 drinks), and she was not a daily drinker.

As with the J.s, the self-recording cards were presented to the N.s at the first treatment session. The data from these cards will be presented and discussed in the treatment section.

The Drinking Patterns Questionnaire (DPQ), described above, was also administered to Mr. and Mrs. N. Five major areas were identified by the N.s as related to Mrs. N.'s drinking: emotional factors, physiological antecedents, relationships with the children, financial problems, and major life stresses.

Mrs. N. was keenly aware of her own emotions, tended to describe them in dramatic terms, and felt that her emotional state controlled her drinking. Mrs. N. reported that when she felt depressed, guilty, nervous, angry, sad, hurt, spiteful, or hopeless, she "had" to have a drink. She recognized that drinking eventually made her more depressed, but she did not effectively use other means to cope with negative feelings.

The second area affecting her drinking—physiological factors—was also connected with Mrs. N.'s exaggerated focus on her own feelings. For a few days before and after the onset of her menstrual period, Mrs. N. would experience abdominal cramps, backaches, headaches, mild nausea, and weakness. Since she was menopausal and cycling at irregular intervals, Mrs. N. was never sure if a period was "coming on." Thus, when any of these symptoms appeared, Mrs. N. would drink to prevent the pain and "sick feeling" she expected to have soon. If her period began, then she felt she had effectively avoided the worst of it.

Her children also represented another set of factors related to Mrs. N.'s drinking. Both children were adopted as infants because Mrs. N. was unable to become pregnant (blocked fallopian tubes). The N.s had gone through ten years of first trying to have biological children and then trying to adopt. As a result, Mrs. N. felt that the children had been spoiled and taught to be irresponsible. Mr. N. did not agree, especially in regard to the son, and felt that the son's repeated trouble with the police (e.g., drinking, drugs, fighting) was merely a result of boyish rambunctiousness. The N.s reported that they often argued about their son, and Mrs. N. would then drink.

During the initial interview, in fact, the N.s' disagreement about their son became so heated that the therapist had to stop them to be able to complete the necessary assessment. Mrs. N. kept trying to return to the subject of the son's transgressions and disrespect for her through the rest of the interview. Another factor related to the children that contributed to Mrs. N.'s drinking was the fear that her children no longer needed her. For example, whenever they would talk about leaving home, she would cry and plead with them to stay. She had concentrated a great deal of her life on raising her children, and worried that she would be useless after they were gone. Mrs. N. felt that her drinking and "sloppy housekeeping" had driven her children away, and, feeling guilty, she would drink some more.

The final set of factors that both the N.s believed triggered Mrs. N.'s return to drinking was the husband's illness. Because of his disability and forced retirement, their financial status was lowered, their bills felt overwhelming to them, he was now home all the time and interfering in Mrs. N.'s domain, and he was depressed and frustrated. Both of them also carried a low but constant level of awareness that his disease was serious and would get progressively worse.

In the financial area, Mrs. N. tried to help supplement their income with odd jobs (e.g., as a waitress), but she was often needed at home to care for Mr. N. (although they disagreed on how much she was needed at home). Neither had thought of or wanted to ask either of the children to help Mr. N.

Also, on the Drinking Patterns Questionnaire, Mrs. N. endorsed several positive consequences of drinking. Most important of these were that drinking relieved her physical discomforts, made her feel more relaxed, helped her forget her problems, and provided an excuse for her failures.

Some of the adverse consequences of Mrs. N.'s drinking were described previously. On both the MAST (score = 42) and the DPQ she described a large array of negative results of drinking: depression; anxiety; withdrawal from others; not liking herself; family arguments; sexual difficulties; "sloppy housekeeping"; occasional blackouts; and possible medical problems (liver disease).

Psychological/Psychiatric History and Current Status

Mrs. N. reported no previous psychiatric treatment. The N.s had been seen by a psychiatrist for an evaluation before adoption of their children, but otherwise neither had sought any help or treatment for emotional problems. As noted above, about three years before, Mrs. N. was treated for alcohol abuse.

Mrs. N. scored within normal range on the Mini Mental Status Examination (Folstein et al. 1975), indicating no significant organic impairment from her alcohol abuse. Also, she evidenced no psychosis or thought disorder when she was administered the Present State Examination (Wing et al. 1974).

The therapist did have some concern about depression in Mrs. N.'s case. Mrs. N. reported feeling overwhelmed by her problems and often hopeless about resolving them. She felt depressed more than half the time, had lost most outside interests except bowling, felt weak and tired, but could not sleep well at night. In addition, she had gained thirty-five pounds in the last six months. She did not express any suicidal plans or ideation.

The decision regarding whether a depressive disorder or alcohol abuse is primary is often difficult and perhaps impossible to make. Depression is quite frequently a concomitant of alcohol abuse. Since Mrs. N.'s depressive symptoms had intensified as her drinking became heavier, our hypothesis was that the alcohol was at least exacerbating the symptoms, if not the actual cause. Other possible precipitants for depression existed too, the most obvious being the onset of menopause and the stresses resulting from Mr. N.'s illness.

Eventually, the decision was made to focus on Mrs. N.'s drinking as the target of choice. We felt that while it was possible that her depression was independent of her alcohol abuse, alleviating the alcohol problems could remove one whole set of complications. This decision was discussed at length with Mrs. N. The therapist emphasized that if work specifically in depression was needed during or after alcohol therapy, a referral would be made and the therapist would help her to follow it through. Mrs. N. agreed with this decision and, in fact, expressed a belief that if she conquered the alcohol problem, she could cope with the rest. She noted that during her previous eighteen months of abstinence she had felt relatively happy.

Marital Relationship: Status and Measurement

The state of the N.s' marriage was assessed before and during therapy through the use of questionnaires and self-monitoring cards. It should be recalled, however, that therapy itself focused only on the drinking behavior and not on the marital relationship.

The N.s' scores on the Locke-Wallace Marital Adjustment Test (Locke & Wallace, 1959) were disparate. Mr. N. (score = 102) rated their marriage as "happy" and felt they had few areas of conflict or disagreement. He saw them as solving most problems by mutual give and take. He did note that they also had very few interests in common, and that he likes to stay at home while she prefers to be on the go. However, he felt that if he had his life to live over, he would marry the same person.

On the other hand, Mrs. N. (score = 64) rated their marriage as "unhappy." She felt they shared no interests at all, that they frequently disagreed, that Mr. N. "just gave in" on most decisions, and that they had many strong conflicts about their children and about sexual relations. Although discussion of the issues was limited by the treatment protocol, it became evident from the questionnaires that the N.s had not engaged in sexual relations for at least six months. Mr. N. did not seem to feel particularly bothered by this, but Mrs. N. was feeling hurt, angry, and frustrated.

Their responses on the Areas of Change Questionnaire (Birchler & Webb, 1977) also reflected this general disagreement. Mr. N. did not even seem aware of Mrs. N.'s feelings about the lack of sexual behavior between them. In addition, although he did recognize their son's problems as an area of conflict between the two of them, he minimized the intensity of this conflict. He focused on wanting her to be a better housekeeper. Mrs. N. was aware that her husband wanted her to cook and clean more. She also emphasized her dissatisfaction with their sexual relationship and their disagreements over the son.

Thus, it appeared that the N.s had a very conflicted marriage and, in particular, Mrs. N. and her husband were not communicating effectively about her desires. While the N.s were told that therapy would focus on drinking, they were also told that if they wanted further treatment for their marital problems after the alcohol treatment, a referral would be made.

The Therapist

The therapist in both these cases (the first author) was a 28-year-old female doctoral candidate in clinical psychology. She had completed all graduate work except her dissertation, and had recently finished an APA-approved clinical internship with specialized training in work with alcohol abusers. In the six years previous to the internship she had also engaged in research and clinical work with alcohol-related issues.

The therapist was supervised on her work in these cases by the second author, a clinical psychologist certified in the state of Rhode Island who has had considerable experience in treatment and treatment research with alcohol abusers. The supervisor is the chief of both the Problem Drinkers' Project and the Project for Alcoholic Couples Treatment at Butler Hospital in Providence.

Having presented both couples and the therapist, we will now describe the treatment of each case.

TREATMENT OF THE COUPLES

The reader will recall that after each couple had participated in the pretreatment assessment sessions (clinical interview with the therapist and two baseline sessions with the research assistant), they were randomly assigned to one of three experimental groups. Both these couples, coincidentally, were assigned to the same treatment protocol in the same therapist's caseload. Thus, the treatment of each couple can be presented in parallel format as they occurred with the therapist. These couples were seen from July 1981 through November 1981. The discussion of the treatment is divided into the units described in the beginning of the chapter.

Sessions 1–3: Functional Analysis

Goals and Methods

The goals of the first three sessions were: (1) to teach the couple basic principles of learning so that they could understand the maintenance of drinking, and (2) to assist the problem drinker in doing his or her own functional analysis of their alcohol consumption.

In the first session, couples were introduced to the rationale for the treatment to which they were assigned. They were told that although they might have other important problems, we would be working in therapy on "one problem at a time." Thus, the focus would be on the drinking itself and discussion of other problems would be limited. The idea was to clear the alcohol out of the picture and allow the drinker to learn to cope with the other problems with a clear head.

Treatment requirements were also spelled out at the beginning of the first session. Clients were to report for sessions with a BAL of less than .05 percent (a BAL of 0.0 percent was preferred), they were to attend all sessions together and were to attempt all homework assignments. The goal of the treatment was abstinence from alcohol, but the therapist stressed that any drinking or urges to drink that occurred during treatment must be accurately recorded.

The self-recording cards, described above, were then introduced and explained. Clients were asked to keep their daily rating cards with them at all times, while spouses were asked to make their ratings at the end of each day.

The functional analysis was explained briefly in the first session, and then couples were asked to fill out the Drinking Patterns Questionnaire (DPQ) (Zitter & McCrady, 1979), described above, for homework. The explanation and work on the functional analysis was continued through the second and third sessions.

The functional analysis is used to conceptualize drinking as a behavior chain. The chain is broken down into different steps: (1) antecedents of drinking (called "triggers" for clients); (2) internal events, called "thoughts and feelings"; (3) the drinking behavior; (4) short-term consequences of drinking (generally positive); and (5) long-term consequences of drinking (generally negative).

Using lists of antecedents from their DPQs and self-recording cards, clients were asked to write out several personal examples of behavior chains. These chains were completed during sessions and for homework. The therapist explained that short-term positive consequences generally maintain a behavior even though the long-term consequences are negative. In addition, it was explained that the long-term negative consequences (e.g., hangovers the morning after) can sometimes serve as triggers for another drinking episode.

It was expected that by the end of the third session, couples would have gained a basic understanding of drinking behavior, and that the behavior chains could serve as a blueprint for planning the rest of the interventions. In addition, it was expected that the clients had by then acquired the habit of self-recording every drink or urge to have a drink.

Mr. and Mrs. J.

Mr. J. reported for each of the first three sessions with a BAL of zero. At the first session he reported no drinking since his hospitalization (by then he had been out of the hospital for three weeks); his wife confirmed this report, as did the self-recording cards.

Mr. J. followed the treatment protocol as described above and Mrs. J. appeared very supportive. They both seemed quite interested in the principles of learning theory that were explained and the personal application of these principles in the functional analysis. Mr. J. remarked during the second session that he felt like he was getting a free course in psychology. The J.s read the handout for this section, asked many questions, and did all their homework.

During the first three weeks of self-recording, Mr. J. reported one to two drinking urges per day. Generally, these urges were rated at 3 to 4 in intensity (moderate), and were related to social activities (e.g., lunch with customers). Mrs. J. also estimated her husband's average daily urge intensity at about 3. Their daily recordings of marital satisfaction also matched well and remained quite high. Mr. J.'s ratings hovered between 6 and 7, while Mrs. J.'s ratings, on a scale of 1–7, were always 7. These ratings were not discussed during sessions.

An example of one of Mr. J.'s behavior chains, developed during these first sessions, is illustrated in Figure 2-1.

At the end of the third session Mr. and Mrs. J. were asked to rate his current ability to resist the urge to drink in the various situations that he rated as most difficult on his DPQ. The questionnaire used was intended to measure the client's perception of self-efficacy. This measure was obtained because previous research (Bandura, Adams, & Beyer, 1977) had suggested that long-term behavior change was related to increased feelings of "self-efficacy." In the questionnaire, the client was asked, "How confident are you that you can resist drinking in the following situations?" A list of personally highly rated DPQ items followed. The client and the spouse on a separate form were to rate, from 10 to 100, their level of confidence that drinking could be resisted in each situation and overall. Both the J.s felt that he could resist all urges to drink but might have some trouble in situations where he felt he needed to be more relaxed with other people or to make a "good impression." Overall, they were both fairly sure that Mr. J. would maintain his abstinence.

Mr. and Mrs. N.

Mr. and Mrs. N. provide a sharp contrast to the J.s. Although Mrs. N. reported to each session with a BAL of zero, she continued to report sporadic drinking episodes during these first three weeks. In addition, the interaction between Mr. and Mrs. N. during the sessions was conflicted, and each threatened the other with dropping out of treatment. They did remain in treatment, however, and satisfactorily completed all assigned homework (the self-monitoring cards, the DPQs, and behavior chains).

Despite conflicts within the sessions, Mr. and Mrs. N.'s daily marital satisfaction ratings remained on the high side of moderate (a mean of 5 on a scale of 1–7). Mr. N. consistently rated his

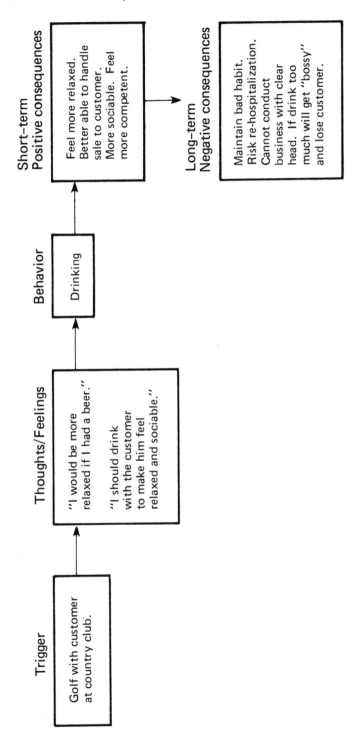

Figure 2-1
Behavior Chains in Alcohol Intake Decision Making: Mr. J.

satisfaction at 5, while Mrs. N. mostly rated herself at 5. It was perhaps clinically significant that on drinking days she rated her marital satisfaction at 4. Because of the treatment protocol, these ratings were not discussed.

At the first session, Mrs. N. reported that she had had two drinking incidents over the past week. Her husband was unaware of her drinking, however, and expressed some anger that she had not said anything until they arrived for the session. This issue came up again when the self-monitoring cards were introduced and explained. Mr. N. felt that he could not report accurately on his wife's drinking because, "She's a sneaky drinker. She lies and lies and thinks she's really getting away with something".

The therapist explained carefully that Mr. N.'s role was that of an outside observer who could help by supplying information. He was not to be a detective, or to interrogate Mrs. N. about her drinking, but instead was to decide, based on his observations, whether she was drinking or not. Mrs. N. was told that she was under no obligation to tell her husband if she drank, but she was expected to report accurately on her cards, and that these data would be discussed during the sessions. Mr. N. agreed to these plans reluctantly because he felt that he couldn't trust his wife. Mrs. N. seemed pleased that she did not have to "tell" on herself. She did agree to report her drinking accurately on the cards.

During the first three sessions, as the rationale and the behavior chain concept were explained, Mrs. N. listened, participated, and completed her homework. However, she often interrupted work in a certain area to explain, "But that isn't my real problem. My real problem is my nerves," or "my real problem is my depression," or "my children," "menopause," or "housework." She would then complain about how bad the problem was that she was discussing, and if not stopped by the therapist, could have continued in this vein to the end of the session.

Initially, the therapist would agree that she was presenting a serious problem, but that the treatment could not focus on all her problems at once, and that she had agreed to begin with the problem of her drinking. An analogy was made in which Mrs. N. was to imagine herself deciding to walk the dog, wash the dishes, and make a cake all at the same time. "You put the dishes in the water, and start to mix the ingredients for the cake. Then you discover that the mixing bowl is in the sink, so you clean that and begin to beat egg whites. Meanwhile the dog is barking to go out, so while you put him out, you let the egg whites go. Of course, they've fallen while you were taking care of the dog. So you come back, try to redo the egg whites, find that the egg whites have spattered on the counter, and now the dog is barking at the neighbor's cat. By this time, you're frantic, overwhelmed, and the dishes, cake, and the dog still need attention."

Mrs. N. enjoyed this analogy and even added some humorous details of her own because it sounded so much like "one of my days." Occasionally referral to this analogy also helped to refocus Mrs. N. on her drinking problem.

The housework still remained an issue. Mrs. N. reported (and Mr. N. agreed heartily) that she was a "lousy housekeeper," and that now that she had stopped drinking all afternoon, she felt overwhelmed by the amount of housework that needed to be done. The therapist suggested that since the house had been that way for the last six years, there was no reason it couldn't remain a mess for another fifteen weeks. Mrs. N. was urged to throw all her energy into the alcohol treatment and to let go of the housework.

Surprisingly, both the N.s agreed to this idea with enthusiasm, and Mr. N. spontaneously offered to pick up some of the household chores (e.g., cooking). Mrs. N. was enthralled with not having to do housework, and even asked if it was all right to go away for a while. She had a cousin who owned a house at the beach. The therapist again emphasized that Mrs. N. could do whatever she pleased, as long as she came to the sessions, did her homework, and focused her energy on staying abstinent.

The following week, the N.s appeared for the session early, and when the therapist came into the waiting room, Mr. N. announced loudly, "What did I tell you, she drank again." Mrs. N. was angered by this comment and the two began arguing as soon as they entered the office.

The therapist intervened with a suggestion that Mr. N. remember the principle of confidentiality and refrain from comments about Mrs. N. until he was in the office. We then quickly moved on to the breath test (BAL 0.00 percent) and a discussion of Mrs. N.'s self-monitoring data.

Mrs. N. had, indeed, been drinking during the past week. The N.s had gone to stay at the beach house, and for the first three days she had been abstinent. On the fourth day, they had gone

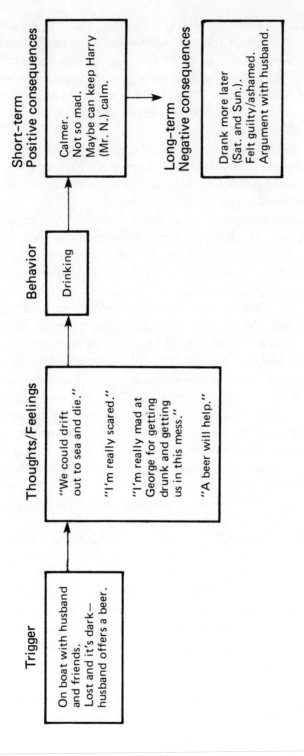

Figure 2-2
Behavior Chains in Alcohol Intake: Mrs. N's Boat Incident

out on a boat with some friends. Mrs. N. knew these people were heavy drinkers, so she brought along an entire cooler of diet soda for herself. She remained abstinent the whole day and was feeling good about this. However, as they were headed back to shore at the end of the day, the boat owner, who was intoxicated, got lost. As they wandered around in the dark, Mrs. N. began to get hysterical, and Mr. N. offered her a beer to calm down. Mr. N. said he felt at the time like the beer was needed. However, he pointed out, "she could have said no if she really didn't want it."

Following this incident, they had argued and had gone home the next morning. Mrs. N. continued to drink the next two days at her sister's house: six beers each on Saturday and Sunday. Mr. N. was unaware of this further drinking, but took pains to point out that she had also "lied" to him again (by not telling him about the drinking). This interaction engendered another heated argument, which the therapist had to stop in order to refocus on the alcohol therapy protocol.

Mrs. N., in tears, said that she guessed she should leave treatment because she could not stop drinking and because making her husband angry was bad for his health. Instead, the therapist urged her to stay and complete a behavior chain related to the boat incident. This example chain is shown in Figure 2-2.

Mrs. N., for part of her homework, also constructed a chain describing her drinking on the following days. This chain is presented in Figure 2-3.

Thus, Mrs. N. was able to see that some of the consequences of the previous day's drinking episode served as triggers for later drinking.

Mrs. N. reported for the third session the following week with a BAL of zero. She had one recorded drinking episode: on Sunday she had had five beers at her sister's house and at home. Her husband was aware of this drinking and was not too disturbed because she had told him about it. Mrs. N. had also had several strong urges to drink on Friday, Saturday, and Monday, but she had successfully abstained. She attributed these urges and the Sunday drinking to "just feeling rotten all day." Since Mrs. N. was still drinking, the therapist pointed out her control over her drinking on abstinent days. For example, it was emphasized that Mrs. N. had, for two weeks, successfully avoided drinking on Monday so that she would have a clear BAL on Tuesday morning (her

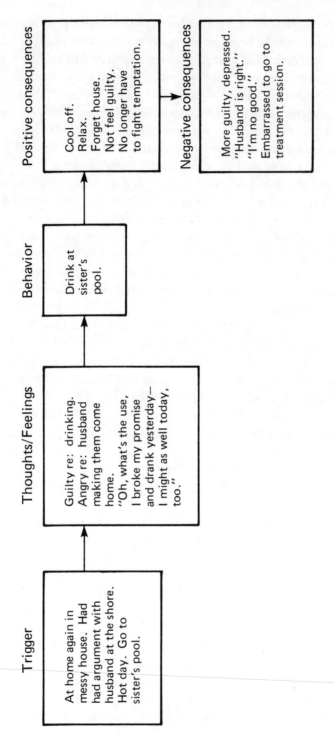

Figure 2-3
Behavioral Chains in Alcohol Intake: Mrs. N's Homework

appointment time). She was urged to maintain that level of control through the rest of the week as well.

Mrs. N., however, was not sure that she could maintain that level of control. She pointed out that she thought that her period was about to begin, her son and daughter were "getting on my nerves again," her house was a mess and she hated it, so she would probably have a drink. "I can't help myself—I know I'll fail," she concluded.

Throughout the rest of the session Mrs. N. continued to try to steer the conversation toward problems that she felt made it imperative that she drink again. For example, at one point she stated, "Well, I can forget the housework, but until I stop having these periods there's no way I can completely stop my drinking." Unfortunately, her husband would spontaneously collude in this, agreeing that she sometimes needed to have a drink.

At the end of the third session, the N.s (like the J.s) were asked to rate Mrs. N.'s current ability to resist drinking in various difficult situations. Overall, Mrs. N. was only 20 percent confident that she could remain abstinent; Mr. N. was 60 percent confident. Both were sure that she could not resist drinking in the face of depression or financial problems. They left on a pessimistic note.

By this time, the therapist was beginning to question the efficacy of the treatment for Mrs. N.'s drinking on an outpatient basis. Since she had not spent even one whole week without drinking, it was not even altogether clear that Mrs. N. had successfully detoxified from alcohol. In addition, two issues were becoming concerns to the therapist. One was the possibility that Mr. N.'s behavior would sabotage Mrs. N.'s efforts to remain abstinent (e.g., offering her the beer, suggesting that she really did need to drink at times). This issue, since it was spouse related, could not be directly discussed during the treatment.

The second issue concerned Mrs. N.'s almost unrelenting attempts to reestablish the agenda of the sessions and to excuse her drinking through the introduction of explosive topics. For example, if Mrs. N. could engage her husband in an argument about their son during the sessions, she successfully avoided working on her drinking. In addition, she could offer herself numerous reasons to drink (i.e., "My son makes me angry"; "My husband won't help me control him.") In part, this problem could have stemmed from Mrs. N.'s lack of distinction between triggers or antecendents to drinking and excuses for drinking. While recognition that drinking behavior has specific antecedents is helpful in treatment (i.e., one can then learn to deal more constructively with those situations), clients can sometimes get the idea that the antecedents cause drinking. Thus, they may feel an argument with a spouse is a reason for drinking. Actual control of drinking is ascribed to outside events. If the argument is instead viewed as an event increasing the likelihood of the urge to drink, the client can then use that incident as a warning to put other coping mechanisms (besides alcohol consumption) into effect. Drinking will then be seen as internally controlled. Mrs. N. was not making this distinction and was viewing antecedents or triggers as excuses for drinking. A decision was made to address this issue as well as the detoxification issue directly in the next session.

Sessions 4 and 5: Stimulus Control

Goals and Methods

In these two sessions, the therapist began to teach specific techniques to avoid drinking. During the first three sessions the client was taught to view drinking as a habit triggered by certain antecedents and maintained by certain consequences. The focus on sessions 4 and 5 shifted specifically to external antecedent events (i.e., "triggers"). Training in "stimulus control" (Miller, 1976) was aimed at teaching the client to alter these triggers, either by avoiding them or by changing them, thus decreasing the likelihood of drinking. For example, if passing a certain bar on the way home from work was a strong trigger for drinking, the client could minimize the risk by driving home on a different street. If the trigger is unavoidable, then rearranging the environment to minimize risk can also help. For example, Mrs. N. used this technique when she took diet soda along for herself on the boat where beer would be served. Another variation on this technique might be to carry only a small amount of cash on certain days to make it more difficult to buy liquor.

Note that in all these examples drinking per se is not prevented. The client could, in all the above cases, still get a drink. The purpose of the technique is to decrease cues for drinking, to make drinking more difficult (less an automatic behavior), and to make maintenance of sobriety a little easier.

These techniques, thus, required some planning to implement. Clients were taught a formal procedure involving problem-solving techniques called "self-management planning." Examples of this procedure will be illustrated for each of the clients.

Basically, self-management planning involved having the client first list the trigger (e.g., driving past a favorite tavern) and then brainstorm various methods of avoiding or altering the trigger. The negative and positive consequences of each method, and the difficulty of implementation, were evaluated. Based on these evaluations, the client was asked to choose one or more stimulus-control methods for environmental antecedents to drinking, and to implement this method systematically through the 4th and 5th weeks of treatment. Homework for sessions 4 and 5 focused on continuing self-monitoring and implementing stimulus-control techniques.

Mr. and Mrs. J.

Mr. J. remained abstinent during these weeks, his BAL was zero for each of the sessions, and he continued to complete all of his homework assignments. Both the J.s continued to rate their marital satisfaction at 7 on a scale of 1–7.

Mr. J. continued to report about two urges to drink per day. In general, he rated these urges at an intensity of 3 (low moderate), although he did have occasional urges rated 5 to 6. These strong urges were associated with social gatherings (e.g., cookouts on the beach) rather than business activities.

Mrs. J. estimated Mr. J.'s daily urge level at an average rating of 2. She also occasionally rated the intensity a little higher (3 or 4) and the days of her increased ratings tended to match his. She also felt that social gatherings were difficult for Mr. J. because he was often embarrassed to explain to friends why he was no longer drinking. (Business associates tended not to question his not drinking alcohol.)

Both the J.s were very interested in self-management planning. Mr. J. remarked that it "came along at just the right time." He was beginning to get very tempted to drink again and this new technique gave him an alternative. One of the triggers he chose to work with was business lunches, since these seemed to occur almost daily. The self-management plan he developed is shown in Figure 2-4.

Mr. J. developed and followed these plans over two weeks. The

Trigger	Plans	+/-	Consequences	Difficulty of Implementing 1 - 10 (easy-impossible)
Business lunch meeting. Everyone else orders drinks.	1. Decide on a particular non-alcoholic drink and be ready to order it.	1. − +	No guarantee; could still order alcohol at the last minute. No have to "stew over" order for a long time.	2
	2. Have breakfast meetings instead (people less likely to drink).	2. + + −	People less likely to order drinks with breakfast. Better for me; I function better in the morning. Some customers might not like to get up early for breakfast meeting.	4
	3. Ask waiter ahead of time to bring a non-alcoholic beverage.	3. + −	Don't have to worry about being asked if I want a drink. Feel "silly" about asking waiter to do my choosing for me.	4
	4. Go to restaurants that don't serve liquor.	4. + −	Can't drink, no choice to make in the situation. Limited number and kind of restaurants to choose from (can't take customers to McDonald's).	8

Figure 2-4
Self-Management Planning Sheet, Mr. J.

plan used most frequently was the first (decide on a particular nonalcoholic beverage) and he soon discovered that he had developed a habit of ordering "tonic with a twist". He also reported being surprised to find that no one questioned him about not drinking. The issue of most concern to Mr. J., his fear that others would think poorly of him, was being contradicted by his actual experiences in such situations.

Mr. and Mrs. N.

Mrs. N. came to sessions 4 and 5 with a BAL of zero, but continued to drink, especially between sessions 4 and 5. Following session 3, in which she had stated that "there was no way" she could completely stop drinking, she managed to get through a week with almost no drinking. Mrs. N. complained, in notes that she began writing on the back of her self-monitoring cards, that she felt sick from her period, that her son "came home in a rotten mood", and that she had gone to the poolside cookout—all without drinking. By Sunday, she reported she had reached her limit and drank one beer (in response to a depressed mood). Then she stopped and didn't drink again because she wanted a clear BAL for the session.

Mr. J. was aware of the drink, and again was not very disturbed about it. "I don't think one beer will hurt," he commented spontaneously. His marital satisfaction ratings continued consistently at "5"; hers were also consistently "4" during these two weeks.

The therapist, in an attempt to shape Mrs. N.'s nondrinking habits, praised her for her resistance to the urges through the week. Mrs. N. seemed quite proud of herself and commented that she felt as though she had gained enough control to stay abstinent. She recognized that her depressed mood was a result of both the hormonal effects of the period and the cessation of alcohol consumption.

Session 4 with the N.s went well. Mrs. N. had done all her homework well and became very involved in the self-management planning material during the session. Mr. N., for his part, sat quietly and listened, refraining from the jabs and negative comments that he often made.

Since the issue of Mrs. N.'s attempts to introduce new and explosive topics seemed to have settled down, the therapist did not make overt mention of it in session 4 (as she had planned to do after session 3). Not surprisingly, this issue was predominant in session 5.

Mrs. N. arrived for session 5 in tears. "I didn't want to come," she said, "I've been really bad." Her short notes on the back of her self-monitoring cards had developed into long essays on her awful condition. For example: "I'm really a mess today. My period is really bad and I hate myself. Maybe I'm losing my mind—I can't cope with anything." When the therapist commented on the notes, Mrs. N. responded, "I just wanted you to know how I was feeling. I'm awful." Mrs. N. had also been drinking: two beers on Friday, four on Saturday, and six on Sunday (once again staying sober on Monday). Mr. N. had also recorded this drinking on his cards.

The therapist's most immediate concerns for Mrs. N. were, once again, detoxification and Mrs. N.'s emotional state. The therapist suggested that since Mrs. N. seemed unable to abstain completely for even a week, a short inpatient stay might be indicated. Mrs. N. reacted with anger to this suggestion, and blamed her drinking on her daughter: "I was doing fine. If she hadn't decided to move out this week, I'd still be okay! I don't need to go into the hospital; I just need to get rid of my problems—then I can stop drinking."

Still angry with the therapist, she continued to argue that, "If we'd just take the time to talk about my real problems, I could stop drinking. These sessions are too short—maybe I should call you on the phone during the week."

The therapist emphasized again that the issue was not a matter of limited time. The focus was on drinking, and would remain there. It was acknowledged again that Mrs. N. had lots of problems, but that the alcohol had to be cleared out of her system before she could begin to try to cope effectively with other problems.

Mrs. N. eventually calmed down and agreed that she would "try" to remain abstinent through the next week to avoid hospitalization. Then she got out her self-management planning homework. One of the triggers she had worked on was "Marybeth [her daughter] saying she's finding her own apartment." Following the format, she had listed several plans for coping with this trigger, all involving trying to keep Marybeth at home (e.g., "I'll try to be a better mother"; "I'll always lend her the car when she wants it"; "I'll try to keep the house clean").

The therapist commented that such plans were not exactly the idea behind stimulus-control techniques, and that perhaps they could talk about Mrs. N.'s feelings about Marybeth's departure and how those feelings related to her drinking. At this, Mrs. N. exploded angrily, "But she can't leave home! I can't let her! I don't want to talk about drinking—I've got to find a way to make Marybeth stay home! That's what I want to talk about!"

By this time the therapist was angry with Mrs. N. and decided to use that annoyance in the session. "Look, Helen, this is really making me mad. Our agreement at the beginning of treatment was to concentrate on your drinking. I don't think I'd do you much good by jumping from one problem to another. If you want to talk about how to avoid your drinking and if you're willing to try to stay abstinent, then I'll do my best to help you. If not, then we'll have to decide on another course of therapy with another therapist."

Mrs. N. started crying at this point and kept saying "I want to leave! I want to leave!" The therapist said nothing. Eventually, Mrs. N. stopped crying, blew her nose, and got out her next self-management plan. Within a few minutes, she was working busily on plans to avoid triggers. At the end of the session she left, still sniffling, with a promise, "You watch—I'm not going to drink at all this week."

Sessions 6–8: Rearranging Contingencies

Goals and Methods

The goal of this section was to help the client learn techniques that would provide reinforcement for efforts to remain sober. The therapist would explain to the client that drinking in the face of negative consequences usually persists because it is reinforced in the short run. Sobriety, on the other hand, is often not and may, thus, be difficult to maintain. In this section, clients were taught how to change the timing and the nature of negative and positive consequences.

Three procedures were taught. One was writing up a list of all the negative consequences of their drinking that they had encountered or expected to encounter if drinking continued. On the other side of an index card, the client wrote all the positive consequences of sobriety. Both these lists were then reviewed three to four times per day, thus reminding the client of his or her reasons for avoiding alcohol.

The second technique was self-contracting for goals to be achieved (usually homework assignments) and specific rewards for fulfilling these goals. The third technique, convert reinforcement (Cautela, 1970), involved vivid rehearsal in imagination of a scene in which the client has a strong urge to drink, but refuses. Following the avoidance of drinking, the client is instructed to reinforce himself or herself covertly (a "pat on the back") for staying sober in the face of temptation.

These three techniques were taught in three sessions (6, 7, and 8) over a four-week period. The time between sessions 7 and 8 was interrupted by the therapist's vacation.

Mr. and Mrs. J.

Mr. J. continued to report for sessions with a BAL of zero, and both the J.s reported that he remained abstinent. He continued to have urges to drink, usually about two per day (business lunches and/or golf). Mr. J. rated the intensity of these urges about 3 (low moderate); Mrs. J. rated the intensity about 2. Both their marital satisfaction ratings were consistent sevens (i.e., "best ever").

Especially because of the contrast she could see between the two cases (the J.s and the N.s), the therapist was becoming concerned that Mr. J. might be "too good to be true." He was quite proud of himself for doing so well and made abstinence such an issue; how might he react if he did have a slip? This issue was discussed at length with Mr. J. in session 7 and he displayed a surprisingly realistic attitude.

He acknowledged that it was possible for him to have a slip since he was still experiencing urges to drink (although he felt it was getting easier to avoid alcohol). However, he would not view a slip as "the end of the world." "I'd have to stop drinking immediately and get back into my routines." he said. "Maybe I'd read my list [of negative consequences of drinking] or something like that."

Mr. J. also continued to complete his homework assignments faithfully, suggesting with a laugh that he should be getting course credit at Brown University for all he was learning. His lists of the negative consequences of drinking included "Health problems, driving (accident), not thinking clearly," and so on. Positive consequences of sobriety included "think more clearly, more harmony at home," and so on. In his self-contract, Mr. J. decided to rehearse his list of consequences at least four times per day, and to use telephone calls to his home office as his cue for this rehearsal.

For one of his covert reinforcement scenes, he imagined himself at a party on the beach with friends. He set the scene as a very hot day in July when his friends had a cooler of beer. Mr. J. imagined himself taking out a beer, opening it, seeing the foam rise out of the can, and feeling the icy cold in his hand. Then he imagined giving the beer to someone else and running out into the ocean to cool off. Finally, he complimented himself: "Whew! You got out of that one! Good job, Ed."

At the end of the eighth session, the J.s were again asked to rate Mr. J.'s ability to resist drinking in various situations. (The format was the same as that used at the end of session 3.) Both felt about 80 percent certain overall that Mr. J. could remain abstinent. The situations they felt might still present a problem included those in which others were drinking and social situations in which he wanted to feel more comfortable. Mrs. J. was especially enthusiastic about her husband's progress, and said that he seemed to be looking and feeling better than ever.

Mr. and Mrs. N.

Once again, Mrs. N. reported to each session in this section with a BAL of zero. Marital ratings continued at about 5 for each partner. Following her promise after the fifth session, Mrs. N. came to the sixth session all smiles. "I did it. I went this whole week without drinking!" Her behavior during this session was very upbeat, and in marked contrast to the previous weeks. When the therapist remarked on this, Mrs. N. acknowledged, "I feel great. I know I'm back on the right road." Mr. N. also smiled and praised her achievement.

However, between sessions 6 and 7, Mrs. N. was involved in a slight automobile accident (not uncommon in Providence) and drank two beers afterward. Actually, this drinking was very unusual for her—she had the beers by herself in a bar by the scene of the accident to calm down. That was the first time she had been in a bar in several years. However, she also handled the slip well by stopping herself after two beers and going home. She told her husband about the incident, and they apparently had a rational discussion about it. She did not drink the rest of the week, despite the fact that her daughter was now actively looking at apartments.

However, after two weeks of fairly good success, Mrs. N., unfortunately followed the common pattern of clients when the therapist goes on vacation. During the two weeks between sessions 7
and 8, Mrs. N. drank two beers on the first Saturday ("near my
period"), three on Monday ("started period, bad hemorrhaging"),
three beers on Thursday ("period continues, depressed, and Marybeth says she found an apartment"), and four on Friday (same as
Thursday). The session was on the following Tuesday.

In the session, the therapist emphasized the escalation of
amounts of alcohol that Mrs. N. drank during the two weeks. Mrs.
N., however, pointed out that she had seen that pattern, and had
stopped herself from drinking Saturday, Sunday, and Monday.
She felt she would be okay and would continue to be abstinent.

Mr. N.'s cards indicated that he knew about all the drinking,
even though she had not discussed it with him. "I can tell when
she drinks now," he said. "She acts drunk—she doesn't maintain
well like she could before." (This meant that she was not able to
hide it well.)

The issue of limiting the work to one problem at a time continued to dominate the sessions. Mrs. N. kept trying to turn the
discussion to her depression, her menopausal problems, her son's
misbehavior, and her daughter's "abandoning" her. She also
started to come to sessions up to a half-hour early, and sat right
outside the therapist's door, hoping that the session would start
early and "we can have a little more time." She persisted in trying
to make sessions run overtime, and once asked the therapist for
an extra session without her husband present, saying, "I just feel
like I need to talk."

The therapist was unsure about the best way to respond to
these maneuvers. On the one hand, limit setting seemed to
strengthen the dependent role that Mrs. N. had taken on in so
many relationships. On the other hand, lack of clear limits led to
Mrs. N.'s being scattered in sessions and not setting any clear goals
for herself. In a way, she was sounding more and more overwhelmed, but she had not yet concentrated on and accomplished
even one important goal: to stop drinking completely.

Because of the previous agreement about the time-limited and
focused nature of the treatment, the therapist eventually decided
to set and enforce some limits. These limits were explained to Mrs.
N. in the eighth session. She was told that sessions would begin

at 10:30 and end at noon, that they would always meet with the therapist as a couple, and that they would continue to focus on alcohol. Regardless of whether they had covered all material by noon, however, the session would definitely end then. Since Mrs. N., when she arrived early, had also been asking the therapist's co-workers to "let her know I'm here," the co-workers were informed of this policy as well.

Overall during these three sessions, Mrs. N. showed some improvement. She was more thorough in completing her homework assignments (e.g., reading her positive and negative consequences list about five times per day) and seemed to have gained a better understanding of how her alcohol consumption was maintained in the face of long-term negative consequences. In addition, she was actively planning ahead for potential drinking situations. For example, she asked her sister to keep ice water in the refrigerator and she drank that instead of beer on the hot days around the pool.

At the end of the eighth session, Mr. and Mrs. N. evaluated her current ability to avoid drinking. Overall, Mrs. N. rated herself as not very confident (about 20 percent confident that she would remain abstinent) but felt she could resist in all situations. (Note that in the third week, there were some situations in which she felt she would have to drink.) Mr. N., in contrast, felt his wife had less control over her drinking than at the end of the third session. He felt she could not resist a drink when she felt guilty, restless, in pain, or in situations in which she had had a family disagreement or financial problems.

Session 9: Cognitive Restructuring

Goals and Methods

In the previous three sessions, clients were taught to modify two classes of cognitions that often precipitated drinking: alcohol-related thoughts, and thoughts about the expected positive consequences of drinking. In this session, clients were taught to modify a third class of thoughts that were functionally related to their alcohol use. If a person's behavior in a social-emotional situation results in self-derogatory, retaliatory, or guilt-related thoughts, then these thoughts can become a part of a chain leading to alcohol abuse. The purpose of session 9 was to teach clients to question the logic of these irrational thought patterns and to replace them with more "rational" thoughts. The procedure used was similar to that developed by Ellis (see, for example, Ellis & Harper, 1961). Clients were asked to write down a specific situation that had gotten them depressed (or angry, or anxious, or whatever) enough to feel like drinking. Below the description, they were to write out all the negative irrational thoughts that led to the conclusion that "a drink would help me." Following these irrational statements, clients were asked to write specific, constructive counterstatements. They were also asked to read each group of statements aloud and discuss how they felt after each one. For homework, clients were asked to repeat this procedure several times in various situations through the week.

Mr. and Mrs. J.

Once again, Mr. J. reported abstinence through the week, with his wife concurring. He had begun keeping track on his self-monitoring cards of how many days it had been since his last drink (96), and planned a celebration for his 100th day that week. Mrs. J. was quite enthusiastic about her husband's accomplishment. Both reported consistent sevens as a daily level of marital satisfaction.

Mr. J. also reported his usual level-three lunchtime urges, but also had a series of fours and fives on Friday evening. The J.s had attended a party that evening and Mr. J., fearing what his friends might say, had ordered nothing rather than asking for a nonalcoholic drink. This situation was used to teach rational thinking, and was outlined on the first irrational statements worksheet.

His irrational statements were:

1. Some of these people don't know I'm an alcoholic; if I order just tonic, everyone will know.
2. If they know I'm an alcoholic, they'll think I'm weak or strange.
3. If they think that, they won't talk to me or be friends with me, and that would be terrible.

He also listed four counterstatements:

1. If I order a non-alcoholic drink, I won't be so tempted to have alcohol.

2. These are my friends; it doesn't matter if they know I'm an alcoholic.

3. If someone thinks less of me or doesn't talk to me, that's too bad. They have a lot to learn about friendship.

4. Even if I order a tonic, they might not think I'm an alcoholic anyway.

This "rational" approach to thinking appealed strongly to Mr. J., and he asked for extra readings in the area. Over the next week he completed several worksheets, and expressed surprise about how much control over his fears this approach gave him.

Mr. and Mrs. N.

Mrs. N., on the other hand, had a great deal of difficulty learning and accepting this approach. For example, she chose a situation in which her son had made an obscene gesture toward her, and eventually developed her list:

1. He shouldn't be that way towards me.
2. I don't know why he hates me so much.
3. Maybe I should have a drink, then he'll be sorry.

It was quite difficult to get her to budge from the idea that her drinking would make her son sorry. "But he'll know it's his fault," she insisted.

Eventually, she was able to see that drinking would not help the situation at all. Mrs. N. still believed, however, that if she drank, it would be his responsibility, not hers. On the other hand, she felt more in control of her drinking, but on the one hand, she still believed that some situations and people could cause her to drink.

During the prior week, Mrs. N. reported one drinking incident, and the event went along with her notion that situations caused her drinking. She had been given a surprise party by some bowling friends. Someone handed her a beer, and she ended up drinking six. In the session, she felt embarrassed to discuss this incident, but pointed out that no matter how well she planned to avoid triggers, sometimes things "just happened." "I did keep myself from drinking the rest of the week," she said, "so I guess I'm learning."

Mrs. N. was also reporting fewer urges to drink because she was avoiding triggers so well. In addition, with Christmas coming, to help with the bills she had taken a temporary job selling jewelry to friends at home through "parties" and over the telephone. Thus, she could still be home to help care for her husband when he needed it. This job also kept her busy and in contact with other women much of the day. Thus, she said, she often went through the day without even thinking about drinking.

The marital satisfaction ratings for both the N.s continued at around 5. At the beginning of the session, when they briefly mentioned the jewelry business and the housework, Mr. N. said that he had been doing almost all the cooking and was helping Mrs. N. keep track of her accounts. She thought he was complaining and said, "Well, you don't have to do all that. That's not your job." "So what is my job now?" he asked.

Session 10: Planning Alternatives to Drinking

Goals and Methods

This session involved review and further practice of the irrational thinking techniques presented the week before. In addition, clients were taught, through role playing and covert reinforcement, some techniques for drink refusal (Foy, et al., 1976). Clients were taught that the offer of a drink could be discouraged both firmly and politely. "No" should be the first word of the refusal, followed by a request for an alternative beverage, as well as perhaps changing the subject. For example, the person could say, "No thank you, I have stopped drinking alcohol. In fact, I'd be pleased if you didn't ask me to have a drink. However, I would like some ginger ale. Would you get me a glass?"

Several typical refusal scenes were role-played in the session, and the clients were asked to practice these scenes covertly at least twice per day. In addition, they were asked to practice refusing a drink in "real life" over the next week, and to write down what happened.

Mr. and Mrs. J.

This session was a usual one for the J.s. Mr. J. had celebrated his 100th day of abstinence and was still going strong. He had done all his homework and more. In addition, Mr. J. learned the drink refusal technique quickly. Because he was skilled verbally, he was able to elaborate on several themes in the role playing, and seemed to respond very assertively to "pushers" (people who insist, for example, that "just one won't hurt you"). He planned a golf situation for his *in vivo* assertive refusal.

The J.s' marital satisfaction scores remained high and they spontaneously remarked at the beginning of the session that therapy had enhanced their marriage significantly. This was a rather interesting comment since it was clear that discussion of their marriage was deliberately avoided in the sessions.

Mr. and Mrs. N.

For Mrs. N., session 10 proved to be a turning point in treatment. She arrived early and weeping. "You don't know how much I want to stop drinking," she cried before the session began, "I try and I try, but it just won't work!"

The therapist immediately checked out Mrs. N.'s BAL (0.00 percent) and her drinking data cards. Mrs. N. was not intoxicated for the session, but had been drinking again. She had not had any urges or drinking incidents for four days after the session. Then, on the fifth day, she started drinking in response to her daughter buying some furniture for the new apartment. What was especially significant about this incident was that Mrs. N. made absolutely no attempt to use her new skills to stop herself from drinking. In fact, she had not done her homework at all.

"I just needed to drink," she said, "I was so depressed." On the back of each self-monitoring card was a long note to the therapist about how depressed she was and how "bad" her children were to her.

At this point, the therapist decided that since limit setting had helped once before, it was time for more. "Helen," the therapist said, "All I've heard from you in the past ten sessions is how you'd like to stop drinking, you want to stop drinking, you'll try to stop drinking—I've never once heard you say 'I have stopped drinking.' Instead, you hang on to every excuse in the book to need a drink. Well, I'm not fooled and I don't think you're fooled either. If you really want to stop drinking you know that you will stop—even if you have to stand on your head in a situation to keep from drinking. It's a waste of my time and your time to sit here each Tuesday and work at cross-purposes. I'm working to help you stop drinking and you're working to tell me why you should continue. Well, I'm not going to do this anymore. If you want to come back next week and you've done your homework and you haven't been drinking, then I'll see you. Until then, I've got other things to do today."

Mrs. N. sat in stunned silence for a few minutes, then Mr. N. stood up and began gathering his things. "Come on, Helen," he said. "She said to go home."

"But can I come back?" she cried.

"You know the conditions," the therapist said.

They left and the therapist spent a nervous week wondering if Mrs. N. would be back. The therapist had felt that the therapeutic relationship was strong enough to sustain the breech, but when Tuesday morning arrived and Mrs. N. had not called, the therapist was not sure what to anticipate.

Mr. and Mrs. N. arrived, however, at the right time, smiling and happy. "She's just like she was before when she stopped drinking!" (after her inpatient treatment) said Mr. N. "Nerves of steel—she's strong, she can do anything when she decides not to drink." It was the most enthusiasm he had ever shown toward his wife.

For her part, Mrs. N. was also quite enthusiastic. She had written on her card each day, "Kept my commitment." "You should have been firm with me before," she said to the therapist, "When someone is firm with me, I do things right."

She had also done her homework thoroughly and had reviewed and repeated some of the previous homework assignments. In the session, as planned, emphasis was placed on learning drink refusal skills. Mrs. N. initially had some difficulty thinking of a situation in which she needed to refuse a drink (since she usually just "helped herself"). The therapist suggested a "bowling night" situation and role-played that interaction with Mrs. N. Mrs. N. was quite enthusiastic, but unskilled in her initial refusals. For example, to the question, "What are you having, Helen?" she replied, "I'm not drinking and don't try to force me into it." After a few practice role-playing sessions, she replied, "I'd like a coke please; I think beer really messes up my bowling."

The other situation role-played in the session involved the party in which Mrs. N. had just been handed the beer. She role-played handing it back and saying, "No thanks, I'll have a coke instead." Thus, the session went quite well and Mrs. N. went home with a promise of continued abstinence from alcohol.

Sessions 11 and 12: Problem Solving and Assertion

Goals and Methods

All too often a problem drinker responds to a difficult situation with an aggressive or a passive response. The purpose of these two sessions was to help the client decide if a particular situation called for an assertive response (by using problem-solving techniques) and to develop an effective, assertive response (through role-playing in session). In these sessions, clients were to plan an assertive response to a situation, role-play their response with the therapist, and then actually perform the response *in vivo*. Also in these sessions, the therapist began a limited discussion of therapy termination and maintenance of sobriety.

Mr. and Mrs. J.

Therapy was beginning to "wind down" for the J.s at this point. Mr. J. enjoyed the assertion training and completed all his assignments, including being more assertive with his boss in regard to the company's treatment of a particular customer. He continued his abstinence and reported now having only one to two mild urges per day. By now, he had told most of his friends about his alcohol problems, and had no qualms about ordering nonalcoholic drinks in any situation. He reported that when he paid attention to some of his friends' and customers' drinking habits, he noticed that they occasionally ordered nonalcoholic drinks also. "I just wasn't aware of it before," he said, "I just assumed everyone drank in all situations."

Mr. and Mrs. J. continued to report high levels of marital satisfaction and felt confident that even without continued treatment, Mr. J. would remain sober.

Mr. and Mrs. N.

Mrs. N. continued to remain abstinent during these two weeks. During that time her weight dropped by fifteen pounds and her affect noticeably brightened. Between the 11th and 12th sessions she actually helped her daughter move to an apartment. "Actually, I've discovered that I like it," she smiled. "Maybe it's about time for Richard [her son] to move out too."

Mrs. N. was also surprisingly adept at being assertive and used her skills to deal effectively with a jewelry customer who had not paid for an order. Mr. N. continued to be enthusiastic about her abstinence and remarked in one session, "Now she's getting back to being the lady I married."

Mrs. N. kept doing her homework thoroughly, and writing on the back of each card at the end of the day, "I kept my commitment." She also continued to read her lists of the negative consequences of drinking and the positive consequences of sobriety. "They help me the best," she said, "but you [the therapist] also helped by being firm with me."

The only concern during these sessions was her reluctance to discuss termination. She didn't want to think about leaving, or about the possibility of having a slip. The therapist's suggestion that "you'll need to know how to overcome a slip" was lost on her. "I just won't have a slip," she said.

Sessions 13 and 14: Relaxation

Goals and Methods

These two sessions were fairly straightforward in purpose. An oft-cited reason for drinking is "to relax," so the purpose of these sessions was to give clients an alternative method of relaxing. Therefore, in session 13, clients were taught deep muscle relaxation (Jacobson, 1938) and were asked to practice twice per day over the next week. In session 14, relaxation via the "letting go" method was taught. Since spouses were not to be taught any new skills, they were asked to leave the room during the relaxation induction in these two sessions. During that time, they sat in the waiting room and read about relaxation. For homework, clients were asked to practice and record their relaxation twice a day and to attempt to relax in some difficult (formerly urge-triggering) situation.

Mr. and Mrs. J.

This was the first time that Mr. J. did not thoroughly complete a homework assignment. He found relaxation quite difficult, and though he practiced for two or three days after the first relaxation training session, he eventually stopped. He said that he wasn't sure if he should call the therapist or what to do. He did do some other homework that week (some self-contracting for being assertive at work) and said he hoped that the other homework would be a good substitute.

"It's good that you're practicing your new skills," the therapist agreed. "But let's try to get some relaxation training under your belt before you conclude that you can't do it." Discussion of Mr. J.'s relaxation practice suggested that the problem was a common one for those attempting to learn to relax for the first time: he was trying too hard. The more he worked to relax, the more tense he became.

Thus, the therapist taught Mr. J. a new method of relaxing ("letting go" rather than tensing and relaxing muscles) and also left him with the paradoxical message: "The first few days you will be *more* tense after practice, but keep going—after that you'll begin to feel better if you keep practicing twice a day." The intention of this statement was to help Mr. J. worry less about how well he was relaxing. Between the 14th and 15th sessions, Mr. J. did relax twice per day and, though not proficient, became more attracted to the idea.

Mr. and Mrs. J. both reported that he continued to remain abstinent to have only occasional mild urges to drink. By now, Mr. J. was almost bragging about his success to friends and basking in the glory of several months of abstinence. In fact, he was beginning to enjoy his new, dashing image among friends and co-workers as the man who conquered his alcohol problem. He found all this attention from others quite reinforcing and added it to his list of positive consequences of sobriety.

Mr. and Mrs. N.

Sessions 13 and 14 were uneventful for Mrs. N. She continued to be abstinent, by both her own and her husband's report. She had few urges to drink even in the face of various legal problems with her son and an illness that left her husband bedridden for a few days. She lost weight, her affect was brighter and her at-home jewelry sales continued to flourish. "I'm making extra money," she said, "so maybe I can just hire someone to come in and clean." Best of all, she felt, was that she had regained a sense of humor that the therapist didn't know she had. "I haven't laughed so hard in years," said Mrs. N. during the 14th session. "I guess I was so busy being depressed before, I never got the joke."

Relaxation was surprisingly easy for Mrs. N. to learn. She was quite suggestible in the therapist's office (this is *not* surprising) and became deeply relaxed right away. She set aside time at home each day and demanded that Mr. N. and her son not disturb her then. She told them both that she was meditating and told the therapist that she liked it "better than the pills I used to take." It seemed that her control of the situation was what appealed to her most.

Mr. N., for his part, kept being enthusiastically supportive. He kept emphasizing how much he liked her "old self."

Control of agenda in the sessions remained somewhat of an issue. Mrs. N., in the 13th session, attempted to spend a great deal of time on her anger toward her son, and then got into an argument with her husband about the son's latest arrest. The therapist eventually regained some direction in the session by pointing out that noon was fast approaching and they still had to practice relaxation. Some suggestions were made to help Mrs. N. deal more assertively with her son and then the relaxation skills were taught. (The session, as promised, ended at noon.)

For the most part, Mrs. N. showed tremendous, if somewhat tenuous, improvement since she had stopped drinking. Their 14th session was postponed a week (Mr. N.'s illness), so by the 14th session Mrs. N. had been abstinent about five weeks.

Session 15: Maintenance Planning

Goals and Methods

The title of this session is self-explanatory. The entire course of therapy was examined with each client and the array of new skills was emphasized. Clients were encouraged to continue to practice these skills on a regular basis, to reread the handout materials often and to remain abstinent. Material on how to deal with slips was discussed and clients were asked to be honest with the research assistant about their slips in follow-up for the sake of science and future alcohol treatment. Goodbyes and congratulations were said at the end, and follow-up appointments were made.

Mr. and Mrs. J.

The material on slips was of special interest to the J.s. Mrs. J. had, one afternnon at lunch, almost ordered a gin and tonic—just to see what it tasted like. "I was really close to having a slip," he said, "I guess I got a little too cocky."

He had gone over his "positive and negative" lists—by now

memorized—and had stopped himself in time. Mr. J. felt the lists and the self-management plans would be most important to his continued maintenance of abstinence.

Both the J.s expressed a great deal of hope for his continued progress and repeated through the last session how much they had liked therapy. Neither had been in treatment before and had decided that it had been a positive experience both for their marriage and for his drinking. Mrs. J. shed some tears at the goodbyes and both said they would "keep in touch."

Mr. and Mrs. N.

Mrs. N. left treatment with six weeks of abstinence under her belt. "I've never felt better—I'm really in control of myself now," she said. Mr. N. agreed heartily. However, Mrs. N. also continued to attribute her success to the therapist. "You should have been firm with me from the beginning," she repeated. "I need to be *told* what to do sometimes."

Because of this expressed desire for limit setting, the therapist encouraged Mrs. N. to consider joining AA. "I already checked that out last week," Mrs. N. replied, "I know a meeting right after my bowling on Wednesday night—maybe I'll go."

The therapist encouraged Mrs. N. to become involved and to seek out an AA sponsor as a means to maintain her commitment to abstinence. However, the therapist also reinforced the idea that the ultimate responsibility for her abstinence from alcohol was on Mrs. N.'s shoulders. "Circumstances and people in your life do not cause you to drink," the therapist reminded her. "In fact some people have found it useful, when the situation looks bad, to contemplate how much *worse* it could be if they were still drinking."

The therapist also reintroduced the subject of slips. What could Mrs. N. do if she, through a momentary lapse, were to drink again? Mrs. N. was very uneasy with this subject. "If you mention slipping," she said, "it's just like in the beginning of treatment when you let me get away with some drinking." Yet again, Mrs. N. was assuming that someone else was responsible for her drinking.

After the therapist pointed out that the commitment to sobriety was in Mrs. N.'s control, an analogy between "slip" discussions and fire drills was made. "We'd all be happy if we never had a fire," said the therapist. "But if you have a fire, you'd better know how to get out of the building fast. You know, you say talking about slips makes it sound like you're planning to drink, but that's about the same as saying that when you have a fire drill, you're planning to start a fire."

Mrs. N. agreed to listen to suggestions about what to do in case of a slip, "but I won't need them," she said. The most important understanding that can come from the discussion of slips is that a lapse in abstinence can—and should—be stopped. "It is irrational to assume that, because you've had one drink, you're doomed to have more," the therapist told Mrs. N. "For example, if you're at a bowling night party and you end up having a beer, that doesn't have to lead to the conclusion—'Well, I've blown my abstinence, I guess I'm just going to keep drinking after all.' Granted, you need to take some positive action and work hard to regain your sobriety, but you *can* do it." Mrs. N. seemed to understand, but continued to deny that slips would be a problem for her.

Discussion of maintenance centered on Mrs. N.'s homework assignments. She agreed to keep practicing her new skills, especially the assertion, rational thinking, and relaxation techniques and to review her handout literature from time to time. She felt that the monthly follow-up phone calls from the research assistant would also serve as reminders and reinforcements for continued abstinence (Sobell & Sobell, 1981). Mrs. N. said that she felt ready to leave and thought she could continue to do well. Therapist and clients parted amicably with handshakes all around.

POSTTREATMENT ASSESSMENT

Drinking Measurements During and After Treatment

Mr. and Mrs. J.

Most of the data about drinking and urges to drink during treatment were discussed above. Overall, most noticeable is the consistency of his urge-intensity ratings. Mr. J. did not drink during treatment, and these reports of abstinence are corroborated by his posttreatment liver function tests (within normal limits). Also, Mr. J. experienced roughly the same number and intensity level of urges from week to week.

Mr. J. completed treatment in November 1981, and is currently participating in monthly follow-ups. He and his wife both report that he has continued to refrain from drinking and he is continuing to practice his new skills. The assertion training, he feels, has helped him considerably at work and he feels more respected by his colleagues. He reports some occasional periods of depression, but for the most part he feels cheerful and has a renewed interest in life and his activities.

Mr. and Mrs. N.

Mrs. N.'s drinking and urge to drink data were discussed at length above in the treatment section. Most notable is that as drinking stopped (after the 10th session), the frequency and intensity ratings of the urges also dropped off.

Mrs. N. also completed treatment in mid-November 1981, and has now gone through the entire Thanksgiving, Christmas, and New Year's season without a drink. In addition, her weight has gone down (30 lbs.) and her GGTP when last tested was at 37 (in contrast to the beginning of treatment when she was at 168; normal range is 0–35). She also reports occasional periods of depression, mostly in connection with her menstrual cycle, but feels that she can cope with these now. "The depression doesn't last as long since I'm not drinking," she says. However, she also reports that she has not joined AA.

The N.s as a couple have continued to have financial problems and Mr. N.'s health is deteriorating slowly. Their daughter has begun to come over to the house sometimes to stay with him while Mrs. N. goes out. Their son has continued to have legal problems, but did recently start work in an auto repair shop.

Marital Measures During and After Treatment

Although marital interventions were deliberately avoided during treatment, change measures are of interest since the marital problems of both couples seemed to be associated with their drinking. Measures of marital functioning included within-treatment daily ratings of marital satisfaction (scale of 1–7, seven being "the greatest ever"), and pre-posttreatment administrations of the Locke-Wallace Marital Adjustment Test and the Areas of Change

Questionnaire. Details of pretreatment data on the questionnaires
were already presented for each couple. Within- and posttreatment
data are presented next.

Mr. and Mrs. J.

The J.s' marital satisfaction ratings during treatment were consistently sevens. Occasionally during therapy either Mr. or Mrs.
J. remarked about their enjoyment of each other or their satisfaction
with their marriage. Because of the ceiling effect (initial highest
ratings), no improvement could be seen on these scores through
treatment, but both the J.s said that their marriage was enhanced
by participation in treatment.

Immediately posttreatment, Mr. and Mrs. J. obtained Locke-
Wallace scores of 120 and 130 respectively. These scores were com-
parable to those before treatment (perhaps a little increased). On
the Areas of Change Questionnaire their responses suggested some
minimal conflict in regard to sexual relations (both wanted to have
sex "slightly more often"), sharing the events of the day (she
wanted more from him), and expressing feelings (he wanted her
to express more). Otherwise, they appeared in agreement on most
issues. Finally, in rating the changes in their marriage during the
months of treatment, both noted a positive change in the number
of arguments they had with each other ("a lot fewer").

Mr. and Mrs. N.

The marital changes seen with the N.s were more varied and
difficult to interpret. Mr. N.'s ratings during treatment never varied. He consistently rated his satisfaction at 5 on the 1–7 scale. Mrs.
N.'s scores ranged between 3 and 6. Specific drinking days were
usually given low satisfaction ratings (i.e., drinking and marital
satisfaction seemed related). For the most part, however, Mrs. N.'s
average weekly rating was about 5. Between sessions 4 and 5 (the
week the N.s' daughter decided to move out), Mrs. N.'s average
rating was 4. The average rating then went back up to 5.

The ratings remained at this level until after the tenth session
(confrontation with the therapist and Mrs. N.'s commitment to
abstinence). Her average weekly ratings then began to decrease
slowly until they hit 4.0 in the last two weeks of treatment. Thus,
total abstinence seemed associated with a slight increase in her
marital dissatisfaction.

One would predict from these daily data that the global measures would show that Mrs. N. felt that her marriage got worse during treatment, while Mr. N. felt it stayed the same. This turned out to be a wrong prediction: Mrs. N.'s Locke-Wallace score rose by a large 51 points (64 to 115). She felt that their marriage had vastly improved. She reported much less conflict about sexual relations and less conflict about the children and housework (although they did still experience conflict in these areas). Mr. N., for his part, scored somewhat lower on the Locke-Wallace (102 pretreatment; 89 posttreatment). He listed housework, the children, and sexual relations as areas of conflict (in the pretreatment phase, Mr. N. had only seen their children as an area of disagreement).

The results of the Areas of Change Questionnaire mirrored those of the Locke-Wallace. Both agreed they wanted fewer arguments about the children and housework. Both agreed they wanted sex more often.

Since the marital issues could not be specifically addressed or discussed by the therapist, only educated guesses can be made about the course of the N.s' marriage. It seems possible that after Mrs. N. stopped drinking, she slowly began to communicate more of her desires, wants, and needs to her husband. This communication may have led initially to some open conflicts and unhappiness (note her lowered satisfaction ratings) but at the same time, Mr. N. became aware of her feelings for the first time. Thus, at the end of treatment, he saw their areas of conflict more clearly, while she, having begun to satisfy some desires, saw their marriage as improved. This interpretation may be wrong, but because of the nature of the research group, it is the best we can surmise.

PROGNOSIS?

So, where do the N.s and the J.s go from here? At the time of this writing, both couples' marriages look stronger, and the problem drinking has stopped. In regard to the latter, though, a prediction for the future is difficult to make. Mr. J. is only now reaching his sixth month of abstinence. Mrs. N. has been abstinent for about ten weeks. These results suggest a hopeful prognosis, but only time will tell.

Mr. J.'s therapy course went fairly smoothly. Perhaps because of his previously moderate level of drinking, his good support system, and his high level of motivation, he would have done well in any of the three experimental groups. Since Mrs. N. had so much difficulty, however, some considerations should be given to what benefit she could have derived from different treatment. For example, since she had had so few weeks of abstinence before she left treatment, scheduling two to three "booster" sessions might have helped to allow Mrs. N. more time to learn her skills. It is difficult to say, however, whether or not she would have done better with a more spouse-involved treatment. Perhaps dealing early with some of the marital problems would have been helpful, but considering how difficult it was to keep Mrs. N. "on target" with one problem at a time, it might actually have hindered treatment of the alcohol problem.

For all of their differences in therapy behavior, some interesting commonalities emerge when considering Mrs. N. and Mr. J. The most striking is how much the "commitment" of abstinence changed their drinking habits. Both agreed that therapy was helpful in strengthening this commitment, but both saw the commitment as the most important factor in avoiding alcohol in the future.

Mr. J.'s course may be smoother than Mrs. N.'s. His life has settled back down into a predictable and "traditional" course that both the J.s profess to like very much. In addition, since he made the "commitment" before treatment even began, he has already gone through a fair number of situations without drinking. This repeated practice is important when one is learning a new set of skills.

In their last session, the J.s were asked to make a rating of how certain they were that he could remain abstinent in various situations. Mr. J. was 80 percent certain that he could remain totally abstinent in the future and felt that the only time he'd be really tempted to drink was in social situations in which he wanted to "feel more comfortable." This seemed a realistic point of view. Mrs. J. reported that she was 100 percent confident that he would remain abstinent. She agreed that he might be tempted, but believed that he wouldn't give in, in uncomfortable social situations.

Mrs. N.'s course may be more difficult. She still has many conflicts and problems in her life (e.g., financial, son's legal problems), and her husband is slowly losing his health. Eventually, he will need intensive nursing care. Since Mrs. N. is so dependent upon others for strength, it is unclear how she will react to the increased troubles of her husband. It is to be hoped that by that time she will have developed solid enough coping skills to continue without alcohol.

In addition, Mrs. N. has not been abstinent for very long. She just may not have learned enough from therapy to maintain her abstinence.

On the other hand, Mrs. N. has noted a considerable number of positive changes for herself as a result of abstinence. She feels happier and stronger; she has lost weight and her liver function has improved; she feels her marriage has improved and her husband is giving her more support. Because of Mrs. N.'s prior complaints of depression, the therapist gave some consideration to a referral for the N.s at the end of treatment. However, the N.s both said that they did not want further treatment. Mrs. N.'s depression had lifted quickly following cessation of drinking and her increasing ability to cope with her family and financial situation. Both the N.s reported that during her previous eighteen months of abstinence, Mrs. N. had been reasonably cheerful and had evidenced no problems with daily functioning. Therefore, the therapist agreed to hold off on a referral, but said she would provide one if the N.s called back.

The final self-efficacy measure from the N.s suggested that both had a high level of confidence that Mrs. N. will remain abstinent in the future. She was 100 percent confident, while he was about 90 percent confident. Both felt that her only area of difficulty might be if she gets into a severely depressed mood.

CONCLUSIONS AND COMMENTS

The purpose of this chapter was to present in detail two contrasting case histories involving problem-drinking treatment with a couple. In both cases the spouse was asked to participate as an observer only, and treatment was directed at the problem drinker. Nevertheless, variations within this treatment package produced some profound and we hope long-lasting changes for the couples in terms of the drinking and their marriages.

Follow-up with these two couples plus the forty-three other couples in the research project will provide interesting data about how best to involve the spouse in the treatment of problem drinking. However, the history of each couple in their own right provides an interesting and informative perspective on spouse involvement in treatment.

REFERENCES

Bandura, A., Adams, N., & Beyer, J. Cognitive processes mediating behavior change. *Journal of Personality and Social Psychology*, 1977, **38**, 125–139.

Birchler, G. & Webb, L. Discriminating interaction behaviors in happy and unhappy marriages. *Journal of Consulting and Clinical Psychology*, 1977, **45**, 494–495.

Cautela, J. Covert reinforcement. *Behavior Therapy*, 1970, **1**, 33–50.

Ellis, A. & Harper, R. *A guide to rational living.* Hollywood, Calif.: Wilshire, 1961.

Folstein, M., Folstein, S., & McHugh, P. "Mini-mental state": A practical method for grading the cognitive state of patients for the clinician. *Journal of Psychiatric Research*, 1975, **12**, 189–198.

Foy, D.; Miller, P.; Eisler, R.; & O'Toole, D. Social skills training to teach alcoholics to refuse drinks effectively. *Journal of Studies on Alcohol*, 1976, **37**, 1,340–1,345.

Jacobson, E. *Progressive relaxation.* Chicago: University of Chicago Press, 1938.

Locke, H. & Wallace, K. Short marital adjustment and prediction tests: Their reliability and validity. *Marriage and Family Living*, 1959, **21**, 251–255.

McCrady, B. Conjoint behavioral treatment of an alcoholic and his spouse: The case of Mr. and Mrs. D. In P. Nathan & W. Hay (Eds.), *Clinical case studies in behavioral treatment of alcoholism.* In press.

Miller, P. *Behavioral treatment of alcoholism.* New York: Pergamon Press, 1976.

Paolino, T. & McCrady, B. *The alcoholic marriage: Alternative perspectives.* New York: Grune & Stratton, 1977.

Selzer, M. The Michigan Alcoholism Screening Test: The quest for a new diagnostic instrument. *American Journal of Psychiatry*, 1971, **127**, 1,653–1,658.

Sobell, L. & Sobell, M. Frequent follow up as data gathering and continued care with alcoholics. *The International Journal of Addictions*, 1981, **16**, 1,077–1,086.

Sobell, M.; Maisto, S.; Sobell, L.; Cooper, A.; Cooper, T.; & Sanders, B. Developing a prototype for evaluating alcohol treatment effectiveness. In L. Sobell, M. Sobell, & E. Ward (Eds.), *Evaluating alcohol and drug abuse treatment effectiveness: recent advances.* New York: Pergamon Press, 1980.

Sobell, M. & Sobell, L. *Behavioral treatment of alcohol problems: Individualized therapy and controlled drinking.* New York: Plenum, 1978.

Wing, J., Cooper, J, & Sartorius, N. *Measurement and classification of psychiatric symptoms.* New York: Cambridge University Press, 1974.

Zitter, R. & McCrady, B. The Drinking Patterns Questionnaire. Unpublished questionnaire, 1979.

3

Family, Family on the Run, Who is the Fastest and the Most Fun?

Pauline Kaufmann,M.S.W., C.S.W.

AN UNWANTED CALL

I had one of those terrible days. I felt pressured, pushed, and wilted. Finally the day was over, and then the telephone rang.

"Frank told me to call you—I'm going crazy." My first impulse was to say, "Now there are two of us!" But I managed a "What's up?"

She, Joanne, had just wrecked her boyfriend's apartment; she couldn't stop crying and she was just around the corner—could she see me?

The voice was childlike, the desperation real, and I lactate easily. I invited her to come up. Within minutes she was in the office. A pale, tall, young woman with a tear-stained face. Her pinaforelike dress slightly awry and her stance sweet, compliant, and piteous. As she sat down she volunteered the following information rapidly and nonstop. She was twenty-six, a writer, and divorced. Recently she started drinking. She doesn't think she has a drinking problem. She was worried that she couldn't remember wrecking her boyfriend's furniture. He described it to her. She was worried about the memory loss. Everything else was okay.

Joanne had gone to a neurologist. The findings were negative but the occasional incidents of memory loss recurred. She described a number of incidents, all of them happened when she was out partying and drinking. I tentatively labeled them blackouts. She accepted this, and questioned by me, gave the following family information.

CAST OF CHARACTERS AND FAMILY SCRIPT

She described a "very close family." Mother, father, and the five children, all live home, all of them are talented, and all work in theater or in theater-related jobs. They have a twenty-room house, four floors, and a swimming pool in the basement. An elevator was installed when their mother, Liz, broke her back. Hank, the father, has five dogs and a driver who lives in the house. The driver, Frank, also cooks and cleans. They have two cars, a Jaguar and a Bentley.

Mother used to be a singer in a band. She is very beautiful but has become very heavy. She has been using drugs for pain and sleeping ever since she broke her back, seven years ago. She runs an antique shop.

Hank produces film commercials. He is under constant pressure and will have two or three cocktails at lunch to relax. He likes Joanne to have lunch with him. Over their cocktails he confides in her and finds this very helpful. Joanne is a scriptwriter. Between outside assignments she writes the scripts for Hank's commercials. Teddy, their brother, does the camera work. He is a "brilliant cameraman."

Willa is the most troublesome of the siblings. She had been married for four years. She and her husband drank heavily and used cocaine, quaaludes, and marijuana. Three years ago when Willa could not be reached on the telephone, Liz and Hank became very anxious. They broke into her apartment and found her semi-comatose. She was rushed to the hospital where she was detoxed. After her release, the family insisted she get a divorce and come back home.

Joanne had been married for a year when she was twenty. She had eloped with a Catholic boy. When her family insisted that he convert to Judaism and he refused, Joanne got a divorce. He was a heavy drinker but only drank beer.

Cathy is a singer and an actress. She is unemployed. She did occasional acting jobs for Hank's commercials. She was the only one who could ease her mother's back pains. She frequently massaged Liz's back and gave her pain medication. Her bedroom adjoined Liz's. Hank slept on another floor. Cathy frequently slept in her mother's bed when mother's pain was unbearable. Mother and she would share a bottle of wine when either one could not sleep.

Bobby was straight, he was beautiful and bright. He had just entered college. Sometimes he would smoke pot or use quaaludes when he went out, because he was shy.

I had been on a nonstop family trip for over an hour. Joanne's tears had long since stopped and she was exhilarated as she described her "exciting talented family."

She concluded by saying, "You can see that we are a very close, caring family." I agreed that they were very close and suggested that she ask her entire family to come in since they must be concerned about her blackouts.

We set a time for the following week. Joanne volunteered that she would call me if she had difficulty getting the family together.

Extricating The Therapist

I sat down with a drawing pad and began doodling and making charts. Finally, I came up with some family patterns that began to make sense out of dogs, swimming pool, twenty rooms, alcohol, quaaludes, cocaine, pot, cars, and Frank, the driver and cook. Charting gave the material a quasi-simplicity and order that made it possible for me to put it aside and get ready for bed.

The number five kept plaguing me—five children, five dogs; clusters were beginning to form—Mother, Cathy, Bobby, Teddy, Father, Joanne, Willa, Frank the driver. (see Figure 3-2). And then there were the five dogs. In this family everything had to be even. Mother had three children on her side, father had two and Frank. The explicit battlefield was the five dogs, the implicit one, the children, was denied.

Before I could solve the entire situation, I fell asleep.

Session 2: Who Does What to Whom?

The entire family arrived, laughing and talking. The seating arrangement gave a clear picture of the family alliances.

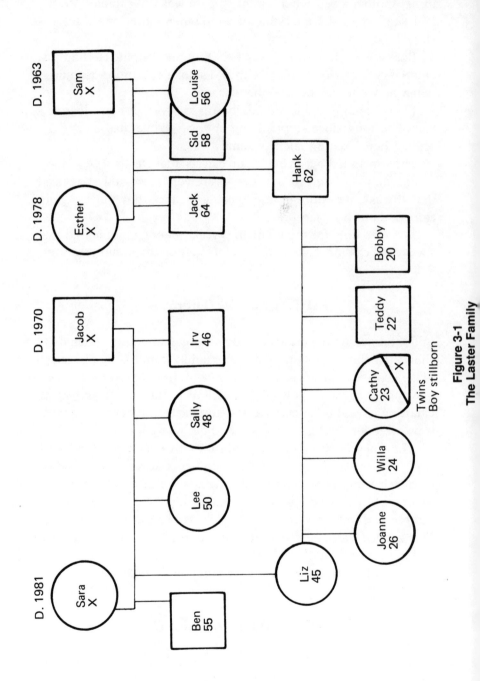

**Figure 3-1
The Laster Family**

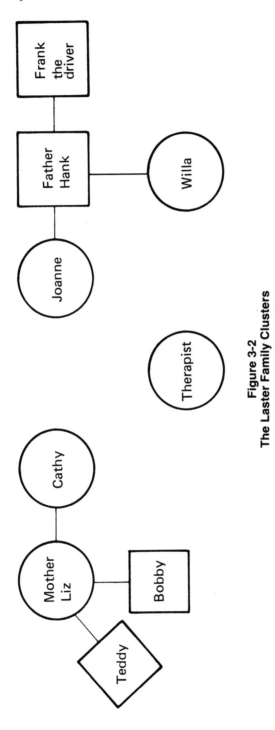

Figure 3-2
The Laster Family Clusters

Liz took charge, graciously and competently. She thanked me for seeing Joanne. They were worried about her memory loss, but felt that it was not serious.

I looked puzzled and asked, "Her blackouts?" Mother continued. Her own illness had been very hard on the family. She had been bedridden for over a year with excruciating pain. Only her family's ministrations pulled her through. To this day Cathy was the only one who could ease her pain.

Therapist: What about Hank?

Mother: He's a dear, but he's very overworked and tired.

Willa: (who had been sitting with her head down) And cranky and mean.

Joanne: Lay off Willa, you know how hard he works.

Teddy: Let's not start that again.

Bobby: Dad's all right, just a little tense.

(Cathy moved closer to her mother and remained silent.)

Therapist: Let's get back to who helps you when you're in pain. Hank, what about you?

Hank: She won't let me touch her. Cathy is the only one who can help—sometimes Teddy can. My wife's pain is so intense that I moved into another room so as not to disturb her. Cathy sleeps with her when she really hurts.

Therapist: There seems to be a great deal of pain and tension all over the family. Liz's back, Hank's tension, Cathy's worry over mother, Willa's not belonging, Joanne's blackouts. Everyone has tried alcohol and pills and that helps for a short time. I'm concerned that if we deal with Joanne's blackouts it will throw the rest of the family out of gear.

The therapist reframes the problem as a family problem. A covert suggestion is made that Joanne's drinking serves to maintain the family homeostasis.

Willa and Joanne in the dialogue that follows seem to have accepted the reframing. Hank holds on to the structure of Joanne as the identified patient.

In setting up the next session for "the heads of the family," the therapist has started the restructuring and at the same time has taken the identified patient off the "hot seat."

Liz: That's crazy. Joanne's memory loss has nothing to do with us.

Willa: Yeah, how about her three cocktails with Daddy?

Joanne: And how about Cathy's bottle of wine with Mommy every night?

Therapist: I suggest that for the time being you don't change anything. I want to think about how best to proceed. For the next appointment, I'd like to see Liz and Hank alone.

Hank: How about Joanne's blackouts? (the first time this word has been used by the family.)

Therapist: I know you're concerned but let's start with the heads of the family.

Session 3: Over and Over and Over Again

The couple arrived, Liz first, followed by Hank some ten minutes late. Liz greeted him by asking if he had been with a slow lunch drinker. Hank ignored this.

I asked about their families of origin, starting with Hank (see Figure 3-3). Hank was the second oldest of four children.

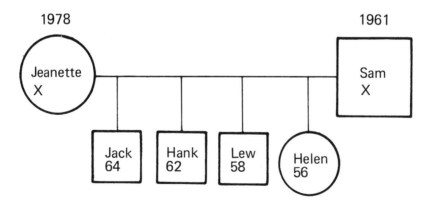

Figure 3-3
Hank Laster's Family of Origin

Jack was a very successful lawyer, married, fathered two kids, both married and doing well. He was his father's favorite. Lew was kind of invisible. He was an accountant, made a living, and was quiet. He had one daughter, a bookkeeper. Helen, as the only girl, was Momma's child, a nice kid, married to a loser. Never was able to have any kids.

Hank was considered a troublemaker like his grandfather Henry. Sam, Hank's father, beat him routinely as the only way to control him. He was frequently told by Sam that he would kill him before he saw him become a drunk and a gambler like his own father. His mother was ineffectual and could not or would not interfere.

When I asked why Hank had accepted the script his father had written for him, Hank looked startled, paused momentarily, and said that Sam was a bastard. But he sure fooled him. He drank occasionally, but he was successful. He made money, had an estate, a swimming pool, and supported everyone in his family.

Hank's role in his family of origin was overdetermined. Named after his grandfather, the hypnotic suggestion frequently repeated, was that he was becoming just like Henry.

The therapist's intervention counters this by suggesting that Hank can reject his father's script. In doing this she legitimizes Hank's anger at his father.

Liz recounted the following about her family. Liz was the second oldest of five children. Her father had died in 1967 and her mother in 1981 (see Figure 3-4).

Morris never married, lived with his mother until her death. He was a sweet guy but a little weird. Liz was both the mother's and the father's favorite. Mother was really the head of the family. It was she who decided that Morris needed to stay home so that she could take care of him. There was nothing wrong with him, he just never grew up. Both Eve and Liz married when they were eighteen. Mother kind of picked their husbands. Don went into his father's plumbing business and ran it. Sid had a bad stutter. The family was not very close except for Liz and her mother. They fought frequently but loved each other. Liz learned how to keep her mother out of her "business."

When asked if any one in her family drank, she said there was some talk of Eve having a drinking problem but her ulcers cured her of this.

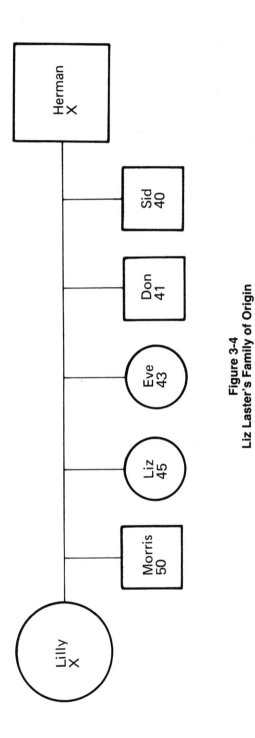

Figure 3-4
Liz Laster's Family of Origin

Therapist: In Hank's family, grandfather drank excessively. In Liz's family, sister Eve drank excessively. What about your present family?

Liz: I don't mind Hank's drinking. I mind his making Joanne part of these "luncheons."

Hank: (with anger) So, I have Joanne and you have Cathy for your midnight ritual.

Liz: It gets lonely in this house and Hank you come home and take a nap. When I go to sleep you're in the swimming pool. Cathy is the only one I have.

Hank: Come off it Liz—every time I come near you, you're in pain. How many times do you think I'll take being turned down?

Therapist: You both seem to have reached an agreement. Liz talks and drinks wine with Cathy to alleviate her pain and loneliness. Hank shares his cocktails, lunch, and tensions with Joanne. Seems pretty even to me.

Liz: Except for Joanne's blackouts.

I told Liz and Hank that I would see Joanne next week. I would see the entire family later that same week. In the meantime, I thought it would be a mistake to make any major changes.

The restructuring continues. The parents had been seen as a couple and now Joanne is separated out to deal with her relationship with Cliff.

Session 4: My Father Loved Me But—

Joanne came in looking attractive and well groomed. She began talking and laughing nervously. She talked about her career, the prospects she had, the possibility of going to Los Angeles. When I asked her about the blackouts, she began to cry.

That only happened when she spent the night with Cliff. The only way they could make love was when they drank. Then they were very tender with each other. Sex was kind of haphazard. The best part was the holding and kissing. Cliff came fast and sometimes couldn't get hard. But that was all right. Sometimes he didn't even try. She told him that the stroking and kissing were more important.

As she said this she began to cry. I encouraged her to keep talking. Between sobs she told me that when she was little, Hank used to have her massage his back when he came out of the pool. She didn't like to do this because he had his hands between his legs and he moved up and down. He didn't even know she was there and he smelled of whiskey. She knows now that he was masturbating. When she objected to masssaging him, her mother encouraged her to continue by saying how hard Daddy worked and how important it was that Joanne be kind to him.

Somewhere around the age of fourteen Joanne managed to be asleep or out when her father came home. She wasn't angry at him. He was so tired and lonely. She was angry at her mother for telling her to "be kind to him."

Joanne was very frightened of her loss of control in Cliff's house. Did I think the drinking did this? We talked about the effect of alcohol and suggested that she might attend an AA meeting and get some more information. She had the usual misgivings: they were all "bowery bums; not people like herself; certainly few women, except old whores." I gave her the address of a meeting where I knew she would not be too uncomfortable. She was hesitant and I ended by saying that I knew she was very uneasy and that she would survive if she didn't go.

Session 5: The Three Graces

Willa, Cathy, and Joanne came, Bobby was away at school. Teddy refused to come. It was not his problem. During the week he had moved in with his girlfriend and wanted no part of the family problems.

Cathy: Joanne has gotten religion. All she talks about is AA. She has all of us as drunks. Shit, she can't even make it as a drunk without the family.

Joanne: Lay off, Cathy. I'm going because I feel better. You do what you have to do.

Willa: One down and one to go.

Therapist: (repeating the phrase) One to go?

Willa: Sure, there's always Cathy.

Therapist: Cathy?
(Joanne bursts out crying.)
Willa: I'm sorry Joanne. It's me. I'm scared.
(Joanne puts her arm around Willa. Cathy moves further away.)
Therapist: Cathy, you seem to be out of it.
Cathy: I'm not interested in this shit. Willa always gets into the act.
Therapist: If Willa gets in, you get out?
Joanne: Come on Cathy. You know Willa is always out. If Willa comes with me that doesn't mean you and I aren't close.
Therapist: Three's a difficult number; it breaks up badly.
Cathy: Willa, I'm feeling lousy—it's not you. Suddenly our great family is not so great. Hell, it's one big mess.

Cathy's statement indicates that the old homeostasis is no longer operative. The three daughters are experiencing different degrees of stress. Coalitions are formed and reformed in an attempt to create a new homeostasis.

Session 6: The Fragmented Lens

Liz arrived with Cathy, followed by Willa; Joanne and Hank arrived separately.

Liz: A lot has happened. Willa has moved out to an apartment in Manhattan that we keep for our business associates.
Therapist: (to Willa) How did that come about?
Willa: I seemed to be in the middle of everyone—I wanted my own middle. I've gotten a couple of writing jobs that will pay for groceries. Besides I can't bring a guy home to this zoo.
Hank: All right Willa shut up.
Liz: And now Joanne wants to move back to her old apartment in the city.
Hank: It's another apartment that I pay rent on for out-of-town business associates.
Cathy: And his little secretaries.
Joanne: All right Cathy you're not helping.
Therapist: Joanne you're in a terrible position.

Joanne: (looking startled) You mean taking sides?

Therapist: You're in the middle. Is that where you want to be? (Joanne moves closer to Cathy.)

Liz: Everything is happening too fast.

Therapist: Let's see if we can slow it down. These changes are too fast for comfort. I don't think you can maintain them. Bobby's at school. Teddy's at his girlfriend's. Willa's moved out, and now Joanne.

Hank: Well, Joanne's still in the house.

Joanne: Dad, don't do that.

Hank: Your mother needs you.

Therapist: And you?

Hank: Is it because of me? Listen, Joanne, stay—I wasn't drunk at lunch. You don't have to have lunch with me.

(Hank's voice is beseeching and he has tears in his eyes. Joanne looks at Hank and then at her mother.)

Liz: Joanne, please stay.

Joanne: (looking at her mother) I'll see both of you but I want my own place.

The restructuring is going too fast. The family needs support as they struggle with pathological alliances. Willa is on her own, Liz's pleading with Joanne to stay is motivated by her fear of having to examine her relationship with Hank if Joanne leaves.

Therapist: I think that Joanne's moving out is her way of trying to keep her mother and father together.

The next day there was a call from Cathy. She asked to see me.

Session 7: The Lonely Runner

Cathy arrived in jogging clothes. She was having a hard time. She missed Joanne and Teddy. She rarely saw her father. She found herself being very irritated with her mother: her constant eating, her holding on to Cathy, and never giving her room. Cathy found herself running away all day. She had tried to move back to her old room on the floor above, but her mother was afraid of being alone. When Cathy spent the night out, her mother complained of her sleeplessness.

Cathy: It's not that I don't love her, but it's like a damned prison. So I stay away with friends.

Therapist: With friends?

Cathy: Well not exactly—a couple of guys I sometimes shack up with. They're not important. We "smoke" together and if I'm drunk enough we have sex.

Therapist: Drunk enough?

Cathy: Yeah. No big deal. I don't get a kick out of it, but it's expected.

Therapist: Did you ever enjoy it?

Cathy: I like the beginning and the end. The love making and the sleeping together. I think I'm a dyke.

Therapist: A dyke?

Cathy: Yeah, you know—a lesbian. Several times when my mother slept with me I found myself getting excited. She's so big and soft—like a comforter and smells so good. That's one helluva feeling—my own mother? I don't sleep with her anymore. It gets me uncomfortable. I love her but I have to get away.

Therapist: There's been many changes in the family. I think you might wait a bit. Let's see what the next family session brings.

Cathy: That's a load off my chest. I haven't been able to say this even to myself.

Session 8: Two by Two

This session took place on a weekend so that Bobby could attend. Hank, Liz, and Bobby arrived together. Cathy and Joanne came next, and Willa arrived alone.

Liz: Bobby's here but Teddy wouldn't come.

Bobby: Cathy has kept me current. Boy, the family sounds different.

Therapist: In what way?

Bobby: Everyone's not stuck in a bunch. And it's easier around the house. We laugh more—at ourselves and each other. I used to walk around on cracked glass, but now the floor's been swept. Friday night dinner Joanne was there with her guy; Willa came with some creep (here a playful nudge from Willa) and Cathy brought a girlfriend. Even Mom and Pop sat together.

Therapist: Are you sure it wasn't staged for you?
(Bobby giggled and the three girls joined in.)

Cathy: We're great at productions. You know, "The Last Supper."

Liz: No, maybe the first.

Hank: I tell you it's been different. Liz even cooks. And Cathy has her own apartment upstairs.

Therapist: And you, Hank?

Hank: I think I may take Cathy's old room so that I can hear Liz if she needs me.

Liz: I miss our old talks together—Cathy's and mine.

Therapist: How about Hank?

Liz: Hank plays gin with me when I can't sleep.

Joanne: Hey Mom, "Gin," how about calling it "Perrier"?
(Everyone laughs.)

Hank: Bobby, you talked about everyone else but how about that old girlfriend you brought to dinner?

Bobby: Okay Pops, lay off. She's just a friend.

Willa: Attaboy, tell them.

Therapist: I think he was.

Session 9: They're Leaving—Will They Come Back?

Hank and Liz came alone. They were both very quiet and a little sad. I commented on this.

Liz: I miss the noise, and yes, the confusion. Sometimes it gets dull.

Therapist: What do you do when you get bored?

Liz: I try not to eat. Lately I've started painting again. I used to be good.

Therapist: And you Hank?

Hank: I'm a little anxious. It's like starting over. Me and Liz. But it's different, we're so much older.

Liz: Hank and I have been talking about me taking over some of the talent casting for the commercials. I used to do this.

Hank: She's good at it and it would be her own thing.

Liz: I tried to make a deal with Hank. I would stop the pills if he would stop the cocktails.

Hank: My cocktails don't hurt anyone. I can stop when I want to.

Liz: We're beginning to find some couples in our business associates with whom we socialize.

Hank: It's not like family but it's fun.

A quality of mourning marked this session. Liz and Hank were no longer in an adversarial position. Hank sat closer to Liz and on one occasion leaned over and put his arm around her chair. Liz made a connection between her eating and boredom. She tries to make a quid pro quo deal with Hank. She'll give up pills if he'll give up drinking. When Hank denies his drinking problem, Liz does not retaliate. Instead she shifts to a positive development in their social life.

Session 10: The Same but Different

Everyone but Teddy came. The seating was dramatically but somewhat self-consciously different. (see Figure 3-5).
(Hank and Liz sat close and touched frequently.)

Joanne: It's like a farewell party. I'm leaving for California next month. I have a screenwriting job.

Hank: She'll do well, but I'll miss her. (Liz leans over and pats him.)

Willa: If things go well I'll be going there too. I'm trying to get an assistant stage designer job.

Liz: Fortunately California is not that far away. Hank and I go there for business frequently.

Hank: It's better than nothing.

Bobby: I'll be back on some weekends. Give me the room with the double bed.

Cathy: Okay Casanova. Going to outdo the old man?

Therapist: How about Teddy?

Liz: He's the most talented and . . .

Hank: (interrupts) And the most drugged. I worry about him.
Cathy: He has Betty. She'll take care of him.
Therapist: What about you Cathy?
Cathy: I have a scholarship in one of the really good acting groups. I went to a couple of AA meetings with Joanne. I also went to one with Willa. I need to get that under my belt and then I may share an apartment with a woman friend.

The talk continued with future plans. Everyone had a hard time leaving.

I got up slowly and Joanne asked if she could call me if need be. Everyone smiled with relief and each echoed Joanne. Hank set up an appointment for three months hence—"a Family Therapy Check-Up" he called it. I agreed and shared with them that it was difficult for me to end the sessions with them. I looked forward to the check-up.

It was some weeks before I got back to listening to the tapes of these ten sessions.

I was impressed with the chaos in this family; no generational boundaries, no gender differentiation, no sexual boundaries, no

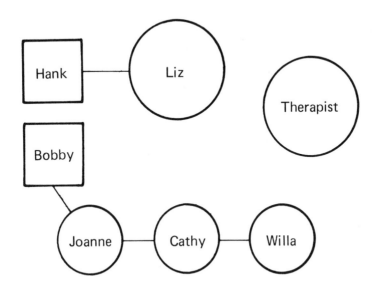

Figure 3-5
The seating arrangement
at the 10th session.

hierarchical structure and the use of chemicals for problem solving. There were frequent comings and goings but no separations and individuation. The sessions took place over a period of four months.

Alcohol and drugs were used to dissolve anger, sadness, fear, and anxieties. The ensuing sticky mass kept the family together and acted as a homeostatic device. Joanne's blackouts overloaded the circuits. The family's anxiety increased to a point where they sought help, albeit for Joanne.

The therapist's frequent warnings not to go so fast, not to change anything, freed the family to try some new alliances. It also allowed them to be oppositional and to take charge in their own way.

A note from Hank and Liz some months later thanked me for being able "to be the mother of them all."

Three Months Later: Reunion

Joanne was on the West Coast working, five months sober and living with a "good guy."

Willa was having a harder time but was off of both drugs and alcohol. She was attending AA meetings four and five times a week.

Bobby was doing well in school and had a steady girlfriend.

Cathy had a "break" in a television series. She was living with an older woman (age thirty-five); the family seemed accepting of this.

Hank and Liz had worked out a relationship where they were good friends. Hank still drank but Liz was not using pills. They were busy and had a good social life.

As the family left, they spoke of annual family therapy check-ups. We left this open with the understanding that any one of the family could call me.

In this family, as in many substance-abusing families, basic pathology is denied. Drugs and alcohol are used to handle discomfort. As the need for the use of drugs increases, the "solution" becomes the problem.

Liz's prescription pills served to maintain her sexual separation from Hank and disguise her substitution of Cathy for Hank.

Hank's drinking served to alleviate his guilt about his sexual promiscuity and his sexual involvement with his daughter.

Joanne's blackouts were the instrument as well as the receptacle for the family's denials.

The coalitions in the family with their mutual dependencies further served to keep this family enmeshed. This enmeshment is reenforced and reframed as an act of sacrifice for the family welfare.

Substance-abusing families have a rare talent at circular movement. They are adept at games without end. Attempted solutions are variations on the theme: "new" solutions become new problems.

The dramatic movement in this family had the intensity of desperation. The therapist's admonitions to slow down served to dilute the intensity somewhat. By the tenth session the family showed some beginning signs of a more functional balance. The family expressed sadness and mourning for the loss of the old "fun and games" but the acceptance of the restructuring had started.

BIBLIOGRAPHY

Berenson, D. Alcohol and the family system. In P. Guerin (Ed.)., *Family therapy, theory and practice.* New York: Gardner Press, 1976.

Fisch, R., Weakland, J., & Segal, L., *The tactics of change,* San Francisco: Jossey-Bass, 1982.

Haley, J. *Problem solving therapy.* San Francisco: Jossey-Bass. 1977.

Kaufman, E. & Kaufmann, P. (Eds.), *Family therapy of drug and alcohol abuse.* New York: Gardner Press, 1979.

Kaufmann, P. Family therapy with adolescent substance abusers. In E. Kaufman & P. Kaufmann (Eds.), *Family therapy of drug and alcohol abuse.* New York, Gardner Press, 1979.

Minuchin, S. *Families and family therapy.* Cambridge, Mass: Harvard University Press, 1974.

Satir, V. *People making.* Palo Alto, Calif.: Science and Behavior Books, 1972.

Stanton, D.M. & Todd, D.C. Structural family therapy with drug addicts. In E. Kaufman & P. Kaufmann (Eds.), *Family therapy of drug and alcohol abuse.* New York: Gardner Press, 1979.

Steinglass, P. Family therapy with alcoholics: A review. In E. Kaufman & P. Kaufmann (Eds.), *Family therapy of drug and alcohol abuse.* New York: Gardner Press, 1979.

Steinglass, P., Davis, D.I., & Benson, D. Observations of conjointly hospitalized "alcoholic couples" during sobriety and intoxication: Implications for theory and therapy. *Family Process* 1977, **16,** 1–16.

4

The Chaotic Flippers in Treatment

Elinor Killorin
David H. Olson, Ph.D.

RATIONALE FOR FAMILY TREATMENT

Chemical dependency is not an isolated dynamic unique to one family member; it is an integral part of a family system. Neither the addicted person nor the spouse is simply suffering from an inadequate personality or a characterological disorder. They are part of their family system and treatment for any problem in the system must deal with the whole unit.

The dynamics of a family system are similar to those of a mobile. Like a mobile, a family is made up of individual unique parts that have some commonness; these parts are connected and hang together in some kind of balance. When units are added and subtracted, these changes affect the whole. Internal and external outside forces provide movement within the system and by doing so increase the dynamics of the parts as well as the whole. Such movement highlights the complexity unique to each mobile. A sudden or strong force will tangle the connecting links, causing disarray to the whole. When the parts of the mobile are not able to hang freely, it affects not only each part but also the balance of the entire mobile. This is the impact that stressful events, like chemical dependency, can have on individuals and their families.

Chemical dependency does become part of the family system. As such, it becomes integrated into the family unit, achieving a sense of purpose and serving as an organizing theme of the family.

Although there is a significant relationship between chemical dependency and family dynamics, we cannot say there is a direct cause-and-effect relationship (linear causality). Such linear thinking leads to comments like: "Because of Dad's drinking, the family fights all the time. No one ever wants to stay home." Linear thinking could also lead to an opposite conclusion. Because the family is continually on Dad's back to stay home and join them playing cards, Dad escapes by going out and getting high.

By definition, however, linear causality and systems theory are mutually exclusive. Systems theory assumes that all parts support and reinforce the whole and the whole supports and reinforces the parts; therefore, we must think in terms of circular causality. One event stimulates a response, which in turn stimulates a further escalation of a cycle.

A good example of circular causality occurs with the Hansens. Mother and father have been working on their taxes all day. They are both feeling insecure financially but nobody says anything. At suppertime they start arguing over their son Cliff's hair. The arguing accelerates. Mother tells father, "Stop yelling. You're setting a bad example." Father continues. Son Jeffrey knocks over his milk. Mother yells at Jeffrey. Father wipes up the milk. Cliff cracks a joke. Everyone laughs. Mother and father return to the den and work on the taxes, and soon are arguing over father's drinking. What causes what? This family has gone through a sequence of events that has escalated into an argument.

Chemical dependency is similar to Jeffrey's spilt milk. It is a behavior in a series of interactions that supports and is supported by the system. It regulates the family either by serving as an expression of dysfunction or by stabilizing the family system. Steinglass (1) states that drinking enters the system as a sign of stress or serves as a functional part of the system.

Berenson (2) also describes two categories of clients: those whose system is organized around drinking as the problem and those where drinking is seen by the family as being tied in with other system problems. Thus, we have a theoretical rationale to begin to look at the dynamics of the family system and the part the chemical dependency plays within it.

If the therapist ignores the family system issue and merely treats the symptom, recovery, if there is any, will be temporary. If dependency is a sign of stress within the system, eradication of the behavior will be followed by replacement by another symptomatic behavior. If it is a working part of the system that serves to maintain balance, its removal will result in system breakdown unless one also attends to the working dynamics of the family.

An optimally effective treatment program will treat the family system as well as the dynamics of addiction within that family. If we believe that chemical dependency is a symptom of a family system, we must acknowledge two things. The behaviors of all family members are dysfunctional in the sense that the family system is organized around the theme of chemical dependency. Energy, attention, and affect are focused on the ingestion of the chemical or the behaviors of the chemically dependent person. Issues or themes of love, needs, angers, fun are ignored.

The term "chemical dependency" implies an addictive process. We are not always so cognizant of the addictive nature of the behaviors of other family members. Yet their focus on the chemical use and their attempts to regulate and/or cover up such use is addictive, compulsive, and dysfunctional.

In treatment of the family system, the system must be reorganized without the chemical. Sober conflict resolution must be taught. Family members must be helped to interact in their relationships without chemicals. In order for the family structure to be reorganized, the role of the chemical must be understood. If this is not done, the family will either find another symptom to relieve the pressure or the system will break down and become even less functional.

The Family Renewal Center, Fairview-Southdale Hospital, Edina, Minnesota, has developed a programmatic approach designed to meet both aspects of the chemically dependent family. Treatment focuses on each family member's addictive, dysfunctional behaviors as well as on reorganizing the family system.

DIFFERENTIAL DIAGNOSIS

Having ascertained that chemical dependency is an integral part of the functioning of the family system of which it is a part, we must also make it clear that there is not just one type of chemically dependent family. The function of the chemical dependency can vary infinitely. The dependency may function to establish closeness or to provide a rationale for distance. It may be used to start fights or to end them. It may be the thing that keeps the family talking together or something around which a family is silent.

As the function of the symptom varies, so does the family style. Some families are noisy, some are quiet. Some parents impose rules, some children set their own. Some families work together, some have no activities in common. Observation of families at the Family Renewal Center confirms the theory that although many families have a common symptom, the system interactions can take many forms.

Combining the complexities of addiction dynamics and family systems can be overwhelming. The therapist must rely on more than intuition. If there are a variety of family types and a variety of functions of addiction, a conceptual framework can provide a useful tool for understanding the complexity of the family system.

CIRCUMPLEX MODEL: BRIEF OVERVIEW

The Circumplex Model developed by Olson and colleagues (3,4) is based on three independent dimensions that are highly relevant to the clinical and empirical conceptualization of family systems. The two central dimensions are *cohesion* and *adaptability*, with *communication* as the third facilitating dimension. As different individuals have independently attempted to explain, identify, and analyze the dynamics of systems interaction, many have come to the same conclusion regarding the relevance of these three dimensions.

Adaptability is the product of feedback loops identified in systems theory by Von Bertalanffy (5). Haley (6) identified the morphostatic or homeostatic quality of families. Adaptability refers to the system's ability to change its power structure, role relationships, and relationship rules in response to situation and developmental stress.

Cohesion, as defined in this model, is the emotional bonding that members have with one another and the degree of individual autonomy a person experiences in the family system. Bowen (7) refers to undifferentiated ego mass. Minuchin's theory (8) attends to the system structure and he refers to disengaged or enmeshed systems. Wynne (9) describes pseudo-mutuality, or the rubber fence in families.

A review of the literature validates the relevancy of both dimensions, cohesion and adaptability (Olson el al. [3]). Therapists and theorists have found these dimensions of value in describing family system interaction. We will examine ways in which the Circumplex Model can help bridge the gap between theory and research. Language that is relevant to both the scientist and the therapist will enable us all to understand family systems better.

Figure 4-1 is a graphic illustration of the Circumplex Model. By combining the two dimensions independently of each other, we

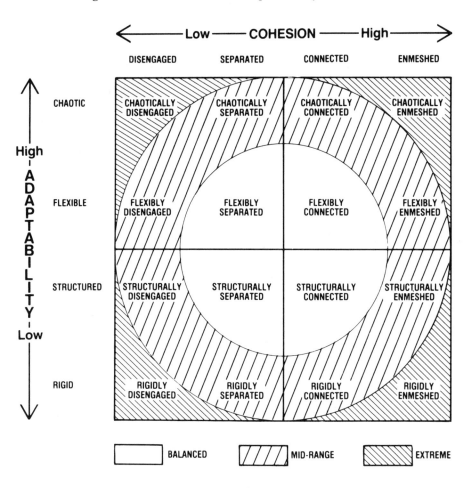

Figure 4-1
Circumplex Model: Sixteen Types of Marital and Family Systems

can arrive at a schematic illustration of *sixteen family types*. There are four levels of cohesion and four levels of adaptability. A family is assigned a position on each of the dimensions and thereby falls into one of the sixteen cells. This allows us to empirically describe and clinically diagnose a family system. Thus, we are better able to understand and treat the family. In addition to knowledge about the family system, the model provides a framework for viewing the many components of the family interaction and for understanding the underlying dynamics of the family. The model helps to clarify and classify the complexity of the family system. And, paradoxically, describing families using the model reveals the vast differences between various types of families, all of whom have problems with chemical dependency.

A chemically dependent family is known to have a problem with addiction to chemicals and dependent relationships. However, as discussed earlier, this is a simplistic view. The Circumplex Model helps to assess the family system on a number of variables and to describe the family as a particular type. Family types differ and the function of the addiction in an enmeshed family is very different from the place chemicals have in a disengaged family. A chaotic family requires different therapeutic strategies from the strategies used for a family that is rigid. As a result, it is important to be able to describe the type of family system.

Using the Circumplex Model in Treatment

The Circumplex Model allows us to focus on the family system rather than on the presenting symptom. By assessing the family on two theoretically valid and relevant themes—cohesion and adaptability—we are able to assess the family typology and to plan our therapeutic strategy in terms of the system structure. When we are working with chemically dependent families we must certainly push the family to look at their behaviors pertinent to the chemical use. The Circumplex Model gives us the entrée to focusing on the system level of interaction.

Thus, there are four essential applications of the Circumplex Model for our work with families. Initially, we can use the model to make a *diagnosis*. Other than the presenting problem, it tells us what else is going on in the family. The family's typology provides important diagnostic information.

Second, an *assessment of the various items* on each of the two dimensions will give us more insight into the family interactional patterns and structural components. We will learn about the system as well as each individual member's part in it.

Third, we can begin to *plan treatment* based on the type of family system. While the therapeutic technique is dictated by the therapist's training and style, the strategy must be relevant to the system.

Assessment on the cohesion dimension may tell us that Mom seems isolated or disengaged while Dad and oldest son have an extremely strong relationship. An intervention strategy might be to unite both parents by means of a parenting task.

In another example, a runaway teenager is seen as disengaged in her family. An assessment of the adaptability dimension will help us ascertain whether she is reacting to a rigid or a chaotic system.

Finally, the Circumplex Model can help us *evaluate our clinical intuition* of the family's progress in therapy. It will provide specific information about system change on each dimension. We can see if there is actual change in the family type: Have they become a more functional family system?

The remainder of this chapter will clarify and explain how the Circumplex Model was used to diagnose, assess, plan treatment and evaluate one chemically dependent family.

FAMILY DESCRIPTION

The Parks family, who shared part of their lives with us, were clients at the Family Renewal Center. The Parks are a family of three persons.

Charles and Anita, the parents, were themselves only children and now have one daughter, Mary. Anita had recently finished treatment for chemical dependence on prescription drugs and had been in and out of psychiatric care. Mary, at age twelve, had been taking care of herself for many years and was an adultified young person. Anita continued to hold down a job during her dependence but had become totally irresponsible and helpless at home. Charles, feeling inadequate in his own right, then felt completely helpless and retreated to his shop in the basement.

Although Anita had stopped using all prescription drugs, was no longer under the care of a psychiatrist, and had been through initial treatment for drugs, the family was still operating as a chemically dependent system. Charles was furious about his wife's helplessness and dependency on drugs. Because of anger and his own helplessness he continued to view the problem as, "If only she would change." Anita accepted the scapegoat position and although she wasn't using drugs, she still felt helpless and dependent. Mary was oblivious to both of them as she continued to manage the family.

Anita's addiction had been functional to the system of organization into which this family had settled. The system maintained itself after the drug use had stopped. We were aware that the drug use had been a symptom of a dysfunctional system and the family was talking about it as if the problem still existed, which in fact it did!

Anita grew up as an only child. Her own mother took care of the invalid Grandma, and was isolated from her husband and daughter. Anita's father retreated from her and worked on his hobbies in the basement. Anita's current family was following the same pattern as her family of origin. Anita's mother had kept her in line by telling her she was inadequate and dumb. Anita recalls: "Mother said I was ugly. I had only two dresses. She didn't want me to be attractive." Understandably, Anita had little sense of self-worth and felt powerless over as well as responsible for the pain in her family. Her isolation increased as she grew up and she eventually found relief from her depression from a psychiatrist. Her first prescription provided immediate relief and began her addictive cycle.

Charles' family was abusive. It was never acceptable for him to express his rage about the many ways he was mistreated. In addition, his feelings of sadness and loneliness were well concealed by the angry exterior. He had, years ago, decided to trust no one, least of all women, in self-defense against abusiveness. Caught in a typical victim-victimizer cycle, Charles' only defense against abuse was to lash out at others. He became the abuser in his own family. Anita, the "willing" scapegoat, let him maintain the distance in their relationship with his sarcastic, caustic remarks.

Being the only child of parents who had not been nurtured and had no self-worth or feelings of love to share with their daughter,

Mary detached from them emotionally and maintained a place in the system by being the one person who set and fulfilled goals. She got supper on the table and kept the family schedule, such as it was, on track. She took the position of parent to the adults in the house.

FAMILY ASSESSMENT USING THE CIRCUMPLEX MODEL

The Clinical Rating Scale (CRS) developed by Olson and Killorin uses the dimensions inherent to the Circumplex Model to elicit information about the family system. It provides a framework whereby the clinician can assess the family. Each of the two dimensions, cohesion and adaptability, is composed of specific variables that are references to various aspects of family functioning. The clinician rates each variable and comes up with a composite score for each dimension.

The variables pertaining to cohesion are emotional bonding, boundaries, coalitions, time, space, interests and recreation, and decision making. Adaptability is described by the variables of assertiveness, control, discipline, rules, roles, and negotiation process.

The variables of the cohesion dimension show a complex pattern in the Parks family (see Table 4-1). Emotional bonding was very low. The family was unable to ask for or receive emotional support from each other. At the same time, they are all highly dependent on each other. They resemble isolated victims hanging on to each other for life support but receiving nothing. Their highly dependent interaction causes them to seek all their support and approval from each other. Because the emotional bonding is low, there is no approval, only criticism and nonacceptance of each other's individuality.

The external family boundaries were closed. There is minimal interaction with people or systems outside the family. One pictures a house with doors closed and shades pulled. Internal boundaries are also closed. All three keep their thoughts and feelings to themselves. There is little interaction with outside resources; there is little interaction within the system.

Table 4-1
Family Cohesion

COUPLE OR FAMILY SCORE	DISENGAGED (Very Low) 1 2	SEPARATED (Low to Moderate) 3 4	CONNECTED (Moderate to High) 5 6	ENMESHED (Very High) 7 8
EMOTIONAL BONDING (Feelings of Closeness)	Extreme separateness. Lack of closeness or loyalty.	Emotional separateness encouraged and preferred. Need for support respected.	Emotional closeness encouraged and preferred. Need for separateness respected.	Extreme closeness. Loyalty demanded. Separateness restricted.
FAMILY BOUNDARIES (External Relationship)	Influence of outside people and ideas unrestricted.	Open to outside people and ideas.	Some control of outside people and ideas.	Influence of outside people and ideas restricted.
COALITIONS (Marital) (Sibling) (Generational)	Weak marital coalition. Poor sibling relationship. Blurred generational lines.	Stable marital coalitions. Stable sibling relationship. Fluid generational lines.	Strong marital coalitions. Stable sibling relations. Stable generational lines.	Weak marital coalitions. Parent-child coalitions. Blurred generational lines.
TIME (Physical and/or Emotional)	Time apart from family maximized. Rarely time together.	Time alone important. Some time together.	Time together important and scheduled. Time alone permitted.	Time together maximized. Little time alone permitted.
SPACE (Physical and/or Emotional)	Separate space needed and preferred.	Separate space preferred. Sharing of family space.	Sharing family space preferred. Private space respected.	Little or no private space permitted.

FRIENDS	Mainly individual friends seen alone. Few family friends.	Individual friends shared with family. Some family friends.	Some individual friends. Some scheduled activities with couple/family friends.	Limited individual friends. Couple/family friends strongly encouraged.
DECISION MAKING	Primarily individual decisions. No checking with other family members.	Most decisions individually made. Able to make joint decisions on family issues.	Most decisions made with family in mind. Individual decisions are shared.	All decisions, both personal and relationship, must be approved.
INTERESTS AND RECREATION	Primarily individual activities done without family. Family not involved.	Some spontaneous family activities. Individual activities supported.	Some scheduled family activities. Family involved in individual interests.	Most activities and interests must be shared with family.
TOTAL COHESION				

Coalitions are weak, as would be suspected from a system with closed internal boundaries. Anita was often seen as the family scapegoat when she was using drugs and/or under psychiatric care; yet Mary and Charles did not form a coalition as much as suffer in isolation from feeling they had to do her work.

The family regulates time and space on both ends of the cohesion dimension. They resemble enmeshed families in that little time alone is permitted. If one member begins an individual project, another will impose a demand that he or she do some project around the house. Because all three are uncomfortable in relationships, two people cannot be together without pulling in the third. "Your time should be my time" is the slogan. They seem most satisfied when Charles and Anita go off to work and Mary goes to school or has the house alone. She, in fact, resents their intrusion via telephone into "her" time and space during the working day.

Space is uniquely divided in this family. All three have separate bedrooms. When Charles gets annoyed with family clutter, he cleans Anita's room. Likewise, she complains about the mess in his. Mary has her own room but sleeps in the living room. Members continually badger each other about the general clutter but no one takes responsibility for clearing it up. Friends either in common or individually are limited. This dynamic increases the isolation of the family.

Interest and recreation are few. Because of the lack of outside friendships, activities are done together. As previously noted, this family is uncomfortable in intimate relationships. They avoid time in dyads. Where two would go, the third is dragged along. Thus, the marital dyad is further weakened. Decisions are made individually in a passive process. Things seem to happen. The family has characteristics of both enmeshed and disengaged systems and seems to flip back and forth.

The adaptability dimension is more consistent and is at the chaotic end of the scale (see Table 4-2). Assertiveness does not exist. The family operates in a passive style. Charles and Anita complain about what they don't like. Mary follows suit in a whiney, blaming style. There is a noticeable lack of control, with very little leadership. Mary carries out what maintenance-level leadership is required. Discipline does not exist, nor do rules. For years the family has been struggling to unpack boxes. There is no way to get this done as the system has no leader or consequences. Role

Table 4-2
Family Adaptability

COUPLE OR FAMILY SCORE	RIGID (Very Low) 1 2	STRUCTURED (Low to Moderate) 3 4	FLEXIBLE (Moderate to High) 5 6	CHAOTIC (Very High) 7 8
ASSERTIVENESS	Passive-aggressive styles of interaction.	Generally assertive with some aggression.	Mutually assertive with rare aggression.	Passive and aggressive styles. Unpredictable patterns.
LEADERSHIP (Control)	Authoritarian. Traditional leadership.	Leadership is stable and kindly imposed.	Egalitarian leadership with fluid changes.	Limited and/or erratic leadership.
DISCIPLINE	Autocratic. Strict, rigid conseq. Rigidly enforced.	Generally democratic. Predictable consequences. Firmly imposed and enforced.	Usually democratic. Negotiated conseq. Fairly maintained.	Laissez-faire: Inconsistent consequences. Erratically enforced.
NEGOTIATION	Poor problem solving. Limited negotiations. Solution imposed.	Good problem solving. Structured negotiations. Reasonable solutions.	Good problem solving. Flexible negotiations. Agreed-upon solutions.	Poor problem solving. Endless negotiations. Impulsive solutions.
ROLES	Role rigidity. Stereotyped roles.	Roles stable, but may be shared.	Role sharing and making. Fluid changes of roles.	Dramatic role shifts. Sporadic role reversals.
RULES	Rigid rules. Many explicit rules. Many implicit rules. Rules strictly enforced.	Few rules changes. Many explicit rules. Some implicit rules. Rules firmly enforced.	Some rule changes. Some explicit rules. Few implicit rules. Rules fairly enforced.	Dramatic rule changes. Many explicit rules. Few implicit rules. Rules arbitrarily enforced.
TOTAL ADAPTABILITY				

shifts are dramatic. Mary carries out a dual parent position, often treating both parents as children. Negotiation is endless, as over the clutter issue. If a problem is verbally solved, no action is taken, hence no solution. A picture emerges of an extremely chaotic family.

Because of the lack of any workable structure, it is theoretically and clinically not surprising that they do not maintain a stable position on the cohesion dimension. They are therefore called "chaotic flippers."

The chemical dependency has facilitated the chaotic style by serving as the scapegoat. Neither Anita nor Charles had to focus on the lack of structure in the family. Roles and rules could not be maintained as "Anita was incompetent." She was either crazy or "doped up on meds." Charles could not possibly deal with such a situation. Neither adult was equipped to lead and the chemical use gave them both an out.

The chemical use also served as a distance regulator. When anyone wished to disconnect, ample rationalization was provided by all the situations promoted by Anita's drugs. When they wished to reconnect, there was plenty to do in taking care of one another.

The Parks emerge, not so much as a new type on the Circumplex Model (see Figure 4-1), but as an example of a highly chaotic system. The therapeutic task is to minimize the chaos so that the family, as a system and individually, has a chance to settle on the cohesion scale. The variables on the adaptability dimension (assertiveness, control, discipline, roles, rules, negotiations, communication process) are in such a state of turmoil that the family cannot maintain any stability on the cohesion dimension. The variables that govern distance regulation in this system (emotional bonding, boundaries, coalitions, time, space, interest, recreation, decision making) are responding to the chaotic quality of the system. On some variables—interest and recreation—the family is enmeshed, and on others—emotional bonding, boundaries, coalitions—they are disengaged. Disengaged and enmeshed patterns are also found in the variables of time and space.

INDIVIDUAL ASSESSMENT

The test results (collected at time of intake) confirm some of the observed dynamics in the Parks' family system. The FIRO-B indicated that Mary is the most active member interpersonally although all of the Parks score relatively low. Mary is exerting most of the control and responsibility in the family (8 on a 9-point scale), father is somewhat responsible (score of 5), and mother is showing no responsibility for relationships (score is 0). Mother wants a lot of affection, she and father express none. Mary wants little and gives a little. Nobody in the family wants to be included in interpersonal relationships and all of them put out very little energy to include others.

These results confirm the flip to extremes on the cohesion dimension. Most scores are very high (12 out of 18) and indicate disengaged people, or very low (3 out of 18) and indicate enmeshment.

The MMPI was given to Charles and Anita. Mary was excluded because of invalid results for her age group. Charles' results indicate a man who is depressed. He overstates his weaknesses, is very withdrawn and retiring, rigid, dependent and a worrier. Anita has a low ego strength, is very depressed, is intraverted with very low energy, and is dependent in relationships. Both partners are seen as individuals who would be expected to be socially isolated. They could be expected to cling to each other for support and out of a sense of "He's (she's) as incompetent in relationships as I am and, therefore, won't laugh at my awkwardness."

The potential enmeshed relationship is offset with the fact that neither person has the skills or the abilities to form attachments and so they have developed ways to push each other away. Anita's role in this scenario is one of maintaining the connection between husband and wife and in reaching out to the outside world for support.

INITIAL TREATMENT SESSION

As a result of the intake interview, a preliminary treatment plan was completed based on the information on the dynamics in the family system. This information, along with client test results, was in the therapist's hand at the initial treatment session.

In addition to Anita's chemical dependency, Charles and Mary's co-dependency was a treatment issue. The family was so focused on the chemical dependency that co-dependency was denied. In fact, the family denied or minimized all items on the preliminary treatment plan. Even when they do acknowledge the issues, they are unable to see them as related to "the real problem" and thus reject them on a "yes, but" basis.

Charles was scapegoating Mary; Charles was projecting hostility and rigidity; Anita was acting helpless and compliant. This confirms the system assessment of the function of the chemical as one that perpetuates Anita's inadequacy. The more "inadequate" she becomes, whether or not she is using, the more rigid Charles becomes in response.

When Anita perceives his rigidity, she increases her helplessness and they are locked into the cycle. The cycle is broken when Charles allows Mary to break into the cycle by scapegoating her. He blames her for everything and focuses on all her mistakes. He could not direct anger at his "helpless wife" so he had to defocus it to his daughter.

Anita fulfills the system dynamics by allowing Mary to take over her role as adult woman in the family. The preliminary treatment plan acknowledges the coalition between Anita and Mary. Charles' threat of physical abuse is not an isolated issue. It could be predicted as a system response to the mother-daughter coalition. Coalitions and angry outsiders reinforce each other. It is not surprising that the couple lists their sexual relationship as a problem.

The therapist lists other problems: no rules or control and a parentified child triangled with the marriage.

Anita (wife): I don't know if I'm crazy or chemically dependent.

Charles (husband): She can't handle anything and it's [hopeless] been going on for years.

Mary (daughter): That's all right—I'll take over.

Therapist: You all seem to have the problem clearly defined and under control.

TREATMENT PLAN AND OBJECTIVES

Based on the diagnostic information and the initial treatment session with the family, the following treatment plan was developed. Tables 4-3 and 4-4 indicate the specific objectives, how they were accomplished, and the desired outcome. The major variables used include variables related to both the chemical dependency and changes in the family system.

The Circumplex Model was used to diagnose the type of family system, to identify the salient characteristics on each of the dimensions and to plan the treatment intervention. Specific treatment goals were established for each of the concepts related to family cohesion and family adaptability.

The assumption is that the current family system is helping to maintain the chemical use and co-dependency in the family. Therefore it was necessary to change the current family system and find a new type of family system that would work for them without the chemical dependency.

Therapeutic intervention continually shifted its focus on different variables related to cohesion and adaptability throughout the treatment process. The goal, however, was to induce change in the family system and help the family develop and maintain a new type of family system.

THERAPEUTIC SESSIONS

Session One

Multifamily group therapy was used as the primary treatment approach for this family. There were, however, two conjoint therapy sessions with the couple, focusing on their sexual relationship.

In the initial family group therapy session, Anita declared herself Mother of the Week. On assignment from the addiction group, Anita had her husband and daughter present her with a self-purchased rose. She then proceeded to state her own worth to the members of the group in positive terms. She broke down and cried. Charles responded with, "She's a good mother. I appreciate her not using drugs." Mary tried to tell her mother that she loves her but acted nervous portraying the fact that she felt inadequate, as if she couldn't say enough.

Table 4-3
Treatment Plan

PROBLEM	OBJECTIVES	HOW ACCOMPLISHED	MEASURED OUTCOME
Family Systems Chemical Dependency			
Chemical Use	Anita does not use chemicals.	Peer Therapy focus on issues of addiction. Family Therapy focus on system response to chemical use.	Sobriety. Attend A.A.
Co-Dependency	Charles and Mary do not focus on Anita's chemical use.	Peer Therapy focus on co-dependency issues. Family Therapy focus on system response to chemical use.	Talk about self. Attend Al-Anon
Family System Adaptability Dimension			
Assertiveness	Each member speaks for self with "I" statements.	Learn communication skills and practice them. A.A./Al-Anon. Step 1 process.	Each person speaks for and about self, not other.
Control	Parents take leadership. Each person makes some decisions for self.	Family Therapy—Strategic Assignments. A.A./Al-Anon. Step 1 process.	Reduced complaints about disorder—tasks get accomplished.
Discipline	Each person takes care of own responsibilities. Parents enforce rules.	Family Therapy—Strategic assignments.	Expectations are clear—infractions get acknowledged.
Rules	Parents set rules for daughter. Each adult sets rules for self.	Family Therapy—Strategic assignments.	Rules are established and made explicit.
Roles	Parents in charge of self and child. Daughter acting in child like role.	Family Therapy—Strategic assignments. Family of Origin work to increase self esteem.	Parents make decisions. Child spends time with peers.
Negotiation	All members to discuss issues to resolution.	Family Therapy—Strategic assignments. A.A./Al-Anon. Steps 2 & 3 process.	Ability to resolve an issue and carry out a decision.

Table 4-4
Treatment Plan

PROBLEM	OBJECTIVES	HOW ACCOMPLISHED	MEASURED OUTCOME
Family System Cohesion Dimension			
Emotional Bonding	Members able to trust each other.	AA/AlAnon. Steps 4 and 5. Work on family of origin in order to reduce shame. AA/AlAnon. Steps 8 and 9. Make amends in relationship issues.	Ability to get needs met in family and from others.
Boundaries	Members able to interact with each other.	AA/AlAnon. Steps 2 and 3. Work on family of origin. Practice reaching out to others.	Ability to share parts of self. Improved self-esteem.
Coalitions	Eliminate scapegoating.	AA/AlAnon. Step 1. Give up manipulative behaviors; relearn role-appropriate behaviors.	Members able to interact in role-appropriate dyads.
Time and Space	Clear awareness of decisions to share space and time and to be alone.	Family therapy. Strategic assignments.	Members have sense of own space and respect other's space.
Interests and Recreation	Each person develops personal interests and support system.	Therapy. Strategic assignments. Groups process. learn new behaviors in group.	Personal friends and activities. Family friends and activities.
Decisions	Members able to make plans and decisions.	Family therapy. Strategic assignments.	Ability to make plans and carry them out.

The addiction group had given Anita a task to propel her into confronting her addiction. She needed to confront the fact that her addiction is covering the pain of feeling inadequate and feeling as if she has no place in her family. Both are symptoms of low self-worth.

Charles took his part as a good co-dependent by continuing to focus on her drug use. Mary's co-dependency flared up as she tried to hold the whole family together. Both will need to deal with their own feelings and their roles in the family.

From a family systems perspective, this session portrayed the picture of a family where all members believe Mother is inadequate and are attempting to cover up and compensate for that reality. After stating that he thought Anita was a good mother, Charles went on to mention that he thought she indulged Mary. He would not acknowledge his anger about that.

At the end of this initial session, the therapist formulated the following plan: Charles needs to become aware of his part in the family. He focuses on Anita's drug use as the problem and denies the fact that neither adult is providing a structured parental coalition. He does not yet see the rigidity of his anger and how he uses it to impose control, since he is too afraid to interact on an emotional level. Anita must become aware of her own self-worth and stop relying on her daughter to meet her needs. The husband-wife bond needs to be strengthened in order to alleviate the parent-child coalition. Mary needs to assume a childlike role and let go of being responsible for Mother.

Session Three

In this session the therapist had Anita do a sculpture of her family of origin. At this point, the system was defining her as the problem and it was believed that her willingness to maintain the victim position was connected to being a victim in her family of origin. Through this experience she became aware of her anger at her own mother. As she began to express that, anger at Charles also surfaced. Charles' passivity was tapped as he became aware of Anita's anger. His defensiveness put him in the role of antagonist as he asked his wife lots of judgmental questions about her anger. Their dynamics escalated as she became enraged at his questioning. Charles' fear of anger was now an explicit therapeutic issue. The therapist decided to let the group support him in his fear for this session, but planned to push Charles to work on his own family of origin very soon. This plan would be worked on in conjunction with what he was doing in his co-dependency peer group.

As mother and father engaged each other, Mary became much less involved in the group, and in fact seemed emotionally to leave the family. The therapist supported the fact that she was detaching from their struggle and talked to her about her social life, which is a more age-appropriate concern.

In the fourth session, Charles talked about his family of origin and the rejection he has felt all his life. Anita complained about her low energy and was given an assignment to take a daily walk. (The chaos of the system was such that to do anything on a daily basis was a real feat.)

Session Five

In this session the dynamics of the family began to change. Charles talked to the group about his loneliness and allowed one of the men in the group to hold him. He became much softer although his fear of being vulnerable was very apparent and extreme. He was still unable to see how his rigidity caused him to be very hostile and defensive in personal interactions.

Anita felt the benefits of accomplishment as she reported that she walked daily, felt physically better, and was losing weight. In one sentence she stated, "I am losing weight and getting angry." She was tired of taking the blame in the family and of being put down by Charles. This change escalated Charles' fear and the therapist used the group to support his progress. Anita's ambivalence about becoming more powerful surfaced as she attempted to deal with Mary on a mealtime issue. She immediately became helpless with parenting her daughter.

Mary talked about her anger at her mother's helplessness and the therapist reframed this to state that Mary wants Mom and Dad to be parents. At this point, it was a double-bind dynamic, in that it was also apparent that Mary did not want to give up the power she had in the family. In addition, Mary talked to the therapist about her pain: "I don't know how to take care of myself when other people hurt me."

Other children in the group were able to concretize some solution to this problem in terms of a school setting. The therapist noted that Mary was working on her steps, that she was giving up control of the family and asking others for help. This child was not able to ask her parents for help but was beginning to trust the therapist and the group members.

Session Six

It became apparent in this session that the structure of the family was changing. Maintaining the change on a behavioral level is a very difficult task for all family members. In the therapy session we focused on Anita's struggles to set dyadic boundaries with Mary. This dynamic is a common outcome of a parent's guilt over her chemical dependency.

Anita continued to state that she is an addict and not a good mother. As part of her first step work* she needed to accept that she can be both. She was directed to talk to Mary about her chemical dependency. After their dialogue she was able to tell Mary that she was going to work on setting parental boundaries and to start parenting rather than pleasing Mary.

Meanwhile Charles took a leap forward and did some effective parenting in the group. Mary's need for play space became an issue. He was able to change his tack. Instead of harping on the mess in the yard, he came up with a solution. Both were able to have their needs met.

The therapist began to formulate the next step in the treatment plan. As Charles and Anita became more effective parents, Mary would feel less powerful. She had been spending time and energy keeping her parents together. As they began to do this themselves, she needed to work on developing her own peer support system. The group was helpful in carrying out this task. They helped Mary set goals and supported her ability to communicate with her parents.

During the next two sessions, all members of the Parks family were less active in group. They reported slow, steady progress, were actively involved with other group members, but took no time for themselves. The therapist read this as a period of stabilization, made that awareness explicit, and allowed it to continue.

*The twelve steps of AA.

Session Nine

In this session, Anita firmly told Mary that she was in charge as parent. Mary verbally retaliated but Anita held her ground. Charles was much less hostile. He seemed to sense that he didn't have to use his anger to attempt to control the family. Mary reported that she was doing much better with her friends. When peers put her down, she had a sense of being able to take care of herself. As she felt more taken care of in the family she could take care of herself at school.

ASSESSMENT OF PROGRESS

At this point in therapy, the chaos of the family system had undergone structural change. The focus was off the chemicals and instead concentrated on roles and control. The parents had established some equality in their power, become more assertive, gained self-discipline as well as discipline of their daughter.

The adaptability dimension was shifting. It is interesting to note that they had not become flexible, or slightly less chaotic, but had moved to the other end of the continuum and were quite structured or even rigid. This dynamic is fairly common. Clients grasp the idea of their power and ability to enforce rules and become focused on that as a way of control.

The therapist's plan now shifted to working on interpersonal relationships on the cohesion dimension. Having obtained some order in the family, the Parks indicated a willingness to engage in this process. They were feeling more competent as they reviewed the positive steps they had taken. This enhanced the individual self-worth of each and they were becoming willing to engage emotionally with each other.

While the therapeutic focus was on the adaptability dimension of the system, Charles and Mary's co-dependency was relevant to the way they attempted to exercise control over Anita. This was a maladaptive response to the needs of the family. They were unable to control her chemical use, they did not acknowledge her strength, and they were unaware of the source of disruption to the system. The drug use was a symptom of the chaos, not a cause. Obviously, sobriety did not restore order to the family.

In terms of the cohesion or relationship aspect of the family, the co-dependency was still an issue. Blocked from focusing on Anita's drug use, Charles and Mary now needed a new way of finding a place in the family and relating to each other, to Anita, and she to them.

The ninth step, whereby family members make amends to each other, is a point to begin this process. This step enables them to say, "My relationship to you, not your behaviors, is of importance to me." In addition, it is a way to put the past behind them and to learn new ways of connecting without controlling each other.

We will follow this process in terms of the family's recovery in sessions ten through twenty.

REINFORCING CHANGE IN THE FAMILY SYSTEM

As her mother began to become more vulnerable, Mary also permitted herself to risk vulnerability in her own relationships. She followed in her mom's steps by telling her dad she was angry at him. Charles, unable to handle his daughter's anger, became visibly agitated. The therapist used this interaction to direct him into working on his own family-of-origin issues.

He quickly accessed the information that he knew it was not safe to be angry in his family when he was a child. The shame, which Charles carried as a victim of abuse, became clear. With his shame, rage, and hurt on the surface, Charles retreated on an emotional level and the family system reverted correspondingly. Gains they had made in structuring their chaos were temporarily suspended as the family retained its homeostatic system.

An analysis of this common treatment dynamic suggests that Charles' intrapsychic conflict became too threatening for him. Perhaps the system had changed too fast. Improving the level of structure on the adaptability dimension had allowed some chance for closeness on the cohesion dimension. Charles made the family's statement: "We are not ready." At this point, the family was stuck. Work could not proceed on even the adaptability dimension as family members were fearful and untrusting. It also became clear that Charles' basic lack of trust was a deterrent to his work on his

Table 4-5
Reinforcing Change Using the AA Model

	Charles' Co-dependency	Mary's Co-dependency	Anita's Chemical Dependency	System Issues
EXPRESSED BEHAVIORS (Step 1)	Anger and helplessness regarding Anita's drug use.	Overresponsible/helplessness regarding parents' lack of control and unwillingness to parent.	Drug use. Feelings of incompetence. Unwillingness to assume responsibility.	Chaotic behaviors.
UNDERLYING ISSUES (Steps 2 & 3)	Sadness at not being valued.	Sadness at not being valued. Inability to trust.	Low self-esteem.	Lack of intimacy.
THERAPEUTIC INTERVENTION (Steps 4 & 5)	Shame-based personality. Needs to learn trust.	Parentified child. Needs to give up control.	Shame-based personality. Needs to learn trust.	Work on levels of shame. Develop self-esteem and competency.

AlAnon steps. Steps two and three depend on a willingness to reach out to others for support and to believe that others are inherently competent. Charles' life experiences told him this did not work for him. Anita, initially, took risks to trust others with positive results, so her step work was progressing with less difficulty. Mary's step work remained ambivalent; she couldn't decide who was right: Father or Mother.

AA/AlAnon: Steps 1–5

1. We admitted we were powerless over alcohol—that our lives had become unmanageable.
2. Came to believe that a power greater than ourselves could restore us to sanity.
3. Made a decision to turn our will and our lives over to the care of God *as we understand him.*
4. Made a searching and fearless moral inventory of ourselves.
5. Admitted to God, to ourselves, and to another human being the exact nature of our wrongs.

The preceding overly simplistic schema demonstrates the impact of the AA/AlAnon steps on the intrapsychic and system therapeutic process. Step 1 interrupts behaviors that have been self-perpetuating and dysfunctional. Steps 2 and 3 provide a rationale and vehicle for reaching out to others, establishing trusting relationships, sharing the innermost self with others, and teaching that others are competent to care for themselves. Steps 2 and 3 also deal with the subtle differences between effective parenting and too much or too little responsible care taking. Steps 4 and 5 prescribe behaviors that allow clients to admit behaviors over which they feel shame, which will help turn shame into guilt. This activity enhances self-worth and trust in others.

Charles continued to express his resistance to change. The group confronted him on not wanting to hear the issue of the "junk" in the house again since no one in the family was doing anything about it. Charles became vulnerable and openly stated, "I can't throw out stuff because a lot of it belongs to Dad and he never threw anything out." Knowing that Dad was deceased, the group immediately picked up the thread that Charles was really saying, "I can't get rid of my Dad." The group was, at this point, more effective in getting Charles to accept the importance of working on his family of origin than the therapist had been for weeks. (Their sensitivity of timing is often overwhelming.) As Charles earnestly began to work on issues concerning his parents, and Anita continued to work on hers, Mary attempted to pull the system back to homeostasis by becoming increasingly more active on her helpless/overresponsible merry-go-round over the next several weeks. The process thus far looks like Figure 4-2.

The family was now able to stay pretty much in the inner circle. Resistance surfaced but they did not retreat to a dysfunctional system; they stayed engaged in the therapeutic process.

Marked change occurred after several more weeks. Having dealt with their own shame and abandonment issues, Charles and Anita were willing to take more risks to be intimate with each other. Increased trust allowed them to implement anew the structural changes begun earlier. They maintained rules and consequences cooperatively. Their traditional orientation resulted in a quite highly structured system. This, however, allowed for clear differentiation of roles: mother, father, child. Clear role expectations seemed to increase the trust level each had for the others.

Soon after the family had stabilized, they began to again show resistance to the therapeutic process. Old issues were brought to the group to be rehashed. Yet there was a difference: the old issues did not have much potency to them. We became aware that the Parks family was getting ready to terminate. The issue of sexuality had not been resolved so Charles and Anita met with us for a series of individual sessions.

Interestingly enough, Mary raised the issue by insisting that her parents go away to a hotel for the weekend and she would stay home. She was attempting to force them to occupy the same sleeping quarters. Explicit boundaries were set in group and maintained by the couple sessions, sans their matchmaker!

Lack of sexual contact had been maintained by their system of flipping between diffuse boundaries and rigid boundaries, and by their lifelong accumulation of resentments. Sexual contact was initially controlled by the therapeutic structure. "When" and "where" assignments were tentatively followed until the clients felt capable of setting their own structure. They will probably never meet their daughter's fantasy wishes but sex became an issue they were capable of negotiating.

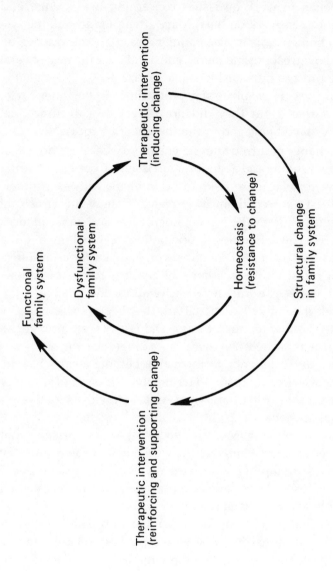

Figure 4-6
Family System Inducing and Reinforcing Change

TERMINATION PROCESS

Throughout the therapeutic process, the therapist had gone in and out of the family system, mostly as part of a therapeutic decision, sometimes without being aware of that process. Termination must, therefore, include the therapist terminating her or his role in the system. We were aware that we had provided a lot of organization to an initially chaotic family. This task was explicitly handed over to them in full. In addition, we had supplied a social support system to a very isolated family.

As part of the termination process, the Parks were supported in developing and maintaining their own individual and family support network. Group therapy would no longer suffice as a social activity. It was less easy to withdraw the personal support that had been important to the self-esteem of all three people as well as to their sense of a family identity. This is a gift we can give to the family to take with them, with gratefulness that each one knows the value of another's friendship and support.

OUTCOME EVALUATION

Anita and Charles were given support in their family therapy group to express their anger at each other. This went extremely slowly at first but they were actually able to become more assertive and to talk about what they wanted. It became evident that they were distressed about the lack of structure in their home, and so they were helped to develop and carry out plans, rules, consequences.

Each accomplished task bred confidence in their abilities to get things done. When Anita stuck to a plan to walk two miles each day for a week and lost ten pounds, she was able to tackle some parenting issues. Mary had to be explicitly restrained in the sessions from exerting control and doing her parents' work. Our therapeutic task was to help Mary find her place in the family as a child. She wanted the nurturing but resisted giving up the control.

As the Parks became aware that they could affect change in their system, they were able to talk about the issues on the cohesion scale. The family was given contracts to spend time in dyads, even if it was uncomfortable, and to stay out of each other's bedrooms except by invitation. Thus, interventions were made on both extremes of the cohesion dimension. The goal was to help the Parks be aware of how to make choices when they want to connect or when they want space. They gradually learned how to enjoy a more intimate relationship for a short period of time. The end result was that they began to function as a more *separated family system*.

As the chaos diminished and the parents regained power, they have moved to a more *rigid structure*. As they previously flipped on cohesion, they later flipped on adaptability. The passive style that led to chaos was not their preferred style. They did not choose a lack of structure. It was more as if they had insufficient skills to make choices. At this point they seem to prefer clear rules, with Charles in control in a very traditional system.

At the end of treatment, it was clear that they were now functioning more like a *rigidly separated* family. This type of family system seemed to be more functional for them at this time and it fit comfortably with them as individuals. How long this type of family system will be useful is an open question but it is hoped that they now have more resources to use when change is needed in their family system over time.

Feedback from Anita

Two years later, Anita wrote that she was no longer looking for a cure, life was not without problems but she was coping and very proud of herself. She had joined several social organizations, was involved in a speaker's bureau and getting regular promotions. She touted Mary's accomplishments, both socially and academically. The letter indicated that she and Charles did not have much intimacy, did a few things together, but mostly went their separate ways.

This later assessment in terms of the Circumplex Model indicates a continuing level of separateness in the family. This is marked improvement from their extreme positions of enmeshment and disengagement prior to treatment. They seem to be neither controlling (enmeshed) or ignoring (disengaged) with each other. Mary and Anita have definite personal accomplishments which would indicate a diminished chaotic environment and more positive self-esteem. Achieving a position on a speaker's bureau is a marked achievement for Anita. Mary's social involvement indicates age-appropriate role concerns, not those of a parentified child. The tone of the letter was thankful and warm as spoken by a woman who had the ability to be intimate. Change in all individuals and the system indicates a positive development of trust.

REFERENCES

1. Steinglass, P. Family therapy in alcoholism In B. Kissim & H. Begleiter (Eds.), *The biology of alcoholism*, Vol. 5. New York: Plenum, 1976.
2. Berenson, D. Alcohol and the family system. In P. Guerin (Ed.), *Family therapy and practice*. New York: Gardner Press, 1976.
3. Olson, D.H., Sprenkle, D.H., & Russell, C.S. Circumplex model of marital and family systems I: Cohesion and adaptability dimensions, family types, and clinical applications. *Family Process*, 1979, **18**, 3–28.
4. Olson, D.H., Russell, C.S., & Sprenkle, D.H. Circumplex model of marital and family systems II: Empirical studies and clinical intervention. In John Vincent (Ed.), *Advances in family intervention, assessment and theory*. Greenwich, Conn.: JAI Press, 1980.
5. Von Bertalanffy, L. The theory of open systems in physics and biology. *Science*, 1950, **3**, 23–29.
6. Haley, J. The family of the schizophrenic: A model system. *Journal of Nervous and Mental Diseases*, 1959, **129**, 357–374.
7. Bowen, M. The family as the unit of study and treatment. *American Journal of Orthopsychiatry*, 1960, **31**, 40–60.
8. Minuchin, S. *Families and family therapy*. Cambridge, Mass.: Harvard University Press, 1974.
9. Wynne, L. et al. Pseudomutuality in family relations of schizophrenic. *Psychiatry*, 1958, **21**, 205–222.

5

Helping the parents to survive:

A family systems approach to adolescent alcoholism

David J. Huberty, M.S.W.
Catherine E. Huberty, M.S.W.

As family therapists, we tend to believe our clients. So much so that we went back to the Brandon family years after terminating therapy in an effort to collect their subjective appraisal of what happened in their family crisis so that we could prepare this chapter. Their perceptions and interpretations became our criteria of what to include and how to reflect on family therapy. If their assessment of therapy was that it was helpful to them, then it was a success. If it was not helpful in their eyes, then family intervention and therapy failed. Kaufman (1) describes mimesis as a process in which the therapists adopt the family style and affect as reflected by the members' actions and needs. He emphasizes that this process is frequently done unconsciously by therapists. As writers, we wanted more consciously to become a part of this family's perception of what happened in family therapy and to discover what it meant to each of them and to the family unit.

To do this, we spent twelve hours reinterviewing family members four years after termination and in doing so, together we examined the process of family therapy with the aid of hindsight. Their perceptions revealed information and memories of treatment that we did not have. What we thought had been pearls of wisdom and monuments of therapy were, at times, insignificant. At other times, the family vividly recalled phrases and innuendos of which we had no recollection whatsoever. Their thoughts about different segments of treatment are briefly summarized in their "Reflections Four Years Later" interspersed throughout the chapter.

In examining and evaluating the process of family therapy, we became more aware of our style as therapists and of ourselves as a couple. We are grateful to the Brandon family for sharing themselves with us once again as they allowed us to reenter their family and for allowing us to share their story here.

PARTICIPANTS

One therapist couple: Dave and Cathy, co-therapists who are also married to each other.

One family: The Brandons*: one set of parents, Keith (Dad) and Betty (Mom); and two siblings: Tim, age 18 at the time of therapy (now age 22), and Tina, age 16 at the time of therapy (now age 20),the identified patient.

Ghosts: All others involved in the family therapy process inasmuch as they were talked about although never present at any session. This included an occasional friend and cousin, a pusher or two, several boyfriends, a few teachers, but mostly grandparents (living and deceased), and uncles and aunts.

PERSONAL BIASES OF THERAPY

While our attitudes about individuals and families permeate this chapter, we hope to make these ideas clear by directly stating our philosophy of alcoholism and family treatment so that the rest of this chapter can be viewed in this context.

Bias #1: For our purpose in family therapy, any distinctions between "alcoholism" on the one hand, and "drug dependency" on the other, are essentially meaningless.

The essence is *dependency*. This dependency is the identified

---

*Brandon is a pseudonym for a real family name. First names have also been changed to protect anonymity. Details of some incidents have also been slightly altered to protect anonymity and to enhance illustrations.

patient's preoccupation with getting drunk or high, intoxicated or ossified, or whatever the term may be. It includes obsessive-compulsive patterns of chemical use as well as peer relationships that expect and support getting loaded on *any* mood-altering substance. This essence of dependency is our concern and focus.

For several reasons that we have outlined elsewhere (2), we will hereafter talk of "chemical dependency" instead of alcoholism or drug abuse. Since the *urge* to alter one's mood is our primary focus, rather than which specific chemical is used to do it, total abstinence from all mood-altering substances is the ultimate goal and this goal is always a backdrop to family therapy. With any couple or family, we continually make the specific point of asking, "Has there been *any* use of *any* mood-altering substance since our last session?" or, "Is any family member suspicious of any use whatsoever?" Harbored suspicions become infectious to trusting relationships in families. Furthermore, we believe that "family therapy" can only take place while there is essential abstinence from all mood-altering chemicals. When relapse to any drug occurs, our focus is quickly shifted to "chemical dependency counseling" in immediate efforts to interrupt the chemical use. Therapists who ignore or gloss over recurring chemical use too lightly while otherwise doing "brilliant" family therapy seriously err as the family will predictably fail to reintegrate or get better under such conditions. This process is even more complicated with adolescents. Many otherwise competent and well-meaning therapists lack training in diagnosing and treating the specifics of adolescent chemical dependency and therefore fall victim to an "enabling role" of doing family therapy while allowing the chemical abuse to continue and progress (3).

Bias #2: Whenever there is an acting-out adolescent, and especially where alcohol or drugs are involved, we may assume an exaggerated and unhealthy parent-child coalition, a divided marital relationship, resulting in secrets within the family as well as one or more siblings being "left out." When this occurs, family process is predictable: As a unit, the family is guided by a rational desire for ongoing stability. The behavior of the family can be viewed as homeostatic since it readjusts itself to any behavior in order to maintain some sense of equilibrium as an interactional unit. As a result of defused boundaries, cross-generational coalitions, overinvolvement in trying to "fix" the adolescent, and a divided marital relationship, parents conveniently fail to see that they play supporting roles in the drama. Their already low self-image is further damaged by their inconsistent methods of relating to the adolescent. As the chemical dependency becomes more pronounced and more dramatic, parents tend to see their child as a public symptom of their parental imperfection and they begin to defend themselves separately by blaming each other. At this point the alcoholism or drug dependency serves as a giant wedge that further splits parental structure as well as splitting the marriage relationship. Acting-out, chemically dependent adolescents can stimulate a conflict between married partners as the adolescent attempts to move from their control toward independence (4, 5).

While we were quite familiar with the above description of family homeostasis from past experience, the pattern initially did not seem to fit the Brandon family very well. Although somewhat confused by this, our belief was that whatever patterns of family equilibrium existed, they probably needed to be almost blindly interrupted first and understood later. Operating on this premise, Dave's initial assumption was that Tina needed to enter a hospital to get time away from home so that she could at least have the opportunity to learn new behavioral patterns away from the restricting expectations and sanctions of her family. Likewise, he assumed that the parents needed time to rest, to cry, and in their case, to pray. After Tina's hospital treatment, we felt that the marital relationship then needed time and special attention separate from total family therapy. Our efforts in working with parents are aimed at having the husband and wife see their marriage relationship as a priority rather than just focusing on their parenting roles. Since we discovered this in our own marriage, we share this with married couples who are our clients.

Bias #3: We oftentimes do more therapy by accident than by design. While we may have some specific goals about where we want a family to go in therapy, the innuendos of technique, probing questions, or brilliant interpretations are uncharted in any particular session with a specific family. Hope, encouragement, compassion, respect, trust—and liking the people we see in therapy—tend to cover up or forgive the mistakes that all of us as therapists inevitably make.

Dave's first meeting with the parents at our Alcohol Detoxification Center included some "accidental therapy": as Betty recalled, "We were so impressed with the compassion we received. As we were leaving our first session with you, you stopped us at the front door and expressed some hopefulness for Tina and that was very encouraging—we needed that!" Of course, I had no recollection of stopping them at the door and it occurred to me that if I had had to go to the bathroom, I simply would not have stopped to add any encouraging comment. Certainly, it was *not* planned as any great therapeutic gesture but nevertheless, was seen that way by them and I was credited as being a sensitive and competent therapist (which is not a bad way to begin an influential therapeutic relationship).

Bias #4: Siblings need attention/prevention. Coleman (6) has alerted us to possible "infectiousness" of drug and alcohol abuse from sibling to sibling. She cautions that "even the ever-widening group of professionals who are using family therapy to treat drug addicts have failed to give much attention to the effect of siblings on drug-using behavior." We did look for symptomatic behavior in Tim without doing a formal chemical-dependency assessment and we did monitor his chemical-use patterns. While there was alcohol abuse on Tim's part, our expressed cautions to everyone in the family to monitor his use by sharing their concerns openly in sessions seemed to be the level of attention that his alcohol use required. Our greater concern was his isolation from the intense family process that had taken place with Tina's discovered chemical dependency, intervention, and hospital treatment. Tina had received a lot of attention during inpatient residential hospital treatment and Tim was ignored even more. Mom had a clear sense of this as she recalled telling her husband, "We have another one at home . . . we'll lose him if we don't get over our depression!" In therapy, we made specific efforts to involve Tim again in this family.

Bias #5: All treatment efforts must be consistent with inner-core family values. We suggest to other therapists and we remind ourselves that we should trust our instincts regarding sensitive family values. For whatever reasons, we must not trample on them and not worry about discovering the "whys" until later. When the need arises to confront these values or to interrupt family patterns that are based on inner-core values, it must be done carefully and with a relationship of trust. We immediately sensed the few sensitive values that needed to be respected in the Brandon family:

1. Anger expressions were foreign to the entire family.

2. Religion and spirituality had deep tradition in this family system. As a result, four-letter words would be offensive and clearly contraindicated in all sessions. Also, the spirituality of Alcoholics Anonymous was consistent with their religious spirituality and perhaps made the orientation of the inpatient treatment phase more readily palatable to Tina and to her parents.

3. Firmly rooted in Mom and Dad's family of origin was the accepted position of the father as the head of the household and family leader. The issue of paternal control needed to be nurtured most of the time and only cautiously confronted in family therapy. Our efforts to reinforce Mom and Dad's equality in parenting decisions had to acknowledge and yet cautiously expose this value of Dad's position as final authority. Therapy interpretations that would challenge this value and parenting pattern had to be very gentle. Any such attempts that were overly aggressive would be quickly rejected or sabotaged by the strong paternal authority that was well accepted in the marriage relationship. As therapists, our tendency is generally to support a greater equality between marital partners in presenting parental limits and controls. However, just as family therapists must be cautious about cultural differences in family patterns, we need to be sensitive to the culture of the family itself.

4. Another consistent value that happens to fit with this family is their emphasis on sickness or illness as an acceptable dysfunction—as opposed to the view that their daughter was a "bad person" or a "juvenile delinquent." Our philosophy of treatment with the Brandons—from our Detox Center to the hospital facility and on to outpatient family therapy—emphasized the "disease concept" of chemical dependency. Only much later in family therapy did we discover Mom's childhood history of hospitalization at age four and that she had been bedridden for one year at age ten. Mom's sensitivity to the concept of illness allowed her to be open to accepting Tina's chemical dependency as a disease state.

Bias #6: Marital therapy with a therapist-couple has unique advantages. As a married couple who happen to be counselors, most of our work together has been with parents of adolescent alcohol and drug abusers. We believe our married status provides unique role modeling for couples in both their marital and parental relationships. Another therapist-couple has described this modeling: "Although there may be some advantage in a male and female therapist-team who are not married to each other or in a therapist-team of the same sex, there is a certain camaraderie, a special mutual understanding, which exists when the therapist-team is also a marital team. Such a team is able to reveal itself as individuals *and* as a therapist-couple during the course of therapy" (7). By disagreeing sharply during sessions and demonstrating that disagreements need not be catastrophic, they receive a message of hope, optimism, and normalcy. We firmly believe that things can be changed without one partner winning and the other losing, and several of our parent-clients have voiced their appreciation of having a therapist-couple who have had and continue to have problems that were and can be solved (or perhaps remain unsolved yet still negotiable).

Bias #7: Therapy should be fun. Once adolescent chemical dependency has been uncovered in a family, we can assume that parents have been in debilitating emotional pain for a long time. While parts of the therapy process also will be painful, family members have a desperate need to enjoy each other's company again and yet need help to do this. We encourage family members to have fun together and we structure fun times in homework assignments. We also attempt to interject humor or to recognize humor in painful situations. Projective techniques are often helpful in doing this. For example, early recollections of the parent's childhood were designed to provide an atmosphere of growth and enjoyment as well as a tool to assist the parents in sharing that very special part of their lives with their children. Sentence-completion exercises were used "just for the fun of it."

Phases of Treatment

The Brandon's story includes four distinct phases: (a) Mom and Dad discovering Tina's chemical abuse (six days); (b) detoxification, diagnosis, and family intervention (five days); (c) inpatient treatment for adolescent chemical dependency (six weeks); and (d) outpatient family therapy (five months).

A. Discovery Stage

More important than the details of how Tina's chemical abuse was discovered is the pattern of her parents' responses. Although Tina experimented with alcohol and pot as early as age twelve, her parents had no solid suspicions until she was sixteen. Betty recalled: "She had bought a car, with our permission, of course. We had loaned her some money with the idea that she would pay it right back. We were kind of busy and didn't get around to collecting. Things weren't going too well, especially between Tina and her dad and we knew something was wrong but couldn't put our fingers on it. Keith suggested that I try to get the money from her and so I talked to her about it. She didn't have the money and that seemed kind of strange to us because she had made quite a bit of money in the summer (it was now early November) and we didn't think she had spent it all. So I pressed her for it and, I guess, I said 'what have you been spending it all for?'. Finally, I asked her if I could see her checkbook and she said, "No, my checkbook is private!' I don't think I had ever asked her something where she had flatly come out and said 'no' like that before. I was appalled but tried not to show how shocked I was. I continued, 'I know something is wrong and I want you to tell me what it is,' but she continued to refuse. I told her I loved her and said 'no matter what you've done I will love you.' She replied, 'I don't think you can take it!'."

The communication between Mom and Tina was fairly open and direct. Tina's response was an ambivalent invitation to Mom to probe more. Tina obviously could have covered up much better had she really wanted to. Tina then confessed, "It's pot." In Tina's sophistication in business but her naivete in the drug world, she had paid for some drug purchases by check. Mom gave a short lecture about how "It's not legal and it is opposed to everything we ever taught you," etc. Tina remorsefully agreed and readily promised she would quit. In reflecting back, Betty knew that as soon as Tina promised so easily, she knew she didn't mean it.

Because of the close relationship between Tina and Mom we might expect Mom to protect Tina from Dad as well as to protect Dad from the hurt of knowing of Tina's drug use. Parental unity, however, was clearly communicated to Tina as Mom told her, "I will talk to your Dad tonight about this." It was not a threat of discipline but rather a message that there would be no covering up from one parent to another. "Keith and I talked and we prayed together—we completely talked it over. But we didn't know quite what we should do."

The next day, Dad had occasion to want to move Tina's car but with her "confession" as a guide, he suspiciously looked for "something" and found three long plastic packages of what he presumed was marijuana. Dad left the bags in the glove compartment of her car and locked it up again. Given Mom's reliance on her husband for security and major decisions, she told him, "Do whatever you think is best," a supportive gesture with a double edge of "I'll let him do the dirty work!" (not consciously intended, of course.) Dad asked Tina to go with him for a ride in her car and he drove her directly to the police station.

Dad explained: "I wanted to get it all out in the open. The police officer was somewhat stunned. I guess they had never had a parent drive their kid there with the glove compartment full of drugs before. I asked him to completely search the car. In addition to the three plastic bags, they found a half-empty quart in the trunk and some empty beer cans. As they unwrapped the plastic bags, they also found some folded pieces of tin foil. The officer asked Tina what they were; she, of course, replied, 'I don't know—I'm keeping them for a friend of mine whose parents would be mad if they knew he had this (an excuse so common that it's probably inscribed on all high school bathroom walls from New York to California).' Police drug analysis later analyzed it as cocaine."

Dad's response was consistent with his controlling "head-of-the-household" personality but also with his insights. From several years of teaching in a state prison he knew that parents covering up was destructive. Tina was incensed at Dad but not at Mom, perhaps because he did the dirty work. Objectively, it was less important *what* Mom and Dad did or *who* actually did it, but that they did something immediate, dramatic, and firm!

Under questioning, Tina gave the police the name of one pusher and some answers but she was sufficiently vague to feign compliance while not being very helpful.

Once back home from the police station, Tina's parents demanded that they all clean up her room together. Mom outlined that "she came with us and we just went through everything . . . paraphernalia, pot pipes, blotter acid, some pills."

After taking an inventory that included twenty four tablets of blotter acid, Dad was recounting and found only twenty three (he was always precise in matters of business!). When he confronted Tina, she replied, "You must have miscounted." He firmly said, "No, I didn't." She went to her purse and returned the one that she had taken, explaining that she thought she would need that one later because this whole thing was upsetting to her. That gesture—"right in front of us"—helped Mom and Dad realize the extent of her preoccupation or need to get high. Since Tina had inherited Dad's preciseness in matters of business, Keith and Betty also found an account book of drug sales and a diary of drug experiences which revealed to them just how deeply she had been involved in the local drug scene.

Reflections of the Discovery Four Years Later:

Betty: I think Tina is still angry at Keith to this day for taking her to the police station as he did. I don't think she really understands the hell that we went through! Yet, the hardest thing we did was cleaning out her room. We had always been very, very careful of her privacy otherwise we would have discovered it [drug use] long ago. There is just no way to describe the hell that that day was . . . she had violated our trust, she had lied to us and so we felt that we did have the right to do what we did.

Tina: That's the most upset I've ever seen her [mom] . . . she had said, "I don't want to look in your room." . . . Dad was very mechanical about it. He asked to see my arms. I really felt bad that they might think I was a junkie.

Keith: I felt pretty confident about the decision to take her to the police. For me the hardest thing I ever did was to look at her arms—I was so afraid of what I might find, but there were no needle marks.

Tim: In junior high I noticed that she was hanging out with people with a drug reputation and that she was lying to Mom and Dad sometimes. One time I remember that she had a party and some kids were smoking grass in the basement while Mom and Dad were gone. I broke it up and got them out of there mostly because I didn't want my parents to be hurt. It was much later that I realized for sure that she was using . . . in about the ninth or tenth grade. We had different friends and so I didn't know for sure before that. I knew she was dealing about a month before my folks found out. I was scared she would be caught. She was using and not doing well in school, and I was worried about her future. That day when Dad and Tina got back from the police department I asked her what happened and she told me "Dad busted me." When I asked her what she was going to do now she said she'd quit using for a while and then probably use later. I felt disappointed. I was afraid for her. Through it all, though, I think I kept her friendship and a good relationship with her. I was glad she got busted and I hoped it would go all the way . . . so *something* would happen so she wouldn't go back to using. But I was really scared what it might do to my folks.

B. Detoxification and Intervention

After that fateful Saturday of "spring house-cleaning," Tina asked to be taken to a local detoxification center. She had known other kids who had gone there and they had said it wasn't so bad. Besides, about this time she wanted to get away from the awkward embarrassment and pressures at home and the reminder of hurt parents. Tina had no particular goal of straightening out but she did acknowledge a vague need for help of some kind. While this ambivalence is characteristic of adolescent development, it is even more true of adolescent chemical dependency and needs to be understood as such. Also, Tina knew she could smoke cigarettes there and couldn't at home. At this point her parents did not know she smoked at all. Although cigarettes seem like a comparatively minor issue, since Keith's father had (recently) died of lung cancer and Keith himself had been treated for cancer, Tina was not about to risk repercussions of any more surprises with Mom and Dad.

"It was a puzzlement to me why she wanted to go to the Detox Center. . . . I always thought that was a place for drunks to dry out," Keith recalled. "I called the Detox Center on Sunday and asked if it was possible to check in somebody and the nurse said, 'No, not unless the police bring them in.' I felt brushed off and was given to believe that the center was not what Tina thought it was. I kind of wrote that off thinking Tina did not know what she was talking about and that this was another con game. So Monday morning we called the Mental Health Center and made an emergency appointment with a psychologist. After a short session, this psychologist, I think his name was Tony, walked us next door to the Detox Center for an admission which then went very smoothly. We were feeling a lot of pressure and, frankly, it felt good to have her there—secure and safe. We felt we had to keep her from using and there she was locked up and we could rest." Betty too breathed relief: "I loved her but I was hurting and humiliated and I couldn't stand to see the sight of her right then! We cried a lot but never raised our voices at her."

At the time of Dave's session with Tina and her parents, on Tuesday afternoon, the nursing notes briefly outlined the chemical-use history as reported by Tina: marijuana, cocaine, and some barbiturates (her alcoholism was later diagnosed while she was in residential treatment). By itself, the drug history was not necessarily diagnostic of chemical dependency although it certainly documented abuse beyond mere experimentation. During our sessions, I made no attempt to make a *precise* diagnosis of alcoholism or drug dependency. It was clear enough, however, that she was so deeply involved in the local drug scene that hospital treatment would be necessary to interrupt the pattern of habitual use and drug sales. This need for treatment away from her parents in a residential setting was confirmed by seeing how close she and her mother were in contrast to the anger and contempt she displayed toward her father. Tina's anger and contempt, more clearly than the drug history, convinced me that any counseling short of residential treatment would predictably result in failure. Therefore, the plan for residential treatment was *not* based on an exact diagnosis of a pathological dependency on chemicals but rather on a sense of family disruption—of the tension and conflict in the parent-child relationships.

In my first interview with Mom and Dad and Tina together, my sense was that Tina appeared compliant enough to go to residential treatment if her mother told her to. Mom, feeling hurt and betrayed by Tina, seemed shaken enough to follow whatever the "professionals" recommended. It was Dad who I sensed needed to be "hooked" into moving in that direction. He appeared distant, perhaps hurt but rigidly firm, maybe even mechanical. I knew I had to make something happen with him; he was the key to the intervention and referral. I tried to develop rapport by asking what

I already knew from the nurse's notes. "How did you all get here?"
A simple enough question designed more to allay my apprehension
about how to approach Dad than anything else. Mom did most of
the describing. As I needed a sense of who Dad was, I asked him
some questions directly but he would answer somewhat awkwardly and his wife would finish the answers for him. As I gradually sensed more hurt than anger on his part and became more
sure of how deeply hurt he must be, I chanced one technique—the
only technique that came to mind that might "hook" him. I simply
asked, "Do you love Tina?" This always seems to be a safe question
to ask a parent. Surely, any self-respecting, "good" parent trying
to protect his self-esteem should automatically reply, "Yes, of
course!" Luckily, he did. I asked him how long it had been since
he had told her, "I love you." He hesitantly admitted that it had
been quite some time, perhaps several years. I quietly asked him
if he would like to tell her that now. He was not prepared for this.
("Shouldn't this counselor be asking her about her drug use and
extract some names of pushers and promises of being good?")
Awkwardly, he glanced at her; "Tina, I do love you!" he announced. With more certainty, I pushed: "How long has it been
since you have hugged Tina?" His fear showed in his quivering
smile, "Not since she was a little girl." When I asked if he would
be willing to do that now, like an explosion, this father who had
"been really mechanical about it all" was devastated by emotion,
reduced to tremulous sobs, rushed the distance of four feet to
Tina's chair, aching to hold her. He clutched his arms around her
head and shoulders.

Tina sat limp and listless in the chair with no apparent emotion
while her father shook in tears. His one risk of emotion and her
unprepared shock of flat rejection is my first and most vivid memory of this family.

Mom, the powerhouse in the family, sat by as I did, feeling
helpless in this still volcano and shockwave of emotion. Yet, Dad's
tears are what I had hoped would happen and knew needed to
happen so that this family could begin to do something with their
chaos. As Keith shook in his tears, I *knew* Tina would hug him
back. When she didn't, *I* felt angry at her. "How could she be so
insensitive . . . my God, will my daughter some day do the same?"
I personally identified strongly with Keith's pain. My insides, my

feelings were diagnostic—for sure, she needed inpatient treatment!

From that moment, the referral to a hospital treatment program was a matter of mechanics.

Reflections of Detoxification and Intervention Four Years Later

Betty: As we left Tina at the Detox Center, I remember getting in the car, looking at each other and realizing how overwhelmed we were by the warmth and the compassion. I don't think we had expected that. Knowing that they hear this every day, we just had not expected such caring. We expected perhaps an attitude that "here is the juvenile delinquent-type who's done all these terrible things." Of course, Keith's breaking down and crying made quite an impression on Tina, and on me, too. I haven't seen that happen much. He has not done that before or since to that extent in my presence, and that was impressive. I remember saying to Keith, "That was some skillful counseling!" The feeling that we are going to get some help, that somebody knows about it and has had experience and can tell us what to do. One thing that I will never forget, and I will always be grateful for, is that when we were leaving, we said goodbye to Tina, you came and caught up with us and said, "I can see some real hope for her—I'm not saying this to make you feel good, and I don't say this to everybody but I can see that the two of you are united and that gives me hope." It was such a good thing to hang on to! I really appreciated that. That extra little interest in us and Tina and knowing that we needed encouragement.

Keith: I remember hugging Tina and crying! I don't do that much, you know. I even surprised myself. But I felt some hope. . . . I had the sense we had totally lost our daughter and this felt like some glimmer of hope of reconciliation.

With such good therapeutics taking place—Dad's crying, a quick and clear treatment plan, and well-placed morsels of support—we might expect that Tina's perception of the Detox stay was equally therapeutic. It wasn't! But it was perhaps equally eventful.

Tina: After I had given the police the name of one pusher, they had told me not to talk to him or contact him at all! When I got to Detox there he was. . . . God, what irony! . . . One of the guys that I was going out with was in there too. He was discharged about three hours before my other boyfriend came to visit. I remember staff sitting around and watching—seeing me sitting with one guy and then when he takes off seeing me with another guy. I was really depressed there, though. I felt really guilty, really bad about hurting my folks—especially my mother. I do remember my Dad crying—that's the *only* time I've seen him cry. I never ever saw him shake and cry like that—I was really tense, I did not know how to react. . . . I don't think I reacted at all—I think I just sat there and felt really uncomfortable. I've never seen him emotional at all. He might say that he's angry but he never shows that he's angry or that he's feeling anything. He always appears to be in the same mood.

During the two-week waiting period of inpatient treatment, I negotiated with Tina's parents for her to stay in Detox a total of five days and then return home to await an open bed in the hospital. We contracted for her not to use any chemicals while at home and invited her to return to the Detox Center if she needed to (if she was afraid of using or if her parents had any suspicions of any use). They needed the reassurance that that option was immediately available. Tina was home two days and almost begged to return to the Detox Center. Wearing pajamas in the Detox Center for a few days did not look quite so depressing anymore!

Tina: My Dad took off from work and stayed home and watched me like a hawk. I couldn't even get out of the house to go to the grocery store. I was dying for a cigarette and couldn't get out of his sight. He kept picking at me too. He wanted to know every little thing that I had ever done wrong. He kept searching for information. I think he felt very helpless and that the only thing he thought he could do was to watch me to make sure I did not go out and buy drugs.

Mom was really supportive of me going into treatment and Dad really felt responsible for what happened to me. Tim came to visit me once but we were distant and very different at that time. He would always tell me that I shouldn't be using drugs. He knew everything practically and was concerned about me. He always asked me how I was doing but he never threatened to tell my parents. (Tina did return to the Detox Center for another four days and then a bed opened up at the inpatient treatment facility.)

Tim: I was relieved she was in Detox and really glad she was going to treatment. But, I was disappointed that she said she'd use again when she'd get out. And then when she told me one of her boyfriends got some acid into Detox for her I felt really down and disappointed.

Mom (speaking for Mom and Dad): "We cried a lot and were depressed when Tina was in Detox. The shock of it all! In our talking we did decide that we have another one to be concerned about at home—if we're depressed all the time, we're going to lose him. . . . We tried hard to be cheerful but it was hard. Our greatest fear was that she might run . . . and never come back, or even commit suicide. It was a terrifying time.

C. Hospital-Based Adolescent Chemical Dependency Treatment

St. Mary's Hospital (Minneapolis) Adolescent Chemical Dependency Unit was one pioneer in hospital-based treatment of adolescents with chemical dependency. What started as a narcotic and other drug detoxification unit in 1972 had rapidly changed by 1974 to provide specific programming geared to adolescent chemical dependency treatment (8). While my two-hour assessment of the family at the Detox Center may have validly pointed in the direction of hospital-based treatment, one of their goals in the hospital would be further diagnosis.

The initial two weeks were in an intensive locked evaluation unit in order to differentiate the substance *abuser* (who has considerable *choice* over the use of chemicals) from the chemically dependent adolescent (who has lost the element of choice and judgment of whether or not to use chemicals). One method for such differentiation is noting significantly greater conflicts between one's values versus one's behaviors in the chemically dependent adolescent. Tina's drug history and value conflicts fit the pattern of the chemically dependent adolescent. The extent of her alcohol abuse was also uncovered through routine administration of the Adolescent Alcohol Involvement Scale (9). Her score of 61 alerted the hospital staff to dig deeper in uncovering the specifics of her alcoholism which had been really overshadowed by her other drug usage. After ten days she was transferred down the hall to the unlocked primary treatment unit for an additional four weeks. This multidisciplinary team staff provided a consistent therapeutic milieu to minimize manipulation of individual staff members by patients.

Consistent with Bias #1 above, the philosophy of the St. Mary's Adolescent Chemical Dependency program emphasized that while there is typically a drug of choice, dependency is always expanded to include all mood-altering substances; such an emotional dependency on an altered state of consciousness has no respect for the pharmacopoeia but rather is an intimate emotional attachment to getting high.

Based on the disease model of adult alcoholism, the program presented didactic material to educate adolescent patients and parents in the disease concept. The hospital's program philosophy is heavily steeped in Alcoholics Anonymous with emphasis on the 1st Step of AA: "We admitted that we were powerless over alcohol [and other drugs] and that our lives had become unmanageable." An acceptance of this "powerlessness" (loss of choice and judgment) was a primary goal of treatment. For Tina, however, it was not so much AA while in hospital treatment that was significant. Rather, what "hooked" Tina or "convinced me to stay straight" was what happened to her when she got out. "I really liked my AA group and really felt close to them after I got involved in AA back home. In contrast to not feeling close to anyone when I was using . . . they cared about me in AA. That's what really kept me straight."

What was most important about her hospital stay was her hostility. Tina had wondered what treatment would be like. She was apprehensive and scared but someone had assured her that, "All I would have to do is go there and read a bunch of books and come out—really easy! So when I went there I was expecting to just sit around and talk to people and read some books. When I got there my roommate, who had been there three weeks, had told me that she was planning to go straight and how much good she had gotten out of the program. I couldn't believe that anybody really wanted to go straight. I just expected that they were all going to try to bullshit their way through and that's what I was going to do. I was really hostile for the first four weeks. I felt very different from everyone else—I just couldn't express myself as others did. I had a hard time explaining how I was feeling. I didn't know what they wanted me to say and I was so out of touch with my feelings. I felt really helpless! I was trying so hard to cooperate but I just didn't understand what they wanted. I wasn't saying the things that they wanted to hear. For four years I had felt practically nothing and I was mainly concerned with saying whatever they wanted to hear from me. I finally started to get in touch with my anger after about three and a half weeks. It was a turning point when I stormed out of my chair during one group and screamed at one of the counselors. He had called me a slut or something and I started shouting obscenities at him. I got good strokes for that. I still didn't understand why they had wanted me to yell but he provoked me until I did and then it felt so good. That was the turning point."

Family or parent involvement on Sunday night was a didactic lecture in large groups of nearly eighty people (patients, siblings, parents) followed by AlAnon for parents only. Monday night was a three-hour therapy group of parents with their adolescents (four to six families per group).

The turning point for Mom and Dad was "one of those dreadful Monday nights." Those groups were terrifying for Betty: "All day I would dread those Monday nights, they were *so* painful and I shook, I was so afraid of what would come out. The night we finally hit bottom Tina had been there three weeks and a counselor said, 'Tina, I think it's time for you to share with your parents the extent of your drug use.' I thought we knew it all but it was astounding. Up until that time she had maintained that she had smoked a little pot but that she had not used any other stuff—that she had been keeping it for other kids. And we had believed her! As she went through the litany of the variety and quantity and the extent of her dealing, her dishonesty really hit us and we had this picture of a totally degenerate daughter. Up until that point she had not been making good progress—she had been *so* dishonest, even in treatment! That was the absolute bottom for us—the utter hopelessness—it hurt so deep."

From that point on, for the remaining two weeks of treatment, Tina and her parents began to progress. Yet, they all had so far to go and were so vulnerable to old patterns—Tina to use and medicate her feelings, and her parents to try to control.

Reflections of Hospital-Based Treatment Four Years Later:

Betty: I remember my own anger, especially at God. It all seemed so unfair. Here we didn't drink or smoke, our family was intact, and we didn't set that kind of example. There were other families there where they did set such an example and yet our daughter was in the same place. We did meet another couple, though, a Lutheran minister and his wife, and their case fit us more closely than many of the other families. It was hopeful for us to meet another couple with such a strong faith as we had."

Keith felt angry too and although he couldn't express it directly, he could clearly identify it.

Keith: I remember a father saying to his daughter that she would buy anything on the street corner from a "junkie" with complete trust and yet have no trust in her own father. That really caught my attention—that the affection and trust of a child could so easily be manipulated away from a parent. I felt empathy with that father. "Lace it to her," I thought. "Tell her how it is to be a crushed father!" He summed it up well: "You kids have had all the fun of getting high and we've had all the grief." I appreciated how frank he was. We received a lot of support from other families and knowing that we were not alone helped.

(Keith's conflict over the "disease model" reflects not only the dilemma of many parents but also the judgmental ambivalence of a broader society.)

The disease theory impressed me! I can see the rationale behind it—that it helps eliminate blame. I bought some of the theory but I had serious reservations. It seems to me that with alcoholism and drug use there is some involvement for which the person should stand accountable. I believe Tina was accountable and not an innocent bystander who happened to "catch a disease" as one catches a cold. But, we were in a situation, desperate for help and we were about to do anything they wanted us to do to help our daughter get out of the situation. I felt as if I were playing some sort of charade whereby I was adopting that [disease] philosophy for a while. On the other hand, I morally could not accept that Tina or anyone else should escape the personal responsibility that they have for their drug use.

Betty: I agree with Keith but I realize that there is such a point where the person cannot help himself. I do think Tina was at that point!

Tina: I do believe it that it is a disease in a way and in another way I believe it is more of a behavioral problem. I don't know if I believed everything they told me. I questioned a lot and I still do. I don't see hardly anybody from that hospital group anymore [four years later]. There is only one that I know that is still straight—that I still see once in a while at NA [Narcotics Anonymous]. A lot of them, from what I have heard, are using again or they've moved east or west. A couple of them died . . . one was a suicide and he was using then. The other one had an accident and he was still straight. The staff did say it was a life and death disease but nobody would believe that . . . maybe it wasn't an arbitrary scare . . . I don't know.

(Betty's hurt, pain, and depression needed some release and she found at least one avenue for support.)

Betty: I cried over everybody's problems because those are the saddest stories I have ever heard. In fact, as long as two years afterwards I would break down crying when I would get a vivid reminder about a family in trouble. The scenes were so moving between parents and their children . . . the emotion that was there, the hanging on and yet still trying to let go. These counselors would tell us to let go . . . to detach. I remember one mother and her son. It was clear they loved each other but he was not going to give up his drugs. I remember her saying to me, "It's so easy for these young single counselors who have never been parents, to say 'let go'—they have no idea what that means!" She was angry at the counselors who would say that and I guess I had that feeling too.

And yet, that's precisely what Keith and Betty had to do: to face their daughter's growing up, that they couldn't do much to really control her ever again. Whatever decisions she made—good or bad—would be hers to make. "Hitting bottom" for them was the dreadful realization that (to paraphrase Step 1 of AlAnon), "We are powerless over Tina and her chemical use."

Letting go of Tina was one thing, letting go of the hurt and anger was something else.

Betty: The dishonesty was always the worst. I could tolerate almost anything else. It makes one feel angry and betrayed. I had trusted her and she let me down all the way. I thought I had forgiven her right from the start but even two years later I discovered I was still angry . . . I still had not "let go." It was more of a spiritual battle for me. I realized I hadn't really forgiven her. I then asked Tina for forgiveness—for my not having forgiven her. She was very accepting of any feelings of anger on our part, although she'll never completely understand all that we went through—but she does seem to understand more and more as she matures."

Tina was also critical of some of the counselors: Some of the things [techniques] were unethical. I don't know about the signs we'd have to wear—I suppose they had a purpose but I don't think I got much out of my signs: "Confront me when I'm passive"; "I'm an angry, hostile junky"; "I'm always a people pleaser." I didn't really agree with that. I realize I was angry and hostile but I think they put too much emphasis on it. A lot of my anger came out of hurt but they wanted me to be more angry than hurt. I really believe I was more hurt and to express it as anger just didn't fit. The whole group would sometimes get down on me and pick me apart and I don't think that was too ethical. I suppose I needed something like that to shake me up because it would have taken a lot for me to want to go straight and it did take a lot, too. I guess it shook me up enough to make a decision not to use but I thought it was gimmicky. The main reason I wanted to go straight was because it hurt my parents.

Tim: I don't remember too much about Tina in the hospital. Mostly I remember feeling left out. I had to work a lot so I couldn't go to the family groups and I wasn't sure I wanted to anyway. I went to one group and Tina was swearing. I didn't know what that would do to Mom and Dad. Then, I did visit her once about two weeks before she came home and was really surprised. She seemed interested and concerned for other kids there . . . about dry parties. There was some indication she might be serious about staying straight.

D. Family Therapy

Tina's minimal progress during most of her inpatient treatment, her father's continued distance or hesitant involvement within the family picture, and her mother's understandable lack of trust all pointed to a strong recommendation by hospital staff for family therapy following discharge from inpatient treatment.

The six-week interval during her hospitalization had been good for me (Dave). My earlier angry feelings over Tina's insensitivity and my strong identification with her father's hurt had diminished and were mitigated by the sense that she had successfully completed an adolescent chemical-dependency program. Also, my ego had been stroked by having this family come back and personally seek me out for family therapy. I had no illusions, however, that Keith's aloofness, Betty and Tina's coalition, or even Tina's drug use had been dented very deeply. What we did essentially agree to was a *beginning* into family therapy, to continue to monitor her drug abstinence and generally improve family functioning. As therapists, we had only a vague goal of trying to realign the mother-daughter coalition, strengthen the father-daughter relationship, and reintegrate the missing mystery son, Tim, back into the family circle.

Session 1: January 4 (½ hour)

First contact with Tina was a brief thirty minutes at *her* request to see Dave alone. This was essentially to refer her to an AA group and to get a quick sense of whether or not she had made any changes. I was curious: "Are we working with a conning little witch who has done a snow job on her parents or is there someone genuine, sensitive, and sincere to work with?" I think Tina wanted to show me too.

I discovered a new person when Tina and I re-met. She was cute, even pretty as she could smile now without the tenseness of hostility. She was pleasant, appropriately cautious, and most of all sparkling with some enthusiasm about what she had learned about herself and her chemical dependency. She was enthusiastic to be straight and sober and she could laugh spontaneously. The intense bitterness, cold, stark depression, and distance that I had so vividly remembered from our intervention session had disappeared. I knew this was no guarantee of what her life might be like three weeks or three months later but it did mean there was a lot to work with. Tina showed me she had the courage and power to change. With this hope, I could look forward to focusing on her parents and other family issues rather than spending all of our energies on confronting Tina. It was an important realization for me that I was no longer feeling judgmental. Instead, I felt eager. This might even be fun!

Sessions 2, 3, and 4: January ll, 20; February l (2–2½ hours each)

These next three family therapy sessions included all four family members. As therapists, we basically had four goals:

1. To increase (enhance) family communication.
2. To monitor Tina's sobriety and deal with any chemical use that might occur.
3. To emphasize Tim as part of this family since he had not been a part of the therapy focus at any other time during intervention or treatment.
4. To challenge the existing patterns of family balance and to strengthen the parental subsystem.

As much of life seems to take on clarity of purpose in retrospect, so too our goals became clearer as therapy progressed and as we reflected back on what evolved during those sessions. Certainly as we shared some mumbled agenda with the Brandons as we began, our stated goals were far less precise and articulate than those written here. We also recall that whatever was going to be achieved in family therapy was uncharted territory and we knew we would have to play it by ear!

To Mom and Dad, family therapy presented a "hope for closeness," a reestablished family unity and a validation that this family will survive—"We haven't lost Tina from our family." Early in therapy, Mom expressed surprise that all four of them could communicate so well: "This is one of the few places we can go *as a family* and leave with a sense of accomplishment." Keith knew that he needed some help in reestablishing a relationship and communication with Tina and he viewed family therapy as a mechanism to achieve that. After all, the head of the family *must* provide such leadership! Betty saw family therapy as a dire need for herself. At the hospital she had been confronted in sessions that left her vulnerable and fragile. Her self-esteem was low and she felt like a failure: Supermom was tarnished! Family therapy was a place where she could continue to be confronted on her controlling issues and on the coalition that she had with Tina and yet do that with an atmosphere of acceptance and respect. She dreaded going to each session because she dreaded "losing control" and crying. Perhaps she feared crying to the point of not being able to stop. Clinically, she was depressed. Family therapy was a milieu to treat her depression.

Tina saw family therapy as a place where she could safely be direct and even hostile to her parents. It was a place where she felt they could let go of her, whereas they could not let go of her at home: "They wouldn't listen to me at home, but they would listen to me at those sessions." She also saw family sessions as treatment for Mom and Dad—"I had treatment but they hadn't—they needed a lot of help!" Tim came willingly but had no idea of agenda or goals. He was mostly curious.

As therapists, we saw family therapy mostly for the benefit of parents: "To help them to survive . . . to help their *marriage* to survive."

Before any confrontations or criticisms, we wanted individual and family strengths to build on. Using a lot of newsprint as a huge visual notepad for all six of us to refer to, we began by asking for an initial description of family members by each other. It was a "brainstorming" atmosphere. Their consensual descriptions illustrate who made up this family and gave us some immediate insights of personalities and family roles:

Keith was described as using big words, very logical, a "feeling stuffer," unpredictable but always cool, advice giver, avoids anger, intolerant, gets headaches, stubborn, head of house.

Betty was seen as sensitive, shows that she gets easily hurt, a pleaser—everyone else comes first, takes responsibility for others' feelings, dependent on children for happiness, a feeling person, a worrier.

Since Tim was a total stranger to us, we were as curious about him as he was about us. He "shows good feelings, bottles up bad feelings; very level, happy; if someone asks about feelings, he distracts and does not reveal them; has a hard time socializing, is worried about what others think about him, doesn't want others to know how he feels, doesn't know what to do with feelings."

Interestingly, Tina was viewed as one who uses conning to get her way, a pleaser, enables mother to be a pleaser, is spoiled, cries easily, protects other people's feelings, gets her own way, intelligent, unsure of self, sensitive, and stubborn.

Using a similar exercise to build more on strengths, we asked both parents to present traits that they liked about Tim and Tina. This was an effort to get them to feel their sense of pride in their children, to verbalize compliments and to have their children express an acceptance of these compliments by saying "thank you." This revealed more about Tim and Tina but also demonstrated Keith and Betty's ability to reach consensus and said something about how free or how inhibited they were in acknowledging the individuality and independence of their children.

With a broader purpose, we used a thirty eight-item list of adjectives to describe character attributes and asked Mom and Dad to rate Tim and Tina as *individuals* either "high," "medium," or "low." While this exercise displayed some additional areas of individual interests or abilities (or lack thereof), it also began to illustrate their cooperation and competition as siblings: for example, Tim was highly competitive, had an unparalleled sense of humor, and was an excellent mechanic and Tina had agreed not to compete in these areas. In exchange, Tim allowed Tina to excel in school, music, and art. In this unspoken "contract" as siblings, they had agreed not to compete with each other for their unique identities in these areas. Our greater interest, however, was to sort out traits where both scored high (intelligent, mischievous, selfish, sensitive/easily hurt, idealistic, spoiled, religious) or both scored low (athletic). We defined these areas as "family values"—values held so strongly by both parents that both children internalized them for their own. Because parents are always aware of rejected family values ("she lied to us!"), our purpose was to help Keith and Betty identify areas where both children were carrying on family values, traditions, and cohesion—a sense of family ethos. Also, to have parents discuss *both* children simultaneously served to realign the sibling subsystem once again to include Tim and provided an opportunity to strengthen the parental subsystem. The grid shown in Figure 5-1 indicates highs and lows while the blank spaces represent medium ratings. Again, all this was charted on newsprint to be used for visual reference in later sessions.

In another session, using a twenty-item sentence-completion exercise "just for the fun of it," we had them share their completed

Figure 5-1
Attribute Rating Grid

	TIM	TINA
Intelligence	H	H
Grades in school	L	H
Hard worker		L
Helped around the house	L	
Conformed		H
Openly rebelled	L	
Tried to please others		L
Used charm		
Mischievous	H	H
Considerate	H	L
Critical of others	L	
Selfish	H	H
Demanded way	L	H
Got way	L	H
Sensitive—easily hurt	H	H
Felt sorry for self		
Complained	L	
Temper tantrums	L	
Competitive	H	
Sense of humor	H	
Idealistic	H	H
Materialistic	H	
Standards of achievement		
Standards of right/wrong		
Standards of behavior		H
Athletic	L	L
Physical strength	H	
Height	L	
Looks		
Masculine		L
Feminine	L	
Spoiled	H	H
Punished		
Number of friends	L	
Musical	L	H
Artistic	L	H
Religious	H	H
Mechanical	H	L

sentences to help them practice talking as a family about nonthreatening issues; this was planned deemphasis of the crisis issues that had been the main source of their communication in the past several weeks. Three brief examples illustrate how we used this technique and how we emphasized the importance of "I" statements in communicating with one another:

I am . . .
  Keith: "afraid for Tina."
  Betty: "sensitive, emotional."
  Tim: "quiet."
  Tina: "a woman."

The trouble with most women is . . .
  Keith: "that they worry too much."
  Betty: "they don't have enough confidence in their own abilities."
  Tim: "they hide emotions."
  Tina: "they depend too much on men."

I wish I could be . . .
  Keith: "more efficient"
  Betty: "more relaxed."
  Tim: "better."
  Tina: "completely self-sufficient."

Sometimes I wish my family (or family members) . . .
  Keith: "[my children] were more religious."
  Betty: "[son] would show he cares about me."
  Tim: "[family] was rowdy."
  Tina: "[my parents] wouldn't be so suspicious [let me make my own decisions]."

We would interrupt and comment or discuss, by saying something like, "How do you feel when you hear that, Mom?" or, "How does it feel to say that out loud, Tim?"

Homework was assigned to realign coalitions, to have fun together, and to enhance communications. Specific assignments served as a conscious extension of family therapy between sessions. For example, we suggested that they hold a family meeting at home to discuss family business such as the week's plans and other family business but *not* to let it in any way become a bitching session. We assigned family members to go out for an evening together in less familiar combinations: Keith and Tina were assigned to go out and do something fun together and Betty and Tim were instructed to do the same thing. In addition, they were to sit down together in pairs to plan it out forty-eight hours in advance.

All of the above techniques firmly emphasized positive family communication, which we were able to do with the Brandons because they had dealt with much of the "shit" during hospitalization. But we didn't forget the "admission ticket" that brought us all together. In the very first session we clarified that each therapy session would begin with: "Tina, since our last session, have you used, even a little bit or just one, any mood-altering chemicals?" We would also direct to each family member: "Do you know of or do you have any, even a little, suspicions that Tina has used any mood-altering chemicals? If so, let's get it out." This was to assure the parents that the issue of relapse to drug use is one area that we as therapists would be responsible for bringing up (so that the parents could let go of the issue more easily) and that we would be there with Keith and Betty to go through it with them—"You don't have to face it alone!" With several weeks of abstinence, we began asking this question less specifically, in an effort to communicate trust to Tina, and we would use it as a springboard to direct communication; "Mom, say to Tina, 'I trust you now but I still get scared.' " Yet we never let go of the importance of monitoring the issue of possible relapse.

Sessions 5 and 6: February 8 and 18 (2–2½ hours each)

Sessions 5 and 6 were conjoint sessions with Keith and Betty without their children. The purpose was to explore their families of origin to discover some roots to their individual personalities and the modeling for their marital and parenting relationships. We also wanted them to see themselves and each other within the context of their family systems and to discover the consistency of their values, attitudes, and relationship patterns from childhood to marriage to parenthood. We elicited data from their childhood and adolescent years to help them rediscover feelings of adolescence, and then to point out similar feelings and patterns in Tina and Tim. Our purpose in not having their children present was to feel more open to confront dysfunctional behavior and coalitions without threatening their parental status or causing them to feel defensive.

The techniques we used were part of the Life-Style Analysis as formulated by Alfred Adler and others. In this context, Life-Style refers to a person's "style of acting, thinking, and perceiving which constitutes a cognitive framework within which he selects the specific operations which enable him to cope with life's tasks. It expresses the central theme through which his behavior can be understood. While he may not be completely aware of his life style, he acts congruently within his apperceptive scheme; the life style forms a unifying principle, a *Gestalt* to which behavior is bound in accordance to the individual 'law of movement.' Through this framework, developed early and remaining fairly consistent throughout life, an individual interprets, controls, and predicts experience" (10).

With this theoretical background, we believed that Keith and Betty would reveal their current attitudes, outlook, and goals through collection and interpretation of family constellation and early recollections. An examination of family constellation included details of birth order, siblings' relationships, achievements and deficiencies, parent-child relationships, and the model of a marital relationship that they learned from their parents.

Thus began the two most significant sessions with Mom and Dad. Because the Life-Style is a fun and fascinating technique, we would have liked to reprint it in full but space (and perhaps reader tolerance) prevents this. We will, however, highlight the areas of insight that developed with Keith and Betty.

Parental Relationships

Betty described her father (and we wrote it all on newsprint for visual reference in Sessions 7 and 8) as "quiet, stable, a loving family man—head of household—his word always went! We didn't negotiate! The finest Christian I've ever known. Church was very important. Appears easy-going but is not; he is very stable, always in control and very kind." And, of course, whom did she marry? Keith is a head of the house, firm, loving, a very strong Christian, quiet, and always in control (particularly of himself and his emotions), which projects a strong image of stability.

Keith perceived his mother as "very competent, had things under control, resourceful, was self-assured, practical, and a teacher." And whom did Keith marry? A competent woman, a teacher with a compulsion to work who appears very self-assured.

Betty's memory of her mother was as a "sensitive, emotional, intelligent, high-strung person who was a very good mother; showed emotion a lot, was deeply involved with her children —maybe too much!" Not surprisingly, Betty learned well from her mother. She sees herself as sensitive, very emotional, a real worrier, who is overly concerned for her children.

Keith's father was a salesman, "taken up with business affairs, traveled a lot and therefore gone a lot." As a result, he was emotionally distant from Keith and his brother Darrel who was one year older; Keith identified "many characteristics of Dad in me—radical in solutions, a redneck when it came to order and justice." Yet, he described his parents' relationship with each other as "fairly warm and caring." Betty, too, described her parents' relationship as "warm, loving, a good marriage. He considered her view a lot and was protective of her; he was romantic and affectionate."

The value in these descriptions for Keith and Betty was to enable them to see how clearly they replicated their parents' models of personality traits and relationship patterns. The reminiscing was enjoyable for them, helped them have fun together, and added strength to the marital relationship while providing insights of a therapy process. Even more significant was the opportunity that family therapy created for them to share the insights of this inter-generational consistency of personality and behavior with their children in Sessions 7 and 8.

Birth order and sibling' relationships

Betty's family
Ron, age 46 (+6 years).
Paul, age 43 (+3 years).
BETTY, age 40.
Carl, age 37 (−3 years).
Dorothy Mae, died at age six weeks (−4 years)

Quick guesses (and guesses were used liberally throughout sessions) suggest that an only girl among all males would be a prized possession, even more so since the other girl in the family died. We might expect then that Betty was treated by her family in a very positive way; being taken care of (especially by males), she might often get her own way and thereby develop a dependent relationship on men. Her need for protection was accentuated by the fact that she was sickly as a child. She had whooping cough and was hospitalized for six weeks at age four and had rheumatic fever at age ten and therefore was confined to her bed for nearly a year. In simply processing these guesses, Mom developed some spontaneous insights. Just as her mother and brothers had protected her, she had protected Tina, almost as if to say, "If a mother doesn't protect a child enough [especially a girl] that child might protect a child enough [especially a girl] that child might even die!"

Betty fit rather well Mosak's (10) description of the Life-Style of a Controller: "The *controller* is either a person who wishes to control life or one who wishes to insure that life will not control her. She generally dislikes surprises, controls her spontaneity and hides her feelings since all of these may lessen her control. As substitutes, she favors intellectualization, rightness, orderliness, and neatness. With her God-like striving for perfection, she depreciates others."

Of course, this family climate of protecting women meshed with Keith's position and role in his family, only it was his mother whom he aligned with since he could not compete with his brother's alliance with his father.

Keith's family
Darrel, age 44 (+1 year).
KEITH, age 43.

This sibling relationship was competitive and achievement-oriented, which was a carbon copy of his parents' relationship as they too had been highly competitive with each other. Keith's life task was that one must work hard in order to have a good chance in a competitive world, such as trying to compete successfully with an older brother. Although Keith was the youngest, his was not a "take care of me" position as we initially "guessed." (Our wrong guesses helped stimulate the insights for more correct interpreta-

tions—another example of Bias #3!) Rather, Keith learned that life
must be taken seriously (as modeled by his father and mother);
marriage and parenting too were serious business and one ought
to be very conscientious and a leader. To take such roles seriously
meant to "do it right!" If he didn't do it the "right way," then, as
competition goes, he will lose. Just as he couldn't quite successfully
compete for his father's approval, perhaps too, if he makes any
mistakes at parenting, he might lose the affection, respect, and
love of his daugher. Not much room for mistakes in Keith's life
and therefore he could not allow or tolerate much room for mistakes
(even of normal adolescence) in his children's lives.

Keith, too, fit into one of Mosak's (10) probable selections of
behaviors associated with commonly observed Life-Styles: "The
person who needs to be right elevates himself over others whom
he arranges to perceive as being wrong. He scrupulously avoids
error. Should he be caught in error, he rationalizes that others are
even more wrong than he. He treats right and wrong as if they
were the only important issues in a situation and cannot tolerate
ambiguity or an absence of guidelines."

Early Recollections (ERs)

As described by Nikelly and Verger (11), "The use of early
recollections is one of the many projective techniques which may
be employed to help assess the dynamics of an individual's personality. As is common with most projective techniques, its use
constitues an art as much as it does science. . . . it can provide the
clinician with a glance at the client's Life-Style. . . . [His] recollection of events and experiences from childhood are selective in his
memory and are used to discover the client's *present* fundamental
view of life. . . . it is not important to a therapist whether the
client's early remembrances are distorted, correct, or whether they
are actually fragments and fractions of his memory. They serve as
a reflection of his inner world and can be used for explaining the
client to himself."

With the Brandons we also used their ERs to help Keith and
Betty explain themselves to their children in Sessions 7 and 8.
Often, recollections themselves are humorous (Bias #7) although
the serious themes in most of Keith and Betty's ERs reflected the
seriousness with which they generally approached life and in par-

ticular their feelings toward life through this span of family crises and therapy.

After writing out each recollection word for word, we would start with hunches about interpretations and would ask Keith and Betty to suggest their own interpretations: "What do you make of this memory?" "What attitude about men (or women) is reflected here as represented by what your father did?" Some of our guesses were thrown out immediately by them but later accepted as useful interpretations after further thought or a reinforcement through a later recollection since repeating themes serve to validate the Life-Style impressions. Basically these Life-Style impressions can be couched in categories of interpretations that reflect: (1) self-concept ("I am . . . "); (2) self-ideal ("I should be . . . "); and (3) their subjective assessments of the world interacting around them (e.g., "Women are . . . "; "Men are . . . "; "Life is . . . "; "Authority figures are . . . ", etc.). Our specific instructions were to give an actual recollection right down to specific incidents or happenings. After going through each ER, they were asked to describe the most vivid moment in the recollection or the "stop-action" (SA) and then describe the feeling or emotional tone connected with this SA. All of this went on newsprint too. Five or six ERs were obtained from both parents. The following examples illustrate the technique and the insights that resulted.

Betty's ERs

1. Age four: "It was after I got home from the hospital [after four weeks] and my baby sister died—she was six weeks old. I still was whooping from the whooping cough. The picture I have is the body of the baby lying on the dining room table. The doctor came to get the baby and the baby was dead and my older brother seems to be in the picture too—I'm not sure what he's doing—just observing maybe. After the doctor took the baby, my mother went upstairs and I went upstairs, too. She was lying on the bed crying and I asked her why she was crying because I didn't understand what had gone on. She said her baby had died."

SA: "The baby on the table."
Emotion: "Not understanding."
Interpretation: Betty was confused and didn't understand. Per-

haps she felt she should understand better, that if she understood better or knew more, then the tragedy would not have happened. Women (girls, females) are fragile, get hurt, are emotional; female children are exceptionally fragile and sickly. Therefore, they need to be protected and taken care of or treated gently and very carefully.

This ER illustrated and provided nonthreatening data to help us understand and later confront Betty's need to control, her emphasis on education ("to understand better"), her sensitivity to issues of illness, and her protectiveness of Tina.

2. Age three: "The day my brother was born at home . . . my parents hadn't told me that we were going to have a baby so it was a complete shock. That day I had been sent to a relative's house. When Dad came to get me he said they had a surprise for me at home. I was *so* excited, but when I got home they showed me my baby brother. I thought the surprise was going to be strawberries and cream and I was disappointed."

SA: "Seeing my baby brother."

Emotion: Disappointment.

Interpretation: Men (males) are relatively unimportant compared with females, or even compared with strawberries and cream! Women (including Tina and Betty) should be treated specially and get what they want. Humor was underscored in the "newspaper headline" we asked her to write for this ER: "Girl will trade extra brother for strawberries and cream." This helped Betty understand her "natural" closeness to Tina compared to Tim; boys, after all, are "extra" (as in "extra baggage," *not* extra special) while girls should be special.

3. Age ten: "I had rheumatic fever and spent a whole year in bed. I never had a bicycle and he [father] wasn't in favor of my riding a bicycle. It was okay for the boys to ride bikes—they had beat-up ones—and I just sneaked off and and learned on my own because I was determined to do that. But my father really didn't want me climbing trees and riding bikes. At any rate, a very good friend—a boy a year younger than me—got a new bicycle and he came and brought it to the window by my bed and I looked out. I remember feeling very sorry for myself. I felt very bad; here he

is with this new bike outside and he can do what he wants to and here I am trapped in this bed. I don't have a bicycle and I can't get up."

> *SA:* "Me in bed, looking out the window at that bicycle he had."
> *Emotion:* Self-pity.
> *Interpretation:* Women are supposed to be "feminine" but also tend to be protected. Men (males) tend to be rough and rowdy, provide security and protection but are also restricting.

With much discussion and more guesswork, we used past data to illustrate present behaviors and personality patterns. Betty's tendency to protect and control Tina and yet let Tim do what he wanted made sense. Also, while Betty's depression (self-pity)—a fragile, dependent form of sickness requiring security and protection from Keith—was understandable by itself given the recent family crisis, it was even more understandable with the added perspective of these early memories.

Keith's ERs

1. Age four and a half: "My parents had a fight over something and she left him. As a result of their fight she took us across the country from Kansas to Seattle. I remember being on the train with my mother and brother and there were terrible storms with lots of thunder and lightning. I remember seeing the rain on the windows and thinking the train might be blown off the tracks. I was really scared!"

> *SA:* "The rain on the windows."
> *Emotion:* Scared.

"Following the train ride, my brother and I ended up in an orphanage in Seattle. The bed my brother and I were in fell down. I remember wondering, 'what had we done wrong and what would happen to us next?'"

> *SA:* The bed falling down.
> *Emotion:* Scared and helpless.

"I also remember coming down a large staircase to breakfast at that place and I saw that long table with about thirty-five kids sitting there. It was a starchy, unfeeling place . . . a strange place with strange food. I hung onto my brother."

SA: "That long table."
Emotion: Apprehensive and scared.
Interpretation: This was really three memories around the same theme. The three stop-actions emphasized the terror of uncertainty and the fear of abandonment, all resulting from one argument: anger unleashed between parents. Keith learned first-hand at age four and a half just how dangerous it is to show anger. He must therefore rigidly control all his angry emotions, but to do so carried the price of severely restricting any spontaneous expression and sharing of other powerful emotions, such as fear, hurt, warmth, and love. Direct displays of emotion were frightfully unpredictable so Keith kept them bottled up inside.

2. Age six: "We had bought a bunch of eggs at the farmer's market. I think we had six dozen eggs in the box in the back seat. My brother and I were supposed to watch to see that the eggs didn't fall off the seat. I believe the box kind of burst so it parted at the seams and these eggs were rolling around in the back seat, and, of course, back under the seat and started breaking. He [Dad] was *really* mad—angry that we didn't take better care of those eggs. He had a way of getting very red in the neck and face when he was angry. He shouted at us and we knew we had done something wrong."

SA: "Dad's red neck and face."
Emotion: Scared and ashamed (we were bad!).
Interpretation: Keith's own interpretation was that "I quickly learned that there was anger right under the surface whenever something went wrong, even if it wasn't really my fault." The message was clear: to protect yourself from the unpredictable anger in men, don't make any mistakes. Not only were Keith's mistakes unacceptable to his father, they became unacceptable to Keith. He must be not just good, but perfect! And, to repeat family history, his children had better not make mistakes either. To make mistakes

is to be bad. Other recollections confirmed his understandable turning to his mother (a woman) for approval, warmth, and nurturing. He learned that women are more predictable, accepting, and not hostile so his trust and reliance on Betty were consistent. The headline he wrote—"The Brandon Boys Do It Again"—illustrated his partnership with his brother and perhaps a reason why he would develop a "buddy" quality of relationship with his son Tim.

3. Age twelve: "There was a rock quarry near to where we lived with empty blasting kegs. I took one home that was supposedly empty. We discovered that if you'd put a match into small amounts, the blasting powder would flare up and make a big puff of black smoke. I was shoving a match into small piles of blasting powder. One time the keg was too close and it blew up. It set off the keg and blew it apart. The lid went way out of sight. I just about blew my head off!"

SA: "The oily, coallike particles of blasting powder in a cone-shaped pile and sticking the match in it."
Emotion: Excitement and fear.
Interpretation: We simply commented to Keith: "And you think drugs are dangerous! You were pretty full of mischief yourself." He could now relate at least to the *feelings* of excitement of Tina's "mischief" and her experimenting in the drug scene. It was a concrete example of hope that kids usually survive even the dangerous risks of adolescent judgments and experimenting: "See Keith, you survived and there's good reason to think Tina will too."

For someone who simply could not in any way understand the attractions of intoxication and the drug scene, this ER bridged a gap and provided some spontaneous insight into the enticement of exciting risks and dangerous fears. Most adolescents enter potentially dangerous situations out of curiosity and seeking fun, not realizing the extent of the dangers beforehand. It is only after experiencing the situation that they realize the full implications of the dangers involved—even the risks of "blowing my head off" ("blowing your mind with drugs?"). Often, it takes the perspective of experience and the wisdom of maturing before we appreciate the folly of our mistakes. We asked Keith, "Do you still play with empty powder kegs?" The analogy was obvious. Perhaps Tina too will learn and survive and grow. Through this memory Keith gained not only understanding but hope.

Sessions 7 and 8: March 4, 17 (2½ hours each)

With Tina and Tim present, these two sessions were for Keith and Betty to share their life styles as developed in the previous two sessions. With newsprint as their notes, this "allowed us to share with our kids things they hadn't heard."

Stories of parents and grandparents, descriptions of brothers, childhood ambitions and fears, fantasy wishes, and early memories provided a sense of tradition, humor, and intergenerational consistency. Dad and Mom exposed themselves as real people, mischievous, hurt, sad; wanting to control, to be the center of attention, and to be taken care of; to be accepted and yet helpless at times, fearful of anger and vulnerable.

For example, Dad's response to another projective question, "What would you do at the fair?" "I'd own the carnival" illustrated how pervasive his control was and also how difficult it is for him just to be silly and have fun. His childhood ambition to "succeed in business" followed the skills of both his father and mother but also paralleled Tina's precise records and diary of drug sales. While painful, this illustrated a sense of family consistency. His work ethic and perfectionism came from his mother's often-repeated sayings: "If a job is once begun, never leave it till it's done." "Be the labor great or small, do it well or not at all."

While Tim and Tina had been aware of Betty's childhood illnesses and hospitalizations and the death of her baby sister, they had not made the connections to her protectiveness of them until they heard her describe a recurring adult dream: "Something's happening to the children—it involves water—the road joins the lakeshore. I can't identify what happens—maybe they get killed. It is a definite fear of losing them!"

In their wishes, both parents listed: "that the children turn out well—spiritually and socially."

The early recollections in particular clarified why there had been an absence of anger expressions in the Brandon family. It made sense that Keith should fear anger. After one blow-up he ended up half-way across the continent in an orphanage not knowing what he had done wrong or what would happen next. He was often the recipient of unpredictable rage. In contrast, Betty had experienced an absence of anger in her childhood so she avoided dealing with anger just as much as Keith, but for different reasons. The result was the same: no anger was dealt with in the Brandon family.

These two lengthy sessions were perhaps the highlight of communication between these two generations. The sessions stimulated sharing of emotion and it was the most open Keith and Betty had ever been in exposing the depths of their personalities with their now-adult children. Their children were more able to understand and therefore accept who these people are, not as parents, but as people. Tim and Tina received them gently and with a new dimension of respect.

Session 9: April 4 (2 hours)

Betty and Keith were seen together again without Tim and Tina. This session was planned to refocus on the present status of how they felt Tina was doing, which was an issue that had not received special attention for two months. We primarily listened and provided encouragement to let go, detach, and trust: to trust in God, to trust that their nurturing, example, and family closeness in the early years of child rearing would pay off, provided they would give their children the freedom and room to grow into themselves and learn from their mistakes. We reminded them that individuals and families need a lot of time—time to grow and time to heal. We outlined stages of grief and loss and explained they were in the process of grieving the loss of their "little children" who would never be "little" or "children" again. We offered our assessment that Tim and Tina appeared to be predictably responsible, spiritual, and successful individuals.

At this point, three and a half months after hospital discharge, Tina's commitment to sobriety and AA was solid, and while we certainly could not guarantee her continued abstinence, we could share our hope and clinical perspective that her prognosis looked exceptionally good. We had their trust so that they not only heard us but believed us.

Session 10: April 18 (2 hours)

Seeing Tim alone was purposeful. We wanted to give him some special attention. Since he had appeared fairly stable from the beginning, we had not felt an urgency to see him alone earlier. Although he was quiet, we had gotten to know Tim and really liked him. He was neat and we wanted to tell him so. We also wanted to check whether he felt as good as he appeared, or whether it was a facade. How much was he covering up? Was he afraid of hurting his parents after he saw what they went through with Tina? What was it like, with his dyslexia, to be second place academically to Tina, especially when education was such a high standard and strong value to his parents? How did he feel Mom and Dad were doing? How depressed was Mom? How distant was Dad? How was Tina doing? Was she sober and straight, as everyone said, or has she been using some? Yes, we needed to validate her statements! We wanted to provide a place for Tim to confess or unload how he felt about her drug sales and prior drug use, how he felt about covering up, how he felt that she was coerced into treatment. Did he really think *total* abstinence was necessary for her and how supportive could he really be to that?

We wanted to let him talk freely without any parental sanctions. By asking him how everyone else in the family was doing, we acknowledged his position and status as being more objective "about this whole thing" than anyone else.

We wanted to allow him to talk about his own drinking privately without parental sanctions or his sister's honeymoon enthusiasm of playing "junior chemical-dependency counselor." We discussed his racing hobby, his several junked cars, his ambitions and plans. It was a special session to acknowledge Tim as a special person with a unique position in this family.

Session 11: April 28 (2 hours)

Seeing Tim and Tina together without parents was to offer them time to work specifically on their relationship together and to offer a setting for sibling-peer confrontation and support. We felt this milieu might stimulate the working out of unresolved issues—past or present drug and alcohol abuse, manipulations and parents, jealousy, whatever might come up.

While the session did not bomb in the sense that it was really bad, it was clearly a dud in that it just didn't go anywhere! Whatever deep secrets we expected to uncover, we didn't find any. They related with us and with each other in much the same way as they had in total family sessions. Tim may have been just a little more spontaneous and seemingly relaxed. We asked questions and encouraged statements whereby they shared their concerns and love for each other. Tina, in staunch AA framework, shared her concern over Tim's drinking. Without appearing defensive, he appreciated her concern but expressed that his drinking was not a problem even though he admitted to being uncomfortable and feeling some conflict and guilt in violating his parents' value of no drinking. Cautiously, we affirmed our sense that his drinking, although not always riskfree, seemed within fairly normal adolescent limits of experimentation. We felt easier expressing this without Mom and Dad there, given their firm antialcohol stance. Tim encouraged Tina's abstinence and affectionately expressed his relief and joy that she was "straight." They talked most freely in this area of chemical use and it was the most direct discussion they had together about alcohol and drug use since prior to Tina's trip to the police station six months before.

Very little else came up but this session did validate the two of them in a peer, more adult-to-adult status, separate from their roles as "children of their parents," as had been implied in the other sessions.

Session 12: May 12 (1¼ hour)

As family therapists, one might think we would plan termination very precisely. Well, we didn't!

With the Brandons, termination was primarily determined by their summer vacation or work plans. For years they had operated a summer "trading post" in a resort area of northern Minnesota and would be leaving within two weeks for the summer. However, they had done well and to terminate now was appropriate. We used the session to tell them clearly that as individuals and as a family unit they had done well. Tina was now straight over six months, she identified strongly with AA, and had survived the critical peer pressures of returning to high school. Keith and Betty had been able basically to trust her again. She had her car and was able to use it freely. Tim, while in his own world of cars, had been involved in his family as much as any eighteen-year-old. Not only did his parents like him, he liked himself and seemed more integrated into the family atmosphere. In this session we reflected on these successes. It was a lighter session, less intense than most, but not without a litany of cautions from us. Perhaps our fears and apprehensions of ending our role as parents—oops!—we mean as therapists, was painful, too. For us to detach and let go and trust they would be okay without us was threatening. We had an investment in them and cared about what happened. It felt nice to be needed too and now they didn't need us anymore.

We gave Tina the name and phone number of a female AA contact in the large city nearest their summer trading post. We didn't want Tina's involvement in AA to be left to the impersonalness of AA in the white pages of the phone directory.

Our main caution to them as a family was to "come back sooner rather than later" if any of them felt a need to process family issues. As a family they never did return.

FOLLOW-UP SESSION

Tina did return two weeks after termination; she came to our house to get four rabbits we had promised her. While this was no great therapeutic gesture, just maybe there was a message that we saw her as more than a kid and client. The concept of treating people as social equals pervades Adlerian theory and we hope we convey this in our therapeutic relationships with people.

Tina also returned the following winter. Dave saw her individually for what she identified as depression. And it was depression too, but very situational. It may have related to school, to being a high school senior and unsure of her future. I asked enough questions about her support system, her sobriety, family functioning, and had her do an MMPI to help rule out anything more pervasive than minor situational depression. I then offered support and suggested that her depression was likely to lift as mysteriously as it came and that I would see her for a month and we'd see how she felt then. After three sessions spread over four weeks she looked and felt better and felt no need to return. At Christmas of this same winter we received a family picture from the Brandons, a "thank you" that still has its place on the edge of our bedroom mirror crowded by other pictures of graduated nieces and nephews.

The next contact came one year after termination in the form of an invitation to Tina's high school graduation reception. We viewed this as both a social invitation and another gesture of gratitude and appreciation. We attended the graduation reception. The appearance was that, as a family, they still looked good. There was no evidence of awkward or tense family relationships. We were introduced to their friends and relatives simply as friends.

Six months later, while attending a conference, Dave had coffee with Tina in another city where she was attending her freshman year at college. She was stable, appeared lonely, but not depressed. She simply appreciated the visit from someone from home.

Reflections of Family Therapy Four Years Later:
Our next contact was to initiate interviews in preparation for this chapter. This was four years from where we started, three and a half years after terminating family therapy. Five hours with Keith and Betty in their home were reminiscent of the pain and humor, hope and growth that dominated the tone of the family sessions. Retaking ERs revealed a *less* controlling Keith and a *less* worrisome Betty, but a continuation of their life goals. While many of their thoughts about what happened in those twenty-five to thirty hours of family therapy have been included in the preceding section describing the content and process of family sessions, each recalled some highlights.

Keith: If anyone had failed in the family I felt I had most. I probably didn't give the leadership I ought to have. Those sessions gave *hope* that we'd be brought closer and understand each other and feel good about our family again. . . . The very idea of recollecting childhood images and drawing inferences from what each of us thought was important. This format allowed us to share some things that probably our kids had never heard and maybe we didn't really realize even about each other.

When asked to rank in order whom family therapy was for, Keith quickly ranked (1) Keith, (2) Betty, (3) Tina, (4) Tim. Betty responded differently, putting herself first: "I felt *I* needed help to cope with the pain." Her ranking then went on to (2) Keith, (3) Tina, and (4) Tim. Her *pain* and *hope* are still very vivid.

Betty: The one thing I didn't like was that I cried every time I went. Everytime before we'd go I'd say, "I'm not going to cry tonight but every night I did!" . . . There was always that dread. I don't like baring my soul and I don't like crying in front of other people and I don't like being out of control of my emotions. . . . There was a dread of what more I would find out about myself that I didn't like. I had already found out way more than I wanted to know about what I didn't like about myself. I dreaded going through it but I looked forward to it knowing it was a place we could go together as a family and say things to each other and be accepted. (Betty then smiled.) The fun was in the remembering [ERs] and in the homework [assigning Mom and Tim to go out together]. I remember what fun Tim and I had—we laughed a lot and had fun. We had always paired off the other way [Keith and Tim and Betty and Tina] and that was just fun! He has a terribly good sense of humor—he's terribly funny!

Betty needed this combination of pain, hope and laughter.

We saw Tina once in her apartment at the university where she was finishing her junior year majoring in Women's Studies. She is bright, competent, and having internalized her parents' value of education, she is likely to complete her plans for a Ph.D. in clinical psychology.

Tina: I don't really remember a whole lot of what went on there but I felt really safe going there. My folks letting go of me was the major thing—it seemed as though they started to let go. There were a lot of things I wanted to work out with them that I couldn't do at home by myself. I felt I could go to family therapy and confront them and they'd listen there. At home they'd just say I was wrong. (But in deciding who the family sessions were primarily for, Tina was clear.) I had been through treatment and had AA but that was the *only* therapy that my folks and Tim had.

We met Tim for a lengthy breakfast session: not to be left out of this family, he first finished two years of vocational school in diesel mechanics and, at this writing, is finishing his freshman year of college. Tim had internalized the family values of hard work and displayed this value through taking extra classes in reading and typing to overcome the handicap of his dyslexia. He is deeply involved in a campus Christian fellowship group, much to the delight of his parents. But, he did this after keeping his distance from church affiliation for three years. Like father, like son! Tim saw family sessions as primarily for (1) Keith, (2) Betty, (3) Tina, and (4) himself. But he was initially skeptical: "I didn't think it would do a whole lot of good. The drug use was Tina's problem and because I had been isolated, I didn't think I had anything to do with it."

Nevertheless, his curiosity allowed him to come without resistance and kept him coming.

> I thought it would be kind of neat. . . . I had never been to a "shrink" before and I wondered what tactics and strategies you'd use. I remember those questions you had all of us finish [sentence completions]. I didn't think you'd get much out of it but I felt the technique must be for a purpose and they did make sense later. After the first couple of sessions I had a lot of confidence and a blind trust in what you were doing. . . . I was amazed at how you got Dad to communicate, to open up and see what he was really like; how the family functioned because of him being closed [emotionally]. Getting Mom to open up was important. To help her see how her striving to be a perfect mother had hindered her in certain ways and how her over-concern for everybody in the family would affect us—we'd try to protect her from being hurt.

Tim was critical too:

> I would have liked to talk more about my drinking. I've quit totally now but I was drinking too much then!

But the most impressionable insight for Tim was:
> How I'll develop in their footsteps, whether I want to or not. I want to be more open about my feelings, not to be so closed off. I've been working on that.

As each family member saw family therapy as primarily for Keith and Betty, we too saw it as primarily to "help the parents to survive" both as individuals and as a marriage. As a family unit, this is a success story; not all cases are! Because this family was generally healthy before chemical dependency, our focus was on working to bring them all together *as a family;* not as they were before the crisis but as a changed system nourished by their painful experiences and their courage to change together.

"I feel they accept me the way I am now"—Tina, which is probably very close to the way they wanted her to be.

REFERENCES

1. Kaufman, E. The application of the basic principles of family therapy to the treatment of drug and alcohol abusers. In E. Kaufman & P. Kaufmann (Eds.), *Family therapy of drug and alcohol abuse,* New York: Gardner Press, 1979.
2. Huberty, D.J. The addict and alcoholic in treatment: Some comparisons. *Journal of Drug Issues,* 1973, **3**, 341–347.
3. Huberty, D.J. & Malmquist, J.D. Adolescent chemical dependency. *Perspectives in Psychiatric Care,* 1978, **16**, 21–27.
4. Huberty, D.J. Treating the adolescent drug abuser: A family affair. *Contemporary Drug Problems,* 1975, **4**, 179–194.
5. Huberty, C.E. & Huberty, D.J. Treating the parents of adolescent drug abusers. *Contemporary Drug Problems,* 1976, **5**, 573–592.
6. Coleman, S.B. Siblings in session. In E. Kaufman & P. Kaufmann (Eds.), *Family therapy of drug and alcohol abuse.* New York: Gardner Press, 1979.
7. Pew, W.L. & Pew, M.L. Marital therapy. In A.G. Nikelly (Ed.), *Techniques for behavior change.* Springfield, Ill.: Charles C. Thomas, 1971.
8. Huberty, D.J. Treating the young drug user. In F. Scarpitti & S. Datesman (Eds.), *Drugs and the youth culture.* Beverly Hills, Calif.: Sage Publications, 1980.
9. Mayer, J.E. & Filstead, W.F. The adolescent alcohol involvement scale: An instrument for measuring adolescent alcohol use and misuse. *Journal of Studies on Alcohol,* 1979, **40**, 291–300.
10. Mosak, H.H. Lifestyle. In A.G. Nikelly (Ed.), *Techniques for behavior change.* Springfield, Ill.: Charles C. Thomas, 1971.
11. Nikelly, A.G. & Verger, D. Early recollections. In A.G. Nikelly (Ed.), *Techniques for behavior change.* Springfield, Ill.: Charles C. Thomas, 1971.

We wish to acknowledge our children, Michael, LaNeia, Christopher, and Kelli. We lovingly hope they will collectively survive our family system and individually have the power to grow from it.

6

Alcohol is Destroying our Marriage:

A Couple in Mixed Marital Group Therapy

Donald A. Cadogan, Ph.D.

SUSAN

Susan came to my office alone. She was an attractive, well-dressed woman, twenty-nine years of age. She seemed to know exactly where to sit. When she spoke she looked directly at me. Susan appeared to be in complete control. There was an air of poise and strength about her. Yet, the tears flowed readily on this meeting, and on many occasions thereafter. This time, however, she was very annoyed by them and kept apologizing. "Tears won't solve anything," she would say. She felt that her marriage was failing and wanted desperately to save it. Her husband's drinking had progressed to dangerous proportions. Inebriated states had become more and more frequent. And his behavior at these times was becoming more erratic and more destructive.

Susan labored under a common misconception. She believed that if her husband Matthew loved her, he would stop drinking. This was especially true she thought, once he knew how upset it made her. Unfortunately, Matthew was an alcoholic. Thus, it was not at all likely that he would stop drinking for her or for anyone else. He would stop only when he himself deeply desired to stop. Obviously, he had not yet made any commitment to sobriety. But Susan felt like a failure. She felt unloved and unlovable. Her life was in a turmoil and her marriage a shambles. Matthew frequently accused her of driving him to drink. And she felt responsible. At times she wanted to run. Yet, she refused to let his drinking destroy her or her marriage.

Susan's story has a familiar theme. Even her entrance into therapy was part of a common pattern. Spouses of alcoholics often come to counseling alone. And they display feelings of guilt, depression, anger, and confusion. Many are willing to discover their part, if any, in their spouses' drinking. Some, unfortunately, are too angry or vengeful for this. Susan, however, was willing to look. She had not yet become mired in a power struggle over her husband's drinking. Unfortunately, she felt so guilty about her husband's alcoholism that it was very difficult to probe this area without evoking more guilt and deepening her depression. To her credit, however, she came to accept the view that if she could have an influence on her husband's drinking, she could also develop an influence on his sobriety. At this point treatment goals were established, and the first phase of therapy for her was begun.

Susan was the oldest in a family of five. She had a younger sister, and a brother younger than both. She described her father as somewhat of a male chauvinist, a rough-and-tumble character who ruled the family with a strong hand. Susan both admired her father and resented him. During her adolescence, Susan's father frequently made mocking sexual comments to her. She found his remarks suggestive and derisive, but most of all humiliating. Susan and her sister both felt that their father preferred their younger brother. However, Susan also described her father as basically a responsible man who was protective of his family. She believed that he did love them.

Susan saw her mother as a dependent woman who lacked self-confidence. Mother foisted much of her family responsibilities into Susan. She often complained to Susan about Father's rude and controlling manner. However, Susan's mother rarely confronted Father about her grievances.

Susan grew into adulthood with a marked ambivalence for her father. Hostility toward him was largely repressed and remained unresolved. Also, she had little respect for her mother. She was aware of feeling guilty about her attitude toward her parents.

Susan manifested an underlying rejection of her female identity, and was sexually inhibited to the point of being dysfunctional. She was able to engage in sexual intercourse, and claimed she enjoyed it, but rarely achieved orgasm. She appeared to resent strong male figures, and felt embarrassed by any display of weakness or dependence on her part. Basically, she was a woman who lacked self-confidence, and wanted to be cared for. Yet, she resented her dependency and needed to be in control. She was accustomed to taking the lead in family and interpersonal affairs. But she harbored much self-doubt and feelings of insecurity.

It was my guess that the kind of husband Susan would most likely choose would be someone who was capable, yet himself needful and lacking in self-confidence. As I discovered, she managed to find these qualities in Matthew.

As we talked, certain questions continued in my mind. Was there an interplay of forces between Susan and Matthew that perpetuated his alcoholism? And if so, what forms did it take? There is some clinical evidence pointing to the existence of personalities or behavioral patterns that are not of themselves clearly psychopathological, but tend to foster the development of psychopathology in those close to them (Bateson et al., 1956). These people can present an emotionally integrated appearance and are capable of adequate and successful functioning, but tend to undermine the self-confidence, security, and self-esteem of others. This influence usually takes place in covert and subtle ways. The subtlety of the influence of pathogenic interaction makes it difficult to detect, and once detected, difficult to substantiate or to deal with. This appears to be one of the qualities that makes such interactions so insidiously destructive.

Carl Rogers indicates that a lack of agreement between what we hear or are told, and what we experience intuitively in our interpersonal relationships can lead to defensiveness, blockage, and an inhibition of our personal growth (Rogers, 1961, p. 339). He claims that congruence between verbal and nonverbal communications is fundamental to a positive and growth-enhancing relationship. However, the pathogenic relationship is characterized by incongruent communication. Negative messages are often transmitted nonverbally, through tone, attitude, bearing, context, or innuendo, but are contradicted simultaneously by verbal statements. In an almost subliminal manner, these individuals can have an erosive effect on the personalities of those around them, and especially on those dependent on them for approval or care.

It is possible that close and continued involvement with pathogenic interaction patterns can produce a variety of psychopath-

ological states, including alcoholism. The symptom complex
associated with these states may vary depending on the coping
mechanisms used, or on the manner of one's attempts to resolve
the experience. The question for us here is: Were these factors
present in Susan and Matthew's relationship?

When working with what appear to be pathogenic personalities,
I often experience the ebb and flow of my own defensiveness
sooner or later. I get a feeling of pressure, an irritating need to
justify myself, well knowing that such justification would be little
appreciated or accepted. Negative transference and countertransference you might say, but I tend to question my adequacy and
even my identity at these times. However, I experienced none of
these forces operating in Susan's relationship to me. If Susan had
pathogenic characteristics, perhaps they would be more apparent
in her relationship with Matthew.

The therapy plan agreed upon included marital therapy. Such
a plan, of course, would require Matthew's cooperation. But getting
Matthew into therapy was another matter. He did not see himself
as an alcoholic, did not wish to stop drinking, and saw the family
problems as all his wife's fault.

I am of the view that trust is at the base of the good marital
relationship. It is also one of the principal ingredients in the therapeutic relationship. However, if we told Matthew that we wanted
him in therapy because he was an alcoholic, we probably would
have failed. Yet, deception would have fostered mistrust and would
have been antitherapeutic. Besides, I would have probably entan-
gled myself in any such deception.

One of the reasons Susan came to therapy was because of
depression associated with marital discord. This fact seemed like
a possible lever to help bring Matthew into therapy. Toward this
end, I requested that Susan inform her husband of the following:

1. That she was depressed and in therapy.
2. That her depression appeared to be intertwined with her
marital difficulties.
3. That she would probably need his help in overcoming her
depression.

To the best of my knowledge all of these facts were true. But
Matthew's entrance into therapy required that I respect his right

to destroy himself with alcohol if he so chose. Actually, this position was not difficult to accept. The fact is that if Matthew wanted to drink himself into oblivion, there wasn't a damn thing I, or his wife, or anyone else could do about it. When I told this to Susan she seemed relieved.

MATTHEW

Matthew came in with Susan on her next session. He was an affable, well-groomed man of thirty-one. He followed his wife into my office and immediately sat next to her. He seemed a bit ill at ease, but managed to mask this with humorous comments. This continued for a time and gave the impression that he was in my office for purely social reasons. I felt drawn to him, and liked him immediately. If I didn't know better I would never have guessed that there were problems between them. The defense of denial is characteristic of alcoholism. It appeared to be operating. I found it necessary to focus our discussion on more relevant issues.

Matthew was the second son of a wealthy businessman. His older brother had always been closer to his father and was now a successful attorney. Matthew himself worked in real estate. He did not believe that he was as successful as his brother or his father, but claimed he was doing the best he could and that it was good enough. Susan said she was basically proud of him, but insisted he could do better if he tried.

Matthew described his father as hard working and ambitious, but seldom home. When his father was home he was aloof and preoccupied with business matters. Matthew's father usually deferred to his wife on family matters.

Matthew's mother was a strong, outgoing woman who tended to be the family disciplinarian. She was proud of Matthew when he was a child and often introduced him as her precious baby. Matthew was close to his mother, but in time became increasingly embarrassed and humiliated by her public displays of smothering affection. He often questioned her sincerity, and felt uneasy around her. However, he spent more time with her than with his father, and felt he and his mother were more alike.

The last factor is not uncommon with alcoholics I have seen in therapy. Research also supports this view. For example, in 1966, Tahka engaged in a research project that disclosed strong similarities between male alcoholics and their mothers. This factor, at minimum, suggests a confusion of sexual identity on the part of these male alcoholics. The mothers in his study were inclined to repudiate their feminine identities and tended to have weak, ineffectual husbands whom they dominated. The mothers in Tahka's study took little pride in their male children except as objects used to satisfy their own narcissistic need to be mothers.

The alcoholics' dependency, which is one of their most frequently observed features, may well be the result of continued interaction with this kind of mothering. Although these alcoholics appear to enjoy their mothers' overindulgence, they also seem to resent the loss of freedom and personal esteem it costs them. As did Matthew, many of the male alcoholics I have worked with have indicated that they felt uncared about by cold and ineffectual fathers, or smothered by controlling mothers.

SUSAN AND MATTHEW

As I watched Matthew and Susan interact, some patterns began to emerge. She was often the accusing parent, and he the rebellious child. Sometimes they would switch places. Susan liked to point out that Matthew had such great potential, yet she frequently pointed to his shortcomings. Ostensibly, she was encouraging him, but the only message he heard was that he was not good enough, and that he would have to change in order to please her. Following this, he would insist that he was not going to do everything that she wanted, including not drinking. She wrestled for the lead and was usually in charge. However, Matthew continued to defy her, and at times even baited her. After a fight they would both withdraw. Then Susan would return and patiently wait for Matthew, but when Matthew did return, she would become angry for having waited so long and would again withdraw. In this way they were often able to get a lot of angry mileage out of just one fight. There were also the mixed messages that I anticipated, but they were coming from both.

Although theories of psychotherapy vary, few argue against

the premise that parental experiences are the bedrock upon which personality stands. The early family experiences of people like Susan can leave them feeling angry, frustrated, and fearful of their inner needs. And the experiences of people like Matthew can leave them feeling inadequate, insecure, hostile, and dependent. Yet, despite the anguish experienced in these early relationships there often remains a need to re-create them, return to them, or in some way reexperience them. For some, pathological family interaction was the principal model of interpersonal involvement, it was the way they learned to be intimate. For others, the need to repeat the experience of a disordered parental relationship seems almost counterphobic, the product of a drive to resolve their difficulties by again facing them. But this time, the individual hopes to come away with a sense of success, mastery, and power.

Alcoholics often appear attracted to partners whom they covertly resent in an apparent effort to resolve their feelings of hostility and dependency. The partners, on the other hand, often appear attracted to the behavioral manifestations of the alcoholics' resentment, i.e., drinking, needfulness, irresponsibilty, and violence, in an attempt to rectify the partners' own disordered familial experiences. Unfortunately, by using the same inadequate coping mechanisms, the experience of defeat, failure, and weakness tends to be reproduced. Their attempts to rectify their conflicts tend only to perpetuate the need for their rectification.

Matthew, like many alcoholics, appeared to select a strong and controlling spouse. His dependence on a strong mate seemed to satisfy underlying needs for security and safety. However, Matthew disliked needing others and secretly resented his marital partner's strength. Often he would act out by drinking in an attempt to assert his independence, and to defy and weaken his partner's control. Unfortunately, these maneuvers were having a destructive effect on his marriage. His marital relationship had become fragile, and tenuous. Thus, insecurity feelings were intensifying.

Susan, like many spouses in such relationships, appeared to be an angry, controlling person who was looking for reasons to justify her preexisting hostile feelings. She found in Matthew's behavior much justification for martyrdom, scorn, self-pity, anger, and controlling behavior. But she also believed that taking charge and mothering Matthew would endear her to him. Unfortunately, her actions were engendering further hostility and inebriative acting out on the part of her alcoholic spouse. The actions and reactions of Matthew and Susan toward each other seemed clearly destructive.

It is important to note that in certain cases pathological interactions can hold a fragile relationship together. The traits in some people can be offset, complemented, or neutralized by the traits of their spouse. Thus, improvement in one partner's disorder could have a deleterious effect on the marriage in that the pathological needs of the other partner might no longer find satisfaction. This seemed a valid caution considering the nature of the interplay between Susan and Matthew.

It should also be noted that in many cases, alcoholic marriages are not, or do not appear to be, selected on the basis of pathological need. In these marriages, alcoholism does not seem to develop as a result of pathological family interaction. Nevertheless, as many researchers point out, family equilibrium is a factor that can also perpetuate alcohol abuse. Once alcoholism becomes established, family role patterns change to accommodate the disorder. Having changed, they solidify and resist efforts to change back. This factor can unwittingly undermine the alcoholic member's attempts at sobriety.

Thus, there were several reasons and cautions to consider in deciding on a family therapy approach for Susan and Matthew. Basically, family equilibrium and pathological family interaction were apparently playing a part in Matthew's drinking problem. However, there was also the possibility that therapeutic correction of their "undesirable" characteristics would have rendered their marriage less attractive. Susan was afraid that any form of submissiveness on her part would be exploited by Matthew. She believed that if her husband was strong like her father, he would abuse his power. She felt safer with, and thus attracted to, men like Matthew who could themselves be submissive. Unfortunately, this factor made it difficult for her to compromise. She also felt needed by Matthew, and thus important to him. At the same time, she admired strength and was attracted to men who were capable and effective. But this made it difficult for her to respect Matthew's dependency and submissiveness. If Matthew became more confident and responsible, but she remained in fear of losing power, the marriage would become less appealing. With these factors in mind, it seems reasonable to assume that Susan would be unconsciously motivated to keep Matthew weak. The subtle put-downs and digs that took place in therapy tended to support this view. Susan seldom missed an opportunity to take the lead and display superiority.

Although Matthew resented and rebelled against Susan's control he also found security in it. It was certainly possible that he would feel insecure if she became less controlling. He might even seek out a relationship with a more protective person. He was probably unconsciously motivated to remain irresponsible and keep Susan in the stronger role.

These were some of the forces at play when therapy began. It seemed clear to me that in order for either one to change and not regress, both would have to change.

In the treatment of Susan and Matthew there were three immediate and pivotal issues: (1) to get Matthew to recognize his alcoholism; (2) to involve him in treatment for himself; and (3) to get Susan and Matthew to recognize their influences on each other's behavior. Although treatment focus was on the family, I found it necessary on occasion to meet with each separately. Since Susan had seen me alone on our first session, I was concerned that Matthew would perceive Susan and me as a unit, and would feel like an outsider or as though we were against him. I decided to see him a few times separately as early in treatment as possible. To accomplish this I simply asked Matthew to come in alone before our next conjoint visit. The reason given was to explore with him his view of the difficulties at home. This was to be done while unimpeded by his wife's presence.

Basically, Matthew had good feelings about male authority figures, and expected to be treated fairly and honestly. Also, he was quite hungry for approval by someone such as myself, and a good rapport developed immediately. I presented myself to Matthew in a nonjudgmental and accepting manner, yet utilized every opportunity to tie his drinking to his home difficulties. I was careful, however, to avoid blaming his wife. Instead, I pointed out how his behavior was influencing his wife's behavior, which he then used as an excuse to drink. In time, he admitted that when he started drinking he had trouble stopping, and that he was becoming worried about his alcohol intake. I mentioned AA to him as often as it seemed feasible, but tried not to alienate him by overzealousness.

I must admit to some concerns about AA. The organization is a good valuable resource, and when possible should be utilized by therapists working with alcoholics. Unfortunately, there are some AA groups that counsel against psychotherapy. As a result, there is some danger that the rapport between the therapist and the alcoholic might be undermined, and thus mitigate treatment effectiveness. I usually prefer to deal with this issue up front, and decided to discuss it directly with Matthew.

As a result of our individual and conjoint sessions, Matthew came to accept that his drinking was a problem. Also through my efforts to link his drinking difficulties with the marital difficulties, I persuaded both Susan and Matthew that his budding alcoholism was a family issue. At this point I introduced the idea of a couples group. They were interested, so I prepared them for it through a somewhat detailed discussion of group therapy with couples.

I indicated earlier that the therapy plan agreed upon included family therapy. Let me be more specific. It is well known that the contemporary treatment of alcoholism can consist of a variety of different techniques and modalities. Present-day treatment approaches to alcoholism include individual psychotherapy, group therapy, family therapy, Alcoholics Anonymous, behavior modification, chemotherapy, and other remedial strategies. These modalities are not mutually exclusive, nor is one necessarily superior to the others. For many individuals the simultaneous utilization of different modalities seems essential to their sobriety. I believed this to be the case for Matthew. In the course of treatment with Matthew and his wife I utilized individual and conjoint counseling, and was able to use the resources of AA. For the most part, however, I used an additional procedure. I am referring here to marital group therapy. Since this was the principal mode of treatment used, I would like to discuss this procedure in more detail before returning to Matthew and Susan and their involvement in it.

MARITAL GROUP THERAPY

Marital Group Therapy (MGT) is a technique that can be utilized in combination with other treatment approaches. There is some experimental evidence to indicate its effectiveness. This approach is basically an admixture of family therapy and group therapy. Like family therapy, it is based on the assumption that the family environment can be a contributing factor in either the development or the maintenance of the alcoholic's malady. Here the alcoholic's spouse is included in the alcoholic's treatment, and is placed in group therapy with other alcoholics and their spouses. Children are usually not included (when children are also present, the procedure is more often called multiple family therapy).

In the pure form of marital group therapy, all group members are either alcoholics or spouses of alcoholics. However, there are some considerations to make when endeavoring to utilize MGT in its pure form. Therapists in private practice usually treat a variety of different problems. Often there are not enough alcoholics with spouses in the private therapist's treatment population to assemble such a group. Thus, it is not always possible to compose the marital group solely with alcoholics. A group consisting of couples who are dealing with a broad spectrum of emotional difficulties may be the only practical solution for the small private practitioner. The question is: Is the "pure" marital group more effective than the "mixed" marital group?

I have had the privilege of working in both "pure" and "mixed" marital groups. One of the advantages of the "pure" group for the alcoholic is that alcoholism is more frequently the focus of attention. However, when other alcoholic treatment modalities are utilized simultaneously (e.g., AA), the problem of alcoholism usually gets plenty of attention. Thus, the advantage of increased focus on alcoholism may be diminished.

The principal purpose of the marital group is to uncover and deal with pathological family interactions that are supportive of the alcoholism or other problems. The therapeutic process is usually more effective when it directly focuses on the destructive interactions that manifest themselves in the group. In dealing with these issues, a "mixed" marital group can be more helpful in shifting group focus from the problem of alcoholism to other important and unresolved problems associated with family membership. Experimental evidence (Cadogan, 1973) indicates the MGT of the "pure" variety is effective in the treatment of alcoholism. Clinical experience, however, suggests that the "mixed" marital group is also effective. The choice is left to the therapist and can be based on his or her preference or on the practicalities of the situation.

Beyond this, it is important to know what factors contribute to success when either form of MGT is used.

In a recent publication (Cadogan, 1979), I described some of the attributes of MGT and how these attributes seemed to be linked to successful outcome. In brief, MGT is a variant of group therapy proper and is effective for similar reasons. In addition, there are certain factors associated with the marital group that render it particularly useful. The following is a summary of these factors:

1. With the spouse included in therapy, pathological marital interaction patterns become more apparent.

2. Group discussion of family or marital problems is potentially more relevant to all members.

3. Marriage is a mutual circumstance in the group and lends itself well to the development of group cohesiveness.

4. Membership in the group is a meaningful event and can provide the family with a shared purpose. This can act as a substitute for any purposes served by the family's problem and can thus mitigate treatment sabotage.

5. Couples in the group can learn to socialize as a family, or as a couple unit.

6. A group composed of couples is potentially more attractive to married members. This tends to increase the group's importance, and thus, its effectiveness.

Aside from the therapist him or herself, there is one other variable that affects treatment outcome. I am referring here to the patients themselves. Usually, grossly disturbed or acutely psychotic individuals are excluded from group therapy until their behavior improves to the point where they will not be a disruptive influence. Extremely paranoid patients, especially those who are aggressive, and sociopathic individuals may also be a disruptive influence. Also, markedly schizoid individuals or patients suffering from a retarded depression can cast a negative pall on the group atmosphere and render it less effective. Other patients who are usually poor group therapy risks are people who are brain damaged, extremely narcissistic, or suicidal. At this point, however, it may seem as though we have excluded everybody.

At the time when I did the controlled study of MGT (Cadogan, 1973), I was unable to discern readily which kind of couple would respond best to group. In reviewing the data, I did not find that age had an influence on treatment outcome. Also, I could not find a correlation between treatment success and problem severity as defined by number of hospitalizations. I determined at the time that the element of acceptance and trust between the alcoholic and his or her spouse was one important factor that was positively correlated with treatment success. But there is another variable that has become apparent to me in the years since that study, a variable that I had not then considered. I am referring to the existence of mutual liking and respect between the couple and the therapist, a positive transference and countertransference if you will. I believe that the verbal and nonverbal communication of this liking and respect from therapist to patient in therapy has a powerful curative affect. Those patients with a low capacity for acceptance and trust might not perceive the genuineness of this liking and thus not benefit from this experience.

Susan and Matthew were good candidates for MGT. Neither was grossly disturbed, brain damaged, extremely narcissistic, excessively paranoid, or suicidal. Also, neither of them was markedly schizoid, or in a a deep, retarded depression.

I felt it was important for Susan and Matthew to like the other members of the group and perceive that they were liked in return. This last point seems important for therapists to remember. If the prospective group member exhibits an offensive personality style, he or she will probably be disliked by the others and will likely experience rejection. This factor has antitherapeutic implications. Unfortunately, we can't always judge this accurately ahead of time. When errors are made and a member experiences rejection, I make an effort to tie this experience to the specific behavior that engendered this rejection. As for Susan and Matthew, I felt affection for and from both. My intuitive sense that there would be mutual liking between them and the other group members turned out to be correct.

SUSAN AND MATTHEW IN MGT

Susan and Matthew spent over one year in MGT. This was an open-ended group in which members would leave when they felt finished and new members would be added at that time. Thus, the composition of the group changed over time and provided Matthew and Susan with a variety of human-relations experiences. These experiences formed a backdrop for Susan and Matthew to draw upon in dealing with their own marital difficulties. I was often amazed at how both could see similarities between themselves and other members. This was true even when the other members were in group for very different reasons.

There were times when the group confronted both Susan and Matthew, and urged them each to accept responsibility for their personal and relationship problems. At the end of one group session, both left feeling angry. Each was convinced that the group was on the other person's side. These mutual distortions were discovered in a later group. The discovery that they both felt guilty, and that this guilt was distorting their view of the group led to a correcting of their misconceptions about the group and about themselves.

The group was never really against them, although members did find some of their behavior patterns troublesome. For example, Matthew tended to smile whenever he felt embarrassed or angry. This was the result of long years of masking his feelings. Unfortunately, it made him look as though he was laughing at the others or that he felt superior. In reality, just the opposite was true. It was not Matthew's intention to offend others, only to hide from them. For a long time, however, Susan had been misled by this ruse. She was quite relieved to discover that others had been similarly deceived. Such confrontations and discoveries led to important changes in Susan and Matthew's reactions to each other.

At this point I believe it would be most instructive if we took a detailed look at Susan and Matthew in one of their MGT sessions. At the time of this session, the group was composed of four couples: Mike and Virginia, Tom and Mary, Jim and Judy, and Matthew and Susan. Let me describe each in brief, and follow this with an illustrated discussion of a single session.

1. Tom and Mary were in their early thirties, and both were teachers. They had been married for five years and had no children. The identified patient was Mary who was experiencing an acute depression. Mostly, she was feeling unhappy about married life. Although she loved Tom, she constantly fought with him, and was beginning to fear that she may have made a mistake in marrying

him. Mary was a bright and capable professional who was held in high esteem by her colleagues. Unfortunately, Tom was very lacking in self-confidence, and felt a need to compete with his wife. Although a capable teacher in his own right, he did not possess his wife's drive. Mary had the stronger personality and tended to take charge. Unfortunately, this rankled Tom, who reacted by being stubborn and oppositional. In some important ways, Tom and Mary displayed interactional patterns that were similar to Matthew and Susan. It was my hope that they would learn much from each other by example. And for the most part this was true. There were times, however, when the two couples supported each other's destructive patterns. Fortunately, there is a self-righting mechanism or positive force in most therapy groups that seems to keep such difficulties in proper balance.

2. Jim and Judy were also both professionals. She was a teacher, and he an optometrist. They had been married for four years, and were in their late thirties. Judy had two children from a previous marriage. The presenting problem was Judy's obesity. There was some concern about diabetes developing. It was quickly discerned that marital discord was playing a role in her weight condition. Also, Jim was a little afraid that he might lose his wife if she became slimmer. Fearing this, he tended to sabotage his wife's efforts to lose weight. At the same time, he also wanted his wife thinner and was concerned about her health. They were both in conflict over this. He was the more forceful of the two, and ruled the family through the use of irrefutable logic. Judy was not as bright, felt inferior, and was easily overpowered by Jim's logical arguments. Over time, she learned to vent her resentments in passive and innocent ways. In many ways, her passive-aggressive manner was similar to Matthew's, and provided a link between the two couples.

3. Mike and Virginia were in their mid-forties. He was a successful business executive and she was a housewife. There were no children. Over the course of their twenty-year marriage she had been secretly drinking and had become a full-blown alcoholic. Her history included blackouts, D.T.s and two hospitalizations. She saw herself as very inadequate and totally dependent on her successful husband. She needed constant reassurance that she was lovable. Mike was a little shorter than his wife, a fact that bothered him greatly. However, he endeavored to compensate for this by displaying an aggressive manner. Unfortunately, this fact created

some marital discord. Also, Mike was not a very affectionate man, but he did love his wife and took good care of her. As a result, a pattern had developed where he would become preoccupied with business, she would act out with alcohol, he would rescue her, and she would feel loved and secure—for awhile. Although Virginia was more seriously addicted to alcohol than Matthew, nevertheless, there were many similarities in their behavioral patterns.

Let us now look at an MGT session with Matthew and Susan during which these couples were present.

On this particular night group was started by Susan. She had been angry at one of the other members for several weeks and could no longer contain herself.

Susan: Mike (spouse of alcoholic member), I have been watching the way you treat your wife and it really bothers me. You talk to her as though she were a little girl who couldn't survive without you being there to order her around. Can't you see how she rebels from it by drinking and acting helpless?

Mike: Wait a minute. You do the same thing to Matthew. You can really be pushy sometimes.

(They both stared at each other for some time. This was the kind of confrontation that I had been hoping for, the kind where the timing and the quality of the experience lead to insight. I wanted to jump in and underscore the similarities between them. Yet, sometimes saying less has more impact. Unconscious processes are often more accessible this way.)

Matthew: Maybe I do drink partly to rebel against her control. I know it causes a lot of trouble in my life. But, I just can't stand the thought of being decaffeinated. You know, like the guy on T.V. (referring to a commercial where the wife switches her husband to decaffeinated coffee). If I'm going to stop drinking, it will be my decision.

Therapist: Well, when do you think . . . *you're going to do something about your drinking?*

I emphasized the phrase beginning with *you're* in the hope of impressing on him that it was his decision. Yet the statement, disguised as a question, pushes him clearly, but subtly, in only one direction. I hoped Matthew wouldn't detect the push and become resistant.

Matthew: I don't know. One of these days I'll quit.

Tom: (Nonalcoholic member) What's the matter with right now. I mean, why put it off?"

(Silence followed. During this time Matthew's brow knitted and relaxed several times. He told us in a later session that Tom's comment made sense at that moment, and was instrumental in his decision to stop drinking. Perhaps he was open to Tom's comment at that moment because he had come to accept that it was truly his own decision.)

Susan: (After some time and with tears in her eyes) I feel so angry and confused right now. I can see that telling Matthew what to do won't work. But I can't trust him to take responsibility. He can be so unreliable.

(Matthew was grinning, but red faced.)

Therapist: Susan, you're a woman of action. Usually I admire that. But sometimes you rush in too soon to take charge. You can come on a bit strong sometimes. Maybe it brings the rebel out in Matthew.

(In starting with a positive comment, I hoped to maintain rapport with Susan. But I was concerned that she would see it as patronizing. Unfortunately, by focusing too much on Susan I overlooked Matthew's possible reaction.)

Matthew: Hey! I'm not that irresponsible. I hate being told that. I'd probably come home on time after work if I didn't feel that Susan demanded it of me. Instead of feeling appreciated when I do the right thing, all I get is a lecture on how I should have done it sooner. I just don't feel special to her, you know. I resent it. She has this attitude all the time as though she's looking down at you. (Susan looked angry. Just as she was about to speak I held out my hand to stop her. I wanted her to listen and not defend herself. She seemed to understand my gesture.)

Mary: (Tom's wife. Both nonalcoholic) I know you're angry right now. But maybe it's hard for her to be in an appreciative mood when you're so hostile to her. (Mary's tone was subdued and sympathetic.)

Matthew: I'm not hostile to her!—She's hostile to me!

Mary: Oh! What do you call deliberately being late for dinner. . . . being affectionate?

(Mary's voice had more fire in it. She was obviously frustrated by Matthew's refusal to hear her. Just as Matthew was about to speak, I jumped in.)

Therapist: Matthew—you tend to jump to your defense whenever anyone tries to tell you something. You're missing a chance to learn some important things about yourself . . .

Matthew: I'm not always defending myself . . .

Group: (Interrupting) You're doing it right now.

(Matthew fell silent for a few moments. He seemed a little embarrassed.)

Matthew: Oh!—is that what you mean?

Therapist: How about just trying to listen when someone is telling you something? *You will have the impulse to speak at these times, but you can resist it.*

(Again I was trying to implant suggestion without provoking resistance. My second statement was an effort to link a likely event [his impulse to speak] with the desired event [resistance to speaking and being defensive].)

Matthew: All right. I can do that.

Susan: I'd appreciate it. It's very hard to talk to you sometimes. You have a short fuse.—I guess I've been pretty defensive at times myself. Although it's hard not to be when you feel attacked. I guess I've been pretty bitchy too. But I'm sort of afraid that if I lose control of things that you'll take advantage of me and ruin my life. You know (to group), what I've just said seems a little ridiculous right now. Matthew and I will have to trust each other if we are going to be happy together.

Therapist: That makes sense. And maybe the trust will grow from your both being trustworthy, and being more sensitive to each other's needs.

Matthew: More sensitive?

Tom: You know. Learn to listen. And don't be so defensive. I guess being considerate is part of it.

(Tom and Mary looked at each other for a few minutes. I hoped that they were recognizing the importance of these qualities in their own relationship.)

Therapist: Matthew. You have indicated that you don't like being told what to do. Several of us here today have offered you advice. How do you feel about that?

Matthew: Well at first I felt insulted, like you were telling me I was stupid or something. But I know I have to be open to other people's ideas, especially Susan's, if we are going to get along. It's always been hard for me to do that. It's like I had to know everything, and always be right. But hell, nobody knows everything.—And we all need each other for something, don't we?

(The group agreed, and was very supportive at that moment. The atmosphere became warmer as feelings of mutual liking and caring were expressed.)

Judy: (Nonalcoholic member) Well, I guess the time is right for me to speak. I have been sitting on something for quite a while. But I have to deal with it. Actually, I don't know where to begin, and I feel like a fool, as though everybody is going to laugh at me and think I am a fool because I don't know how to tell you what's wrong with me.—I feel like a freak because I am overweight. I feel like nobody would like me, and that I am a fool to even think that anybody could. I feel like people would laugh at me if they found out that I wanted their friendship. They would think "Who does that fat slob think she is wanting a friendship?" It's so demoralizing that I have no motivation to lose weight. When I'm depressed I eat. And when I eat I get depressed because I'm keeping myself fat. If I could only lose weight, then I would feel better—not so worthless. But it just seems impossible.

Matthew: Jesus! That's the pits. I mean you're really stuck in it.

Therapist: Christ! You really are in the pits. You're really down and you feel helpless and hopeless. You think of yourself as a fool and as worthless. And you tell yourself that others think that of you, that even we think that of you—that Jim (her husband) thinks that of you.

(I wanted to get where she was, and have her with me when I turned out of it. At this point I hoped that she had heard enough of this depressing talk. I was also afraid that if I continued I would make it worse.)

Therapist: But *you're not a fool.* And no one in here thinks you're a fool, except you. You keep saying to yourself, "I'm a fool. I'm worthless." Then you blame it on your weight, and for failing to keep on your diet, and for not having the right words to express yourself. When are you going to be sick and tired of putting yourself down and feeling miserable because of it? When are you going to be tired enough of it to stop talking yourself into feeling like a fool? Isn't it about time you stopped and told yourself, "Hey, wait a minute! Jim doesn't think I'm a fool. That's ridiculous. I'm as worthwhile as anyone else. And Susan doesn't think I'm a fool. That's ridiculous." And so on around the room, and in the world.

(At this point the other group members spontaneously expressed feelings of liking and affection to Judy. Judy then focused her attention on Susan. It was her opinion Judy was most unsure of.)

Matthew: You know, I just realized something. You can put yourself down for any reason if that's what you're bent on doing. Judy uses her weight, Mike uses his height, and I use alcohol. I mean, I feel like I'm no good because I drink too much. Then I drink because, what the hell, I'm no good anyway. Then I feel like a failure because I didn't stop drinking and I feel worse. Then I blame Susan for putting me down. But I'm just looking for evidence for what I already believe. Unfortunately, she plays right in to it. So I attack her, or else feel I have to defy her. But it's really me. I'm putting myself down. I actually say to myself, "Jesus, what a jerk I am." I am really sick of doing that.

When the session was over, I felt that crucial issues had been dealt with. I had a sense of closure, and it felt good. As the weeks went by, Susan and Matthew displayed increasing feelings of respect for each other. They were learning to communicate honestly and openly. They indicated how helpful it was to be able to sit down at home and discuss their differences. Matthew had stopped drinking, and Susan was resisting the impulse to jump in and take charge. She was becoming more comfortable in sharing control of family matters with Matthew. She was helped to discover that Matthew would not exploit her if she yielded to him occasionally. She also discovered that Matthew disliked his dependency on her. This discovery helped to diminish her need to be needed. Matthew continued to feel he needed Susan, but saw it more as part of an interdependence, i.e., both depending on each other, yet capable of surviving alone. Also, Matthew learned to be more accepting of his mistakes, and became less perfectionistic. In the beginning, however, he did struggle with the self-defeating need to accept his mistakes perfectly, i.e., he wanted never to feel bad about a mistake. Thus, there were times when he condemned himself for feeling bad about a mistake, as well as feeling frustrated by the mistake itself.

I maintained contact with this couple in a variety of ways since they left therapy. Matthew has remained abstinent and has continued his contact with Alcoholics Anonymous. After about one year, they came in for a single therapy session. A resurgence of difficulties in sexual relations had occurred. One session focusing on mutual misconceptions about sexual performance was all that was needed. They have referred several patients to me, all of whom comment on how well Susan and Matthew are doing. I also receive cards from them occasionally. They believe that MGT was very helpful and are thankful they had the experience.

Without a doubt, most therapists would feel gratified when working with such patients. Unfortunately, not all couples respond as well in therapy. And as most therapists surely know, some couples are completely unaffected by our best efforts. However, whether we use Marital Group Therapy or some other family treatment approach, it seems clear that the current emphasis on including family members in treatment is increasing our success and allowing us to reach people who otherwise would have slipped through the therapeutic sieve.

REFERENCES

Bateson, G.; D.D. Jackson; J. Haley; & J. Weakland. Toward a theory of schizophrenia. *Behavioral Science*, 1956, **1**, 251–264.

Cadogan, D.A. Marital group therapy in the treatment of alcoholism. *Quarterly Journal of Studies on Alcoholism*, 1973, **34**, 1,184–1,194.

Cadogan, D.A. Marital group therapy in alcoholism treatment. In E. Kaufman and P.N. Kaufmann (Eds.), *Family therapy of drug and alcohol abuse*. New York: Gardner Press, 1979.

Rogers, E. *On becoming a person*. Cambridge, Mass.: Riverside Press, 1961.

Tahka, V. *The alcoholic personality: A clinical study*. Helsinki: Finnish Foundation for Alcohol Studies, 1966. Distributed in the United States by Rutgers University Center of Alcohol Studies, New Brunswick, New Jersey.

7

To All Appearances: The Ideal American Family

An Anthropological Case Study[1]

Joan Ablon, Ph.D.[2]
Genevieve Ames, Ph.D.[3]
William Cunningham, L.C.S.W.[4]

The case materials presented in this chapter have resulted from study, rather than clinical treatment, of intact, middle-class families in which the mother is an identified problem drinker. Statistics tell us that most of the millions of persons affected by alcohol abuse rarely reach professional clinicians. Ablon's previous research (2) with a "normal" sample of middle-class Catholic families suggested that in that population which appears to be representative of many middle-class families over the country, most families affected by alcohol abuse never seek or receive professional treatment. If forced

[1]The research on which this paper is based was sponsored by the National Institute on Alcohol Abuse and Alcoholism, No. AA 00180-80.
[2]Dr. Ablon is Professor, Medical Anthropology Program, Departments of Epidemiology and International Health and Psychiatry, University of California, San Francisco.
[3]Dr. Ames is Study Director, Prevention Research Center, Family Practices Division, Berkeley, California.
[4]At the time of this writing Mr. Cunningham was Deputy Director for Community Health Programs, Department of Public Health, City and County of San Francisco.

into professional treatment by progressive physical symptoms in the problem drinker or by delinquent acting out by children, families are touched by the treatment world only briefly and ineffectively, and leave as soon as possible with the original problems intact and little respect for the services they have encountered. Ablon's research in homes also suggested that much of what occurs in these families is rarely reported by patients touched so peripherally by professional systems, and will not be perceived by therapists who see the families for only brief periods. Thus, the study reported on here was designed to provide for a comprehensive gathering of data often not available to clinicians who characteristically limit their patient contacts to the physical context of the office and the temporal confines of professional office or clinic hours.

The project was an intensive, in-depth study of family structure and dynamics in eight families with a particular focus on both the explicit and the hidden functions of excessive drinking for the whole family. In addition, the range of social, cultural, and economic factors that impinge upon and contribute to the nature of family dynamics was documented. All of the families studied were recruited from those seeking treatment from several major alcohol programs within a large county mental health system in northern California. The fieldwork was carried out in family homes during periodic visits, lasting from two hours to whole days over a duration of six to twenty-two months. Ablon designed the original project proposal and directed the project, Ames conducted the fieldwork for the study, and Cunningham served as clinical consultant.

The study was carried out through classic methods of social anthropology: a combination of naturalistic and participant observation, and in-depth semi- and nondirective interviewing over as long a field period as possible. In most anthropological studies this is at least a year, but it is often much longer. In the study presented here the family was followed for twenty-two months. The conceptual approach was holistic, and perceived the total family as a functioning system, all members of which must be studied, interviewed, and comprehended. Thus, the aim was for as comprehensive a study as possible with a longitudinal time dimension.

Naturalistic observation, the observation of humans in their natural habitat, is a particularly appropriate approach for studying everyday family behavior in alcoholic households. Rarely have practitioners in any field but child development turned to empirical studies of family life or relationships to supplement their clinical observations. Despite the statements of some few clinicians, as noted below, that therapists can benefit in unique ways from studies of family life, by and large practitioners and their patients live and function in two different worlds. However, just as the principles of therapy have relevance to specific daily life patterns, so the detailed intimate happenings of which daily family life is made have specific relevance for the therapy process.

A brief exposition of the conceptual premises and the methodologies used in this study will be presented below.

THE ALCOHOLIC FAMILY SYSTEM

Orientations in the literature on alcoholism and the family have evolved from an early emphasis on pathological features of individual spouses to a more recent emphasis on interaction within the family unit. (For reviews of this literature see Paolino and McCrady [27] and Ablon (1.)

Ewing and Fox (11) and Ward and Faillace (35) presented the clearest early statements relating a systems approach to alcohol studies. However, the contemporary thrust for studying family systems may be credited to Peter Steinglass and his associates. Steinglass, Weiner, and Mendelson (35, 36), Steinglass (32, 34), Davis et al. (9), Wolin et al. (38), Bowen (8), and Berenson (5) explicated a variety of theoretical and practical aspects inherent in the viewing of alcohol-related problems within a systems approach. The realistic unit for research and treatment is recognized to be the "alcoholic system" rather than the alcoholic family member.

Steinglass et al. (36) presented a model detailing the manner in which family members are involved in an ongoing alcoholic bargain that functions for the maintenance of the system. The authors suggest that family members as component parts of a system "manipulate" other members and adjust their behavior as necessary to maintain a "complementary relationship of psychopathology, needs, strengths, cultural values, etc. within the family"(36 p.405).

Davis et al. (9) from related treatment experiments suggested that excessive drinking patterns may indeed have certain adaptive consequences that are sufficiently reinforcing to serve as the primary factors maintaining the drinking patterns. These adaptive consequences may operate at a variety of levels: intrapsychic, intracouple, or on the family or wider social system basis. For successful intervention, the therapist must determine the specific manner in which drinking behavior serves the adaptive function, and then, once the adaptive consequences have been identified, therapy may be structured around helping the patient manifest the adaptive behavior while sober instead of while drinking, and also helping him to learn alternate effective behavior patterns.

The clinical significance of the efforts of the system to maintain itself were explored in various papers (35):

> From a systems point of view, it is the protection of the functioning system itself that takes precedence over the individual concerns or needs of the members of the system. If the continuation of therapy implies a threat to the integrity or functioning of the system, then therapy will probably be rejected as an alien and dangerous force. It would seem, then, that the task of the therapist is to effect the desirable behavioral changes without appearing as an imminent threat to the ongoing system [pp. 278–279].

In a recent paper, Steinglass (34) has added a developmental perspective to his studies, addressing the long-range implications of alcoholism for families. Steinglass' "family life history" model applies the developmental construct of the family cycle to the unique life history of the alcoholic family. He reports on a study that captured behavior of families in the home and clinic over a six-month period at both drinking and nondrinking phases.

Steinglass' family life history model is built around three concepts: the alcoholic system, the family homeostasis which resists change, and the family alcohol phases, i.e., periods of varied drinking behavior. Steinglass (34) here eloquently presents his premises for the use of the systems model:

> The concept of the alcoholic system is drawn from my earlier thinking about the relation between interactional behavior and chronic alcoholism. . . . It was postulated that in certain interactional systems (families being one of them), alcohol use might come to play such a critical role in day-to-day behavior as to become a central organizing principle around which patterns of interactional behavior might be

shaped. In this sense, major aspects of behavior would be so flavored by the style and consequences of alcohol use as to warrant the term, "an alcoholic system." This term, we felt, was particularly applicable in those circumstances in which families remained economically and structurally intact despite (or to use this different way of thinking, assisted by) the presence of chronic alcoholism in their midst. In such families, during periods of active drinking, we proposed that the family actually cycled between two predictable interactional states, one associated with sobriety and one associated with intoxication. These were not merely differential patterns that the family used in dealing with its identified alcoholic member. These were truly different interactional states at the family level. The repetitive and stereotyped aspect of behavior within the family during periods of actual intoxication, we proposed, might actually be associated with certain aspects of problem-solving by the family, and it might also serve to reduce uncertainty. In this sense, intoxicated interactional behavior might become as habitual as the alcohol consumption itself [p. 213].

In keeping with Steinglass, we too found differing stages of intrafamily functioning when the alcoholic was drinking or sober. Most of the families in our study would be labeled "stable-wet"; this means that they have organized themselves around the alcohol usage as a component of the family homeostasis. The resistance of family members to treatment of and change in the alcoholic's drinking patterns, despite their stated abhorrence of what drinking has done to their family lends credence to the view of a rigid, homeostatic system at work. The premise of our research was that the total family, and in some cases, the extended family system was the appropriate and necessary focus of study.

THE FAMILY HOUSEHOLD AS THE SITE OF CLINICAL WORK AND STUDY

Clinical Home Visits

Bloch (6) has suggested that the clinical home visit is a valuable tool for the diagnosis and treatment of the family as a group. Says Bloch:

The physical household, its contents and the social arrangement for their use are a vast, living and changing representation of the psychosocial life of the family and can be entered into, and joined with, by the clinician in such a way as to complexly reveal the forces operating in the family system [p. 39].

Bloch presented cases in which clinical family home visits provided data that would rarely if ever have come to the attention of therapists in traditional office treatment sessions. Bloch notes that traditional office schedules make home visits difficult and even monetary liabilities, yet he states such visits are very valuable and should be *required* of beginning family therapists.

Several clinicians have reported on actual therapeutic activities that were carried out in the context of the family home. Fisch (12), Friedman (13), Pattison (28), Hansen (14), and Perry (29) all report on such experiences with patients. Hansen (14) went so far as to move into her client family's home for a week. These authors comment on advantages, disadvantages, complications, and new insights for therapeutic intervention that might be gained through home observation. All of these authors concluded that home therapy sessions have great advantages.

Fisch (12) commented:

> It is obvious but important to say that the exploration of family interaction in the doctor's office is artificial, yet most data is [*sic*] obtained in this way. It would be akin to studying the culture of the Hopi by having the tribe move to Columbia University [p. 115].

Nonetheless, clinical home visits remain an anomaly in the mental health treatment world, as do naturalistic studies of families in their homes.

In-Home Studies

The original inspiration for the methods used in this study came from the work of Jules Henry, an anthropologist who carried out naturalistic observation studies in homes, schools, convalescent hospitals, and other institutional settings. One of Henry's chief interests was in mental illness. Henry argued that by actually living in households where mental illness exists, and presumably has developed, researchers may collect important data to provide an intimate understanding of family life for clinicians. Stated Henry (17):

> For many years it had been my conviction that the etiology of emotional illness required more profound study than had heretofore been possible and that the best way to new discoveries in the field was

through study of the disease-bearing vector, the family, in its natural habitat, pursuing its usual life routines—eating, loving, fighting, talking, taking amusements, treating sickness, and so on—in other words, following the usual course of its life [p. 30].

Yet, very few naturalistic studies are available that detail life in "normal" or "pathogenic" homes. Extensive studies of animals in the wild have been carried out by zoologists, anthropologists, and psychologists who have considered the native habitat rather than that of the artificial zoo to be the necessary context for understanding animal behavior. Yet scientists and clinicians who study human behavior have taken strangely little interest in home observation. Family interaction and assessment studies primarily have been carried out in offices and laboratories through observation, measurement, and analysis of family members' performances in artificial games and tasks, despite the fact that some researchers (for example, O'Rourke [26]) have demonstrated a considerable difference in the performance of similar tasks by families when carried out in laboratories as opposed to their homes. Blood (7), Dreyer and Dreyer (10), and Hansen (15) reported on findings of such household-based studies, discussed methodological considerations, and pointed up the potential richness of such research.

Henry's *Pathways to Madness* was based on naturalistic observation in homes of five families of psychotic and autistic children. Henry lived in one home for a week, and he, and in one case an assistant, spent each day from breakfast to bedtime for approximately a week with each of the others, observing in great detail their normal life routine. Henry's vivid descriptions and analyses of family members' actions, interactions, and motivations unfold in a complex portrayal of factors that add up to—rather than explain—the "pathology" of the family. In discussing the significance of processes or conditions proposed by family therapists as being "pathological," Henry suggests that many of these processes may be necessary consequences of persons living together in the American family; they may be inescapably part and parcel of contemporary family life. If Henry's point is to be taken seriously, it holds significant implications for primary prevention *and* therapeutic intervention.

Naturalistic studies are particularly appropriate to provide data on family behavior in the alcoholic household. Because alcoholism affects the total family, in these households all family members may be living within a complexly chaotic world, often denied and hidden as much as possible from even close friends and relatives. A peculiar family "culture" is thus constructed and maintained. Differing family "cultures" may well be found in accordance with the nature of respective health conditions or chronic diseases that occur in families.

The consequences of varied patterns of alcohol usage can be productively explored through systematic observation. Hidden functions of excessive drinking for the whole family may be revealed by observations of family interaction and by progressive informal interviewing of all family members rather than only the identified alcoholic or irate spouse.

The staying power of anthropological studies can be particularly valuable here. Studies carried out over several years with individual families may produce materials on behavioral and structural changes that occur as families deal with drinking problems. Some of the many areas that might be pursued in longitudinal studies are changes in roles and attendant consequences for family life style, and the restructuring of networks within the nuclear and extended family and with nonkin. Likewise, the career profile of the alcoholic family has not been detailed. Jackson, in her early family papers (18, 19, 20), suggested seven coping stages through which she posited all alcoholic families' progress in dealing with their problems. Yet, in the twenty-five years since her writing, these stages have never been tested through the gathering of data on specific families over time. Likewise, Steinglass (34) has suggested that families cycle through wet and dry phases rather than proceeding through the normal developmental stages of family life. Again, the testing of this proposition requires on going systematic research.

Steinglass' recent papers report on his study of thirty-one families who were followed in their homes as well as in laboratory and family discussion settings over a six-month period. Steinglass focused on ways in which the families regulated their "internal environment" by recording such formally quantifiable measures of the families' use of time and space within the home as: time spent together, the physical distances observed in interactions, and the frequency of decision-making verbal exchanges. Major factors emerging from these measurable variables were related to individual or family symptomatology or family phases. The study reported below in the present paper confronts through a qualitative anthropological approach a number of the issues Steinglass has also addressed.

METHODOLOGY

In the larger study from which the following case was taken, family activities were observed, including behavior at meals, doing household tasks, typical leisure activities, and socializing with kin, friends, and neighbors. The families were observed in visits to other homes, in recreational settings, and at specific events such as parties, weddings, and graduations. These latter social situations offer opportunities to observe interactional behavior with kin and significant others. Likewise, many of these situations are prime behavioral settings where normative "social" drinking is in some cases expected and where excessive drinking sometimes takes place.

In-depth interviewing of all family members over the age of eighteen years was carried out. The dominant focus of interviews was on individual and family history and ongoing interaction between family members. A wide variety of detailed materials was collected on individuals including data on early life history, family of orientation, medical history, education, past and present employment record, significant life events, recreation patterns, and past and present social relationships. All contacts with community or private caregivers and professionals were recorded. There was a careful effort to elicit data allowing a correlation between significant social networks that have existed and do exist as drinking patterns have varied. The history and importance of drinking patterns were elicited and considered as they fit into the total scheme of family life and social and recreational activities.

A variety of complex methodological issues arise in planning for naturalistic studies. A chief logistical task in carrying out such a project which has the potential for producing vast amounts of data is the development of a recording system that is able to record observations quickly, accurately, and in a fashion that makes data measurable and readily retrievable for coding and analysis. Barker

(4) and Steinglass (33) have presented their own methodologies for capturing, recording, analyzing, and processing data resulting from naturalistic observation. Lytton (25) has reviewed the methodologies used in numerous observational studies of parent-child interaction, the only area of family studies that has commonly utilized naturalistic observation. In the study presented here, the observer found that a systematic recording scheme could not be followed during household visits because of the sensitivity of family members to the observer's presence and because of the many, often dramatic, ongoing crisis events that took place. The delicate nature of the observer-informant relationship could be shattered by such a deliberate academic activity proceeding in the midst of often painful family interactions or during intense spontaneous outpourings. Descriptions of events were dictated immediately following the observational field experiences. Planned interviews were all taped and immediately transcribed. Observation and interview notes were coded and analyzed, chiefly through definition and analysis of recurrent *themes* that emerge from the data.

Other complexities relating to the data gathered, must be addressed. What effect does the presence of an investigator have on the behavior that unfolds, or is *allowed* to unfold? Does the investigator get a rosy view of family life that is prepared just for her or him? Initially, this may be the case, yet we would argue that, relative to the time the investigator is in the home, phony fronts cannot be maintained forever, and family members will return to their usual behaviors within a few visits. The stability of family systems would offer evidence that this would be the case. Thus, the less obtrusive the investigator, the longer the periods of observation, and the more systematic the attendance, the more "normal" the behavior that transpires will be.

The problematic aspects of field complexities are exacerbated in working with troubled or problem-laden families where the "normal" crises of family life are replaced by severe ones such as those triggered by rounds of drinking or other behavior considered as abusive by other family members. Henry, who carried out the prototypic study in the households of problem families, unfortunately gave us little in the way of methodological accounting of his field experiences (16). We found that a variety of problems haunt investigators who plan to bury themselves in the bosoms of troubled families (3). Recruiting families is a first major difficulty that can create havoc with the original sampling design. For example, while clinic administrators were enthusiastic about this study, finding families who met the requirements was not so simple a task. Intact families wherein the wife-mother is the identified problem drinker are relatively rare in public clinics.

The fact that the mother was the problem drinker also caused considerable problems of extra concealment and difficulty within the home, When the mother is incapacitated by alcohol, a whole different scenario of family life may occur from cases where the father is the drinker. The absence or indisposition of the wife-mother as the pivotal stabilizer of daily life routine may vastly complicate the research scene. Frequently, in times of crisis, and particularly when the mother was very inebriated, often absented in her room, observational activities were so awkward that they became impossible to carry out. Thus, for a number of related reasons, observations quickly took a second place to interviewing as the primary methodology. Long conversational interviews of a "Rashoman" type (i.e., from the perspectives of all family members) became the chief sources of data. Lewis, an anthropologist who has captured Mexican and Puerto Rican family life in an extraordinarily vivid and sensitive manner (21, 22, 23, 24), worked largely through this style of interviewing, and through the taking of life histories which complemented each other in giving varied perspectives on the same events (for example, see *A Death in the Sanchez Family*, 24).

The family described in this case study was followed over almost two years and exhibited a multitude of problems during this period. All family members accepted the presence of the researcher within the household and shared their attitudes, feelings, and perceptions intimately with her. She thus became a trusted friend and confidant for the family. Because most of the families studied dropped out of treatment within a few months after the study began, they characteristically had no other confidant with whom they could share their feelings of anger, frustration, fear, or guilt. Because of the trust in the researcher, such personal feelings were shared to an extraordinary degree. The following account summarizes many hundreds of pages of field and interview notes that resulted from this study.

THE CASE STUDY: A "TYPICAL MIDDLE-CLASS" AMERICAN FAMILY

To all outward appearances, the Andrews family typifies an idealized normative middle-class life style as many people know it or believe it to be in American society. From the very first visit to their comfortable suburban home, the researcher came away with the firm impression that this family represented an intact, child-centered, religiously involved, and achievement-oriented family. Carl and Molly Andrews, an attractive couple in their late thirties, have been married for twenty years. They married young, when they both were still in college, and within four years had their three children.

Carl, a tall, blond, soft-spoken man, although nonaggressive and retiring in his self-presentation, works hard at his job as a real estate salesman. His work takes him away from the house most weekends and almost every evening during the week, a routine that is most upsetting to Molly. He has had a poor sales record during the past two years, and the family was struggling financially. Their income is supplemented by gifts of money, meat, clothes, and automobiles from Molly's mother, and by assistance from the children, who all have part-time jobs to help pay for their clothes and for spending money. Carl's first priority in life is not his job. In terms of loyalty and emotional involvement, his employer ranks somewhere down the line after family, church, and selected community affairs. His social activities center on his children's school, church and athletic events. Since the onset of Molly's drinking problem, he rarely takes her out or encourages social events in the home; he does escort her to church services on Sundays and whenever she is able to go, takes her to early morning prayer service. Sensitive, warm and personable, Carl displayed an anomalous, stoic resilience to Molly's excessive drinking habits and to their related humiliating and frustrating consequences.

Molly, a slight, fair-skinned brunette, stays home to keep house and care for the family, a role she has maintained and enjoyed for most of the twenty years she and Carl have been together. She is a fastidious housekeeper, an excellent cook and seamstress, and a concerned, affectionate, and fiercely protective mother. Twenty years of marriage have not diminished her love and admiration for

Carl; she invariably speaks of him in supportive and affectionate terms.

At the time this study began, Carol, the eldest, was nineteen. She was living at home, attending a local community college, and working part-time. During her high school years, Carol was outgoing and aggressive; she was an outstanding scholar, a cheerleader, an elected leader in school government, and the winner of a "beauty queen" contest. In her home environment she presents a different image. She is a pensive, withdrawn, and oftentimes visibly agitated young woman. Though ridiculed by her siblings and friends for "wasting" her scholarly talents in a local college, Carol chose to remain at home during her first year of college in an effort to avoid further financial pressure on her father and—as the researcher later observed—out of concern for her mother's deteriorating health and well-being. When necessary, and in Molly's absence, Carol assumed the cook and housekeeper role, but for the most part, her crowded social, work, and college schedule left little time for domestic tasks. A pretty, likable young woman, she was popular among her social peers; however, she rarely entertained friends or acquaintances in the house. Before the onset of the drinking problem, Carol and Molly had enjoyed a close mother-daughter relationship. Through all the frustrating, disappointing months of Molly's alcoholism, Carol, more than any other family member, hung on to the memories of her mother's former self—that of a dependable, nurturing parent and companion.

Barbara, who was eighteen and a senior in high school, was, like her sister, an honor student, reigning high school beauty queen, and leader among her social peers. Everyone in the Andrews family agreed that Barbara's personality was similar to the way they remembered Molly's to be, before she developed a drinking problem. According to Barbara, their similarities created conflict when she was growing up, and she never felt close to her mother. Barbara is disarmingly free of spirit, light-hearted, always laughing, a clever tease, and in constant dramatic motion. No one except Molly seems to mind that among all the family members Barbara contributes the least toward the general maintenance of the household. Perhaps this fortunate exemption from menial tasks was related to the fact that she had unconsciously been allocated the much more important and vital role of family comedian. Barbara had a unique ability to clown around and see the humorous side of those recurring, traumatic family episodes that were related to Molly's drinking behavior. She provided a comic relief in an otherwise tense, depressing, and humorless household. To put it simply, Barbara knew how to make the family laugh, a natural attribute which they all recognized and valued. Carl displayed an open admiration and joyful affection for this daughter, and he was noticeably happier and more relaxed in her presence. He often and proudly spoke of her beauty, her "admirable" personality traits, her academic accomplishments and rising success as an aspiring actress. Molly was threatened by Carl's special relationship with Barbara, not in the sense that she suspected any incestuous or inappropriate inclinations, but from a growing realization that Barbara, perhaps unconsciously, perhaps not, was replacing her as the flirtatious, feminine counterpart to her husband's serious, thoughtful nature.

Ron, seventeen, and a junior in high school, was also a high achiever in many areas of his life. He was handsome, popular in his peer group, a good student, an outstanding athlete, and president of the student council. He was a religious, spiritually oriented young man, who at the age of thirteen recognized a "call to the ministry." He was soft-spoken like his father, and remarkably articulate on a variety of current worldly issues. Always loyal and devoted to his mother, he was still confused and noticeably saddened by the radical periodic changes in her behavior. Still, and in the face of repeating excessive drinking patterns, he remained optimistic that by use of spiritual counseling and prayer, he could bring about a satisfactory solution to Molly's drinking problem. With all the opportunities and valid reasons he had to reject his mother, Ron rarely argued with her or spoke to her (or of her) in a demeaning, accusatory manner. During the two-year research period, at those times when Carl withdrew from Molly, Ron progressively moved toward the role of surrogate companion and confidant to his mother.

Up until four years ago, the Andrews family lived in Centerville, a small town located in the heart of the same agricultural valley where Carl and Molly themselves had spent their childhoods. During the years they lived there, Carl never made much money working in his mother-in-law's lumber business, but he and Molly and the children were happy in Centerville. They were leaders in com-

munity affairs and town organizations; Carl coached his son's baseball teams, was active in Rotary Club, and regularly volunteered
to chaperone for school trips, outings, and teen dances. Molly was
the leader of her daughters' "Blue Bird" and "Campfire Girl"
groups, an officer in the PTA and an active member of various
organizations in the Presbyterian Church. In their formative years,
Carl and Molly worshiped in the Presbyterian and Methodist re-
ligions, and their family of procreation continues to be actively
involved in the Presbyterian Church.

There was no history of long-term alcohol misuse in either parent's family. Carl's parents are moderate social drinkers. Molly's
father developed a drinking problem in his early sixties but stopped
when he developed terminal cancer. Molly contends her father was
an alcoholic, but her mother vehemently denies this diagnosis,
explaining instead that his heavy drinking was a "temporary response" to a costly failure of a business venture. Neither Carl nor
Molly has ever been a heavy social drinker. In fact, prior to the
onset of Molly's drinking problem, they were moderate or at best
occasional social drinkers. Carl can recall only one time in his life
when he had too much to drink, and that was at a neighbor's New
Year's Eve party some years ago. Molly had never been intoxicated
nor has she drunk heavily at a social event; she now drinks only
at home, secretly and alone. Her serious problems with alcohol
began four years ago, coincidentally, the family all agreed, with
the time the family moved away from Centerville. Carl resettled
his family in the rapidly growing urban sprawl where they now
live in the hopes of finding a better job for himself, and a wider
range of educational opportunities for his children. After fifteen
years of working for his mother-in-law in Centerville, he wanted
a change. While Molly reluctantly agrees with him that the change
has been for the best, she misses her old friends and the "com-
fortableness" of small-town life. She once mentioned that she knew
by name literally everyone in that town of two thousand people.

In the same year that they uprooted themselves from their life-
time home and social network, Molly's best friend, neighborhood
companion, and confidant was murdered by an unknown assailant.
Even now, four years later, during discussions of either their life
in Centerville or the tragic death of her friend, Molly becomes
visibly upset and often breaks into tears. Although Molly's secret
drinking patterns were beginning to develop before they left Cen-

terville, she considers the move and her friend's death as primary factors precipitating her drinking problem.

The Andrews family now lives in an affluent California suburban neighborhood, or better said, the external fringes of a large metropolitan area. Their housing development is miles from the city, and in fact, their house is on the end of a street that borders the adjoining and rapidly decreasing farm lands. There are few trees in their neighborhood, and for the greater part of the year the general atmosphere is hot, dry, and smoggy. During the weekdays, when husbands and school children are not outside the houses for gardening and recreational activities, the streets are devoid of people, and neighborly interaction is at a minimum. These factors, plus the preponderance of waist-high weeds in the surrounding vacant fields create a kind of desolate and isolated environment for the houses on their street. Molly, who spends most of her days at home alone, often indicated in both words and action that she was lonely here. Because she has been a secret and heavy drinker since their move from Centerville, and is fearful of being found out, she has made no new friends or even casual relations among neighbors or in the community at large. Her social activities are limited to her Bible study group, Ron's school and sports activities, occasional sessions at the mental health center, and the researcher's frequent visits.

Carl bought the house before the family moved to the area, and without consulting Molly. He felt certain she would like the "space-saver" model he had decided upon. Though small in square footage, it boasted five bedrooms and three bathrooms, which offered each child their own room. The living room, which houses a baby grand piano and nothing else, and the large upstairs "family room" are used only on those rare occasions when the children have school or church related activities. The center of activity in the Andrews' household is the large family kitchen, wherein there is a large table, six high-backed dining chairs, a sofa, a lounge chair for Carl, and the television set. But the most striking feature of the room is the "family bulletin board" which extends almost the entire length of the room. This dominating feature of the house is, in effect, an historical account of the children's lives as illustrated through their many awards for various activities and high scholastic achievements. It is also a kind of symbolic display of the Andrews family life style—of their value system, of their beliefs about parenting, family togetherness, mutual support, and community in-volvements—in effect, of what they perceive as the normal, everyday activities of a good life. There are pictures of their son in his Little League uniform with his various teammates for every year he played baseball from age eight to thirteen, and then of his high school teams. There are pictures and ribbons and certificates of Ron's many awards for high achievement in wrestling, swim-ming, football, baseball, school government, Christian Youth Club leaderships, and other church-related activities. There are sections for the girls: Carol is there as the queen of the Valentine's Day Ball, as valedictorian of a graduating class of 1,500 students, as student government officer, and with numerous handsome young men at school dances and parties. Barbara, also an honor student and reigning high school beauty queen, is represented by pictures or documents of her achievements as a competitive tennis player and an outstanding actress. She later won a full scholarship to a pres-tigious university on the basis of her scholarly and dramatic abil-ities. There are scattered pictures of Carl, mostly with his son, wherein he was scoutmaster, coach, chaperone, and companion on fishing and hunting expeditions. Throughout the house, there are many more pictures of the children; the piano serves as a display for an array of pictures of the girls in their beauty queen pageants.

There are no pictures of Molly, which at first seemed a peculiar absence since prior to the onset of her drinking problem, and less than four years ago when they lived in Centerville, she too was active in community and child-centered activities. As the researcher became more familiar with the Andrews household, she discovered that Molly was also an accomplished seamstress and a creative cook. She made colorful curtains and bedspreads in the children's rooms; she also designed and hand-sewed the pretty dresses that adorned her daughters for their beauty pageants, school dances, and graduation ceremonies. During her nondrinking periods, she prepared nutritional, tasty meals, desserts, and snacks. In the sum-mers, she picked the apricots from their backyard tree and pre-served them into jellies or dried fruit. She would plan far in advance of special family events; for example, at Barbara's graduation party (which the researcher attended), she prepared a variety of hors d'oeuvres, hot dishes, and decorative cookies and cakes. Molly never spoke of these things in the sense of accomplishments; she viewed sewing and cooking as ordinary, expected attributes of her maternal-role duties. She was extremely sensitive about the house-keeping situation, for instance, if she had been "ill" (the word she always used for her drinking periods), she would request that the researcher not go upstairs for fear it was "messy" or "dusty." From time to time Carl and once Carol (the eldest daughter) praised Molly's domestic accomplishments. However, the incentive to re-cognize her special talents was more often than not canceled out by the family's preoccupation with her drinking problem. In their view, because of this failing, she did not deserve any praise.

The Andrews, a family of five, by the close of the research period had five automobiles and a house trailer in and about their driveway. Each child upon graduating from high school, in ac-knowledgment of this achievement, received from their maternal grandmother the gift of a brand new, medium-priced automobile of their choice. In his last year of high school, Ron requested, and received, a new truck instead of a car. Carl was also the recipient of this generous gift-giving practice. He received a new car "to assist him in his real estate business." Molly drives the ten-year-old family station wagon; no family member seems aware or even slightly disconcerted by the glaring, obvious truism that the grand-mother has "awarded" every family member with an expensive automobile with the exception of Molly, her daughter and only child.

After the children, the focal point of the Andrews family house-hold is their church. Their weekly church-related activities include: Sunday morning services; Sunday evening prayer services; Tues-day afternoon Bible study (Molly enjoys this group when she is ("well"); Thursday morning 6:00 A.M. Bible readings (Carl attends this and sometimes Molly); the church choir (Ron); Christian Youth Club; and Campus Life. Ron, Carol, and Barbara have all partici-pated in these latter high school organizations which teach and promote Christian principles. Ron, who is considering going into the ministry, is a leader in the youth groups; in the past he has attended church-sponsored camps and now is preparing for mis-sionary work in Africa.

Thus, this household is for all practical purposes, a commu-nication center for the multifaceted lives of the Andrews children, all of whom are outstanding scholars, competitive athletes, ener-getic leaders in school, community and church organizations, and strikingly handsome young people.

MOLLY'S DRINKING PATTERN

During the almost two years of the researcher's relationship with the Andrews family, Molly was a chronic alcoholic: she drank approximately sixteen ounces of vodka a day during her drinking periods (this is her conservative estimate), and she drank it very fast in order to reach the immediate desired effects of partial or total unconsciousness. Molly *never* drank for reasons of increased conviviality or social pleasure. The time of day for drinking varies between the early morning hours to later afternoon. Her usual pattern was to drink for four to five days and then not drink for two to seven days. The longest abstaining period she had over two years was one fourteen-day abstinence, and the month-long period she spent at a private hospital for treatment of alcoholics.

Molly was diagnosed by her physician as epileptic after what she describes as a "seizure" three years ago. Since that time she has taken a prescribed dosage of phenobarbital three times daily—when she remembers to take it. Carl, the children, and Molly's mother do not agree with this diagnosis, and object to the medication. Three times during the two-year study in apparent attempts to take her life, Molly swallowed full containers of phenobarbital pills, twice in the presence of her family. All three attempts occurred during periods of heavy drinking. In an effort to control her drinking, she occasionally takes Antabuse (disulfiram), a sulfa compound which in the presence of alcohol causes nausea and vomiting. She took this in preparation for her infrequent visits to the county mental health center, and in anticipation of the researcher's visits the first few times she visited her home.

Molly is sometimes pretty, energetic, well-groomed, and pleasant to be with; at other times, she is unattractive, puffy-skinned, sallow, unwashed, and generally speaking, very poor company. The changes of appearance and moods are correlated with her nondrinking periods as opposed with her drinking and hangover periods. Whenever the researcher was with Molly, whether she was drinking or abstaining, the researcher was keenly aware of her sense of low self-esteem and of a smoldering anger, which could erupt with very little provocation. Both her immediate and extended family and her therapist from the county mental health center were puzzled by her frequent bouts with depression, her angry outbursts, and her general unhappiness. Her family was puzzled, discouraged, sometimes disgusted, and oftentimes humiliated by her drinking problem. Molly, as of the past four years, lives in a cyclical behavioral routine, moving from the role of affectionate, nurturing wife and mother when she is sober, to a screaming, disoriented, unpredictable stranger when she is drinking.

THE DISCOVERY OF A PROBLEM WITH NO NAME

Molly was a problem drinker for three years—and perhaps a full-blown alcoholic—before her husband, mother and children discovered her secret drinking patterns, or that she drank at all, for that matter. There are several different versions of the discovery. Carl remembers that shortly before they left Centerville, Molly told him "she was afraid she was becoming an alcoholic." At that time he and Molly drank socially on their rare evenings out and occasionally had a drink before dinner. He kidded her about her worries, assured her she was not an alcoholic, and then forgot about it. Carl goes on to say:

> But after that, things weren't exactly perfect. She started having afternoon sickness, she didn't feel good, and she couldn't do things in the afternoon or evening. And then, after we got here it got worse and so then we had many doctors' appointments and physicals and everything, but neither she nor the doctors ever brought out the problem. Whenever she would go to the doctor, she would be O.K. Then we finally had x-rays and found out she had kidney stones and she'd had these kidney stone attacks which were very painful. She refused to see a doctor about that. Then one day the kids called me from work and said she was having one of those deals—a kidney stone attack—and as I now know, she was drunk too—and finally between the four of us, the three kids and myself, we forced her to see a doctor. We put a mattress in the station wagon and forcibly put her in, and I held her down while Carol drove. We got there, and she refused to cooperate with him, refused to take a blood test and was belligerent. He told her, I know you've been drinking, he says, but you'd have to drink an awful lot—if this is a kidney stone—to kill the pain. I asked her if this was true and she said well, she'd had maybe a half a beer for lunch. I later realized she was drinking vodka every day. So that was kind of the beginning of my finding out.

Carl's father later told him he had known about Molly's problem for three years, and the neighbor across the street said she knew about it also.

Barbara claims the family suspected something was amiss on a family vacation camping trip when Molly "suddenly began pestering Dad every other day to drive to some store to buy vodka for 'cocktails'."

Carol, perhaps the most sensitive and astute member of the family, says it was a gradual discovery process; she and her grandmother (Molly's mother) were firmly convinced that the afternoon sicknesses were related to diabetes.

> For a long time, every afternoon, Mom'd just all of a sudden freak out; she couldn't talk, she couldn't do anything. Grandma was here on a six-week visit and we thought it was her diabetes and we'd always try to make her eat this or that, and she'd spit it out, and we'd get *so sick* that she could act like this. My grandma was really worried so she took her down to a private clinic for lots of tests and stuff for diabetes and epilepsy, but she was fine. We even had her checked for stomach tumors—but they couldn't find any; it came out negative. And finally last summer Dad started finding bottles, and he said, I hope it's not what I think it is. And I said What Dad, just tell me. He wouldn't and I made him tell me, you know. He said, well I think she's drinking. That just shattered me, it was inconceivable to me. I just cried and cried and cried. I kept thinking, I mean, I didn't think she'd be drinking because of us kids—and her marriage seemed pretty good. We were so close to the situation, and we were blinded by it. We had no idea it was this!

These and other discussions about the "discovery" left the researcher with the impression that the family would have preferred a diagnosis of advanced diabetes, or epilepsy, or even the hoped-for stomach tumor, to the less acceptable problem of "alcoholism." In fact they never once in the two-year research period referred to their mother as an "alcoholic," or to the condition as "alcoholism." It was referred to as her "deal" or "problem" or "screw-up"; it was not viewed as a health problem. Molly herself, even after having been diagnosed numerous times by various treatment modalities as alcoholic, never referred to herself in these terms. She did refer to her drinking as an illness, however. The family's basic beliefs and attitude about the problem never changed: toward the end of the two-year relationship with the Andrews family, after Molly had conceded to try various medical, therapeutic, and self-help treatment modalities, and when her deteriorating mental and physical condition was nearing an all-time critical state, Carl and the children were still preoccupied more with the stigma-related aspects of alcoholism than with Molly's health. They never viewed her "problem" as an illness or disease.

The family was more comfortable with a moralistic explanation. As Barbara so often reminded the researcher, "The Bible tells us drunkenness is a sin—so I guess Mom is a sinner." Ron rarely verbalized his viewpoints on the problem, but if action represents beliefs, he too preferred moral over medical explanations. He frequently "prayed over" his mother when she was unconscious, encouraged her to speak to their church minister, and brought counselors from the Christian Youth Organization to the home to talk with her or to "treat" her. He disliked and discouraged private and county mental health treatment. He disapproved of Alcoholics Anonymous. Ron was a strong-willed, decisive, and mature young man—and he was preparing for the ministry; the family held him in high esteem. Over a relatively short period of time, he took or was given the balance of power in the family, in the area of decision making around Molly's care and treatment.

A PRETENSE OF NORMALITY (ABBREVIATED VIGNETTE, SUMMARIZED FROM RESEARCHER'S NOTES)

Molly and I made an unspoken agreement at the onset of this study, that she would be home, in or about the house, during my visits. As such, whenever I planned to drive the distance from my house to the Andrews home, I first checked in with Molly. On one particular Saturday morning, my phone rang at 7:30 A.M. and there was Molly's cheerful voice asking me to "come on over" and spend the day with the family. She was ecstatic about her plans to play bridge with a church group that morning; since the rest of the family would be at home that day, she requested that I visit the home this once when she was away; she promised to return early afternoon. I accepted the invitation, and on arrival, shortly before lunch I noticed that Molly's old Plymouth wagon was in the driveway. When Carol answered the door and motioned me inside, I asked whether Molly was still home. Carol said very softly, "Yes, she's here" and with a resigned wave of the hand motioned toward her parents' bedroom at the end of the hall off the kitchen, saying nothing more. This was typical of the family's

*unusual procedures for explaining Molly's absence from the family scene.
On this morning, the wave of the hand was the signal that Molly had been
drinking and was already asleep and "out for the day," or that she was
in her "drinking place" (as Carol once referred to her parents' bedroom),
going through her private ritual of consuming a pint of vodka. I assumed
the latter, because Carol whispered that she'd like me to accompany her
upstairs where we could chat without disturbing her mother.*

*Each member of the Andrews family has stated that since the onset of
Molly's drinking problem, no one of them has actually ever seen, or has
any desire to see, Molly drink; however, frequently—often four days out
of seven—the children come home and find her in the bedroom. Carol
explains the immediate cue: "When I look in, I can tell for sure cause she
lays down on the bed and she rolls herself up in the bedspread and that's
a for sure sign." On any given day that Molly is in her bedroom drinking,
several family members or the whole family may be in the house also, going
about their normal routines. For instance, on this Saturday morning when
Molly never came out of her room, Carl was cheerfully raking leaves off
the front lawn, Carol was doing her laundry with her shampooed hair
wrapped up in a towel, Barbara was everywhere—on the phone, trying
to shock me with her latest risque jokes, teasing Ron about his new girlfriend, or doing her dance routines on the stairway; and Ron, who laughs
and comes to life when Barbara is around, was alternating between working
on something in the garage and organizing a Christian Youth Meeting for
that week. As I was chatting with one person or another, I too found myself
forgetting or ignoring the fact that Molly was at that moment in the process
of solitarily drinking in her bed. However, this happy, almost comic-relief
ambiance was frequently shattered by sporadic, frightful screams from the
bedroom. These sounds always brought me back to the reality of what was
going on here; at one point, knowing that it was "taboo" to open the
bedroom door and physically check on Molly (no one ever did that), I
couldn't refrain from asking "Do you think she is all right?" The family
feigned unconcern, shrugging it off as distressing but normal behavioral
routine for Molly's drinking periods. Carl walked outside, suggesting that
if it bothered me, I should join him out in the house trailer in the driveway
where he was having coffee. Carol's face turned pale, but she kept her eyes
glued to the newspaper she was reading. Ron stood outside his mother's
bedroom for a brief period, then went back to the garage. Later in the day,
and in the course of a second conversation, Barbara finally spoke to my
question: "Yeah, she's all right. She's just, I don't know. I guess she
screams a lot. Like she'll get scared if she knows her door is unlocked or
something. When she's sober, she doesn't care if the door's open. When*

she's drinking, then she gets into these big acts and stuff. Usually no one's home on weekends like today, so she drinks knowing no one will be watching her. Recently we've been here about 50 percent of the time."

I asked, So does your father stay home with her on weekends?

"No," she said, "My Dad goes out and works on weekends."

"Does anybody stay with her?"

"No, we just go and do our own thing, especially now, it's Christmas season you know, and we have to buy presents and stuff."

I was puzzled by the incongruity of the situation, and said, "Now, Barbara, let's go over this again. Molly drinks during the week when she's alone. Sometimes you all leave her here on weekends alone. Are you telling me that if someone stayed here with her—or if all of you did—that she wouldn't drink on weekends?"

I asked, So does your father stay home with her on weekends?
staying just to watch her. Yeah, she wouldn't like that at all. But like if our family's home and she's planning a big meal—you know, a real nice Sunday meal—and everybody's going to be home—or like our birthdays or something like that—she doesn't get drunk on those kinds of days. If there's something that she has to do, if there's a reason the family's all home—like when you came to Sunday dinner that first night for example—and stuff like that—then she won't drink."

I suggested that maybe Molly took Antabuse on those days, to control her craving for alcohol, and Barbara said she didn't know "what Antabuse was for." (This was unlikely, because we had discussed it in an earlier interview.)

"Well," I replied, "it's a pill that you take—it makes you nauseous if you drink. It's supposed to be helpful in cutting off the drinking. It works for some people, for others it doesn't."

She answered, "Well, she's gone for a week without drinking, before she even had that Antabuse in the house, you know. Like when Carol got Valentine Queen, she sewed for a week on her dress, you know without even drinking anything cause, I mean, she knew she had to do it, so she did it. She didn't even drink in the evenings or anything. But as soon as it was done, back to the bottle!"

DISRUPTION OF FAMILY RITUALS

One important family ritual that was radically altered by Molly's drinking behavior was the family mealtimes.

Molly takes her role as cook and provider of nutritious foods seriously, and on her nondrinking days, she prepares thoughtful meals. On these days, Molly rises early, is in a cheerful mood, and makes sure every sleepy family member knows that she is planning a special evening meal; she expects her family to be there at the appointed dinner hour, as they always were a few years back. But the family has by now, for the most part, scheduled themselves out of the house from early afternoon on. They have adapted their working and social schedules to Molly's drinking patterns and the usual norm of "no hot meals." As a result, dinnertime at the Andrews household on those few nights that everyone shows up for the appointed six P.M. meal, has disintegrated into a fighting, yelling battlefield of wills. Barbara calls it the "battle of insults," and Ron views it as "out and out warfare." From the perspective of the researcher, the plan of attack, defensive moves, and rapid retreats were so predictable, the dinner conversation read like a Eugene O'Neill script.

After the family prayer, and sometimes an appropriate reading from the Bible, the family is immediately preoccupied with consuming the home-cooked food; hot meals are, after all, increasingly rare in this household. The arguments are almost always instigated by Molly who takes the few opportunities when the family is together to complain about all the times they are not together. Carl then reprimands Molly for upsetting the children and tries to change the subject. Barbara unfailingly sides with Carl, ignores Molly's comments, and purposely changes the subject. Ron, who is more sympathetic to his mother's viewpoint, makes at least a feeble attempt to acknowledge her complaints, if not in words, then by concerned apprehensive glances or by patting Molly's shoulder. Carol, the quiet, more contemplative participant in these family confrontations, capriciously sides with the more vulnerable party of the evening. Molly gets more agitated, and insulting remarks ensue in rapid succession between any possible combination of dyads and triads. Ron, in his self-appointed role as family mediator, tries to calm the family but ends up yelling at everybody. One by one, the wounded and angry members vacate first the dinner table, and then the house, leaving Molly home alone, usually to begin drinking.

Over the research period, meals remained a major problem, more so for Molly than for anyone else. No one in the family made a major move to take over the cooking role in Molly's absence, although several feeble attempts were made. The family preferred to grab cold snacks from the refrigerator, or on those occasions when Molly had not shopped or prepared food in advance, they would buy fast foods. On one occasion, when Carl withheld grocery money from Molly and took her car keys, Barbara took over the marketing and cooking duties. Molly became so threatened with this intrusion on what she viewed as her most vital maternal-role duty, that she stopped drinking for two weeks, recovered her keys and grocery money privileges, and resumed normal cooking and marketing routines. Then she started to drink again. When Barbara once again tried to step into that role, Molly threatened suicide, so the whole family gave up on meal preparation. Barbara and Carol deeply resented these "power games" as they so accurately called them, and were disappointed when their father backed down with Molly's tantrums and threats. Although they were sympathetic to the reasons for Carl's ambivalence, they felt he was dominated by their mother.

ADJUSTMENTS OF CONVENIENCE

Molly's early efforts to camouflage her growing addiction to alcohol over a three-year span were perhaps for good reason. After the family's "discovery" of her drinking problem, her life fell into a cycle—or an ongoing struggle—between the polar opposites of the nurturing, affectionate, and dedicated wife and mother to a cold, withdrawn, and malcontent problem drinker. Whenever she could maintain sobriety for any length of time beyond two days, the household regained some semblance of "the way it used to be" or the way she wants it to be, which is with Molly in full control of her designated housewife role. In the span of one year, however, the family gradually made certain adaptive adjustments to the drinking—and for their own best interests, not Molly's. As illustrated in the problems around meals, Molly is often confused and irritated by these changes.

One morning, over coffee, Molly talked about recent changes in her sexual relationship with Carl. She was unhappy with Carl's insistence that they have quick, early morning sex as opposed to their former, more satisfying pattern of relaxed, late evening "romance":

I know my drinking has changed the way he feels about me; our sex life isn't as good and it isn't as frequent. But his time schedule has something to do with that, too. He's pretty well decided that sex in the morning is the best time to have it, and I don't agree with the kids running in and out and one thing and another. But that's the only time now when he's not tired—it's funny, I used to be the one that was too tired. I do resent his job—and the times he's gone every evening when I need him most. The most difficult times for me are in the evening.

From Carl's perspective, the early morning sex coincides best with Molly's drinking problem (she might be asleep by 6:00 P.M.) and his scheduled evening appointments to show houses. However, this schedule persisted even when Molly was not drinking, so whether abstaining or drinking, she now spends most evenings and weekends alone. Several times, when Carl could no longer tolerate Molly's behavior, he slept outside in the trailer. Once he spent the night at a friend's home. Since these were the first times in twenty years that Carl had purposefully removed himself from their bed, Molly was threatened, frightened, and angry all at once. Each time that he did this, she made efforts to abstain for several days, clean the house, put on makeup and an attractive dress, and plan a special meal. On one occasion she even bought Carl a new suit. Carl would always respond to these changes, return to their bedroom, and resume sexual relations. On several occasions, they individually assured the researcher that their sex life, albeit not always so good, was stable in spite of Molly's problem.

In an effort to restrain Molly from buying alcohol, Carl often took the car keys away from her for days at a time. Because they live far out in the suburbs where there is no public transportation, this leaves Molly stranded; she has no means of getting to church, Bible study, group counseling sessions, and shopping areas. Before Barbara graduated from high school and was given her own new car, Carl would often give the car to her on those days he was restricting Molly, much to Barbara's delight and Molly's disbelief. One morning, after Carl had left for work, a screaming battle ensued between Barbara and Molly over this issue. Barbara, who was fast becoming as volatile and verbally abusive as Molly, took the liberty of calling her mother a "bitch who didn't deserve the right to drive a car and kill other people." Molly was so taken aback by this presumptuous behavior that she slapped Barbara, and to everyone's surprise, Barbara slapped her back. Molly, overwhelmed with anger, grabbed the first thing she could reach, which was the butcher knife on the kitchen counter. At this point, Ron stepped in and pushed Molly aside, took the knife, and called his father. Molly cried and Barbara ran upstairs. By the time Carl arrived home. Molly had taken several drinks from her hidden supply of vodka somewhere in the house, was sobbing and shaking in a seemingly uncontrollable manner. After receiving an objective account of the story from Ron, Carl told Barbara she was to stay with a friend for awhile, making it clear to the other family members that Molly was becoming a dangerous person.

Barbara quietly moved out the next day; Molly was so guilt-ridden and shaken by this breakup in the family, that she stayed in her room for several days, coming out periodically to argue, "or try to reason" as she put it, with Carl. During the three weeks Barbara was away, and between drinking periods, Molly began designing and sewing Barbara's graduation dress, and planning for her graduation celebration party, which was less than a month away. Barbara returned home several times to make choices on the fabric (an expensive white on white print) and for the fittings of the dress. She came and went in a pleasant, nondisruptive mode, with no apparent animosity toward her mother. Molly had little to say to Barbara; she was more concerned with Carl's withdrawal since the knife episode. She scheduled Barbara's fitting sessions to those times when Carl was home, and kept him abreast of the party plans. He was pleased with Molly's efforts to remain sober, and for making appropriate preparations for his daughter's upcoming important event. Barbara moved back home two days before graduation.

THE GRADUATION PARTY

The party began with a full buffet dinner at 3:00 P.M. and ended around six in time for everyone to attend the graduation ceremonies. The guests included: the paternal grandparents; Molly's mother; Carl's brother, his wife and three young children; two "special" neighbors who were friendly with Barbara; Kaye, an old friend of Molly's from Centerville, and several of Barbara's and Carol's friends. By the time the researcher arrived all the other guests were already crowded into the family kitchen, sampling the array of foods; there was turkey, ham, salads, homemade breads, decorative cookies and cakes, fruit drinks, candies and nuts, all prepared by Molly, and positioned on the long buffet table just beneath the bulletin boards. The researcher noticed that there were some new pictures of Barbara in her latest starring role in the school play.

Barbara, who like her sister was a strikingly beautiful young woman, was wearing the new hand-stitched graduation dress that Molly had finished just the day before. As she received gift checks from the grandparents, she tucked them into her bra, drawing laughter when she commented, "Oh, well, it fills those out anyway." She was in a happy mood, joking facetiously about her struggle to graduate, when in fact she had just been awarded an $8,000 scholarship to a prestigious university.

Ron was very quiet, sitting next to his maternal grandmother who often held his hand. Kaye and Carl were acting as host and hostess, greeting guests, serving food and moving around the room. Molly was conspicuous by her absence. As Carol later told the researcher, when the family awakened at 7:00 A.M. that morning, Molly had already consumed a pint of vodka and was out for the day. Although the family was angry and upset with her, they decided as a group that they would have the party anyway. Carol was upset because she had to take off work and facilitate the laying out of the food. However, after Molly's careful preparation, there was little left to be done. Molly's mother, who arrived the day before, had, according to the family, cried all morning, making such comments as, "What am I going to do? This is my only daughter. How did this ever happen to me?"

Once during the party, Molly came staggering out of her bedroom looking pale and dishevelled; her dress was wrinkled and her mascara smeared down over her cheeks. She said, "Hi, everybody," went to the buffet, stirred the potato salad, and returned to her room. It was a strange, almost eerie three or four minutes: conversation stopped, no one moved to help her when she staggered, or to stop her from moving toward the food table. Everyone sat in silence, even the young children, staring at her as if she were some pitiful, afflicted stranger who had wandered in off the street. After she returned to her room, the party was resumed, and no one said a word about Molly or her condition.

That evening, when the family were all away at the graduation ceremonies, a former acquaintance of Molly and Carl's, a man who was himself a recovering alcoholic, came to the home with his girlfriend and took Molly to a private hospital for treatment of alcoholism. Molly then began a month-long process of physical and therapeutic rehabilitation. Earlier that week, and with Carl's knowledge, she had made arrangements to admit herself to this hospital, but at a later date. She never discussed with the researcher how she happened to go on that particular evening; she may have called the friend from her room.

After a month's stay in that hospital where several different approaches to alcoholism were attempted (private counseling sessions, group sessions, Alcoholics Anonymous meetings, and a few feeble attempts at family therapy), Molly returned home feeling stronger physically and mentally, and with great hopes that she would maintain abstinence from alcohol. After two weeks, she resumed her drinking patterns, and within a month she attempted suicide for the third time in two years.

TREATMENT HISTORY

Over a twenty-two-month period, Molly attempted to get treatment and counseling, sometimes on her own instigation and at other times through her family's encouragement, from the following resources: the alcohol treatment center of the county mental health services, private detoxification and rehabilitation centers, the psychiatric unit of a large county hospital, a private hospital for treatment of alcoholism, Alcoholics Anonymous, and thereafter various meetings with ministers and church-related counselors. In addition, she entered community hospitals for emergency treatment of injuries incurred during automobile accidents and apparent suicide attempts. Although she did make progress with several of the treatment modalities on a short-term basis, overall she was unable to maintain abstinence or controlled drinking.

At the beginning of the field study, Molly was a client at a community mental health center in the alcohol treatment division through which she was recruited. At this center she participated in individual, joint, and group therapy. There were conflicting reports from Molly and Carl on the merits of this program. Molly enjoyed her weekly sessions at this center, primarily because it was "something for her to do," in an otherwise uneventful week. In anticipation of this event, she made efforts to abstain, usually with the use of Antabuse. She preferred the individual therapy sessions to couple or group therapy and felt she was making progress with one particular therapist; she was discouraged on the days that this therapist was not in the center. Molly said that she responded positively to the "women's therapy group," wherein all of the members were problem drinkers; however, she herself was put off by the intimate nature of the topics some of the women discussed, and felt threatened when questioned about such matters in her own life. Carl's comments on this treatment regimen differed:

> Everytime in the past that she has gone to that center, she has come home in a very angry, resentful mood because they had dug up all sorts of things that had happened in the past and in fact, it usually triggered her off into a heavy drinking period. And the few times I've gone with her it has had the same effect on me. I find it to be an unpleasant environment.

In spite of her husband's protests, Molly continued to visit this center intermittently for a one-year period. Carl joined her for only the first several sessions, and then discontinued the joint therapy altogether. The children never attended a family therapy session, and neither Carl nor Molly ever encouraged them to do so.

At Carl's suggestion, Molly tried Alcoholics Anonymous. She attended her first meeting with the wife of a business acquaintance of Carl's. Molly took an immediate dislike to AA for a variety of reasons:

> They all chain smoke and smoke bothers me. I don't like to drive at night. It's too impersonal and too big a group.

Ron was relieved when she abandoned the AA meetings for no stated reason other than he did not want his mother at AA meetings. Carl agreed with Ron, commenting, "AA can't handle Molly anyway; her problems are much too complex for them."

Several times, Molly admitted herself to five-day detoxification units wherein she also received short-term counseling sessions. These privately owned "home-atmosphere" programs served no better purpose than to get Molly away from the house for a period of drying out and rest. On the positive side, these homes provided a kind of last-resort place for Molly when she was most desperate for help; in that respect, these "retreats" were an alternative or escape from the cold, disapproving responses of the family, bitter arguments with Carl, and the periodic compulsions to take her own life. Molly scheduled these sessions following a heavy drinking period during which there occurred a particularly stressful or humiliating alcohol-related episode.

The treatment at a large county hospital was not instigated by the family, but came about routinely after one of Molly's suicide attempts. Originally she was retained there for six days because Carl refused to co-sign her statement that she would not attempt to take her life again, and she then later was sent to the maximum security ward of the psychiatric unit because the regular detoxification unit for alcoholics was full. Upon awakening and realizing where she was, Molly became so fearful of her roommates, and shocked that she had been abandoned by Carl, that she became hysterical and subsequently, like any other patient on that ward, was retained in her bed by force. This turned out to be a frightful, yet ineffective treatment method.

Attempts to get help for Molly from spiritual, church-related sources were a continuous process. Carl and Ron were the leaders in this effort. Carl regularly spoke to his minister about Molly's drinking and related problems, and from time to time he made arrangements for the minister to come to their home to counsel Molly. At other times, he and Molly saw the minister together. From Carl's perspective, these were the most successful couple therapy sessions; yet Molly was embarrassed whenever radical elements of her behavior were discussed, such as suicide attempts and automobile accidents.

Ron arranged for a "Christian counselor" through his Christian Youth Organization. After one such session when a family counselor came to the home, Molly commented:

> I talked to him a bit, but I don't think one day's enough to tell about anything. Ron feels very strongly that I need Christian counseling, not regular counseling. He objects very strongly to me going to see my therapist at the Community Mental Health Center, and my group—and I *need* to go there. Of course, since Carl has taken my car away, I can't go to my sessions anyway.

Molly's most singularly successful treatment process in relation to abstinence from alcohol and a sense of well-being, was the month-long program at an expensive private hospital for treatment of alcoholics. The most obvious reason for the positive results was that in addition to receiving constant attention and care, she had no access to alcohol. This program seemed to offer everything: private therapy, group therapy, family therapy, Alcoholics Anonymous meetings, diet control, alcohol education classes, and a physical fitness program. The cost of this treatment was $6,000 and although Carl's insurance paid for most of it, he was resentful and skeptical of such high-dollar services for treatment of a drinking problem.

The family visited her several times but did not participate in the family therapy. These sessions met only once a week for a period of two hours and were not private. They were set up as multiple-family group sessions; that is, there were many families present. The minister from their church and his wife also visited Molly. Molly enjoyed this "retreat," as she called it, and returned home at the end of the month's stay in an improved physical and mental condition. She was happier, more relaxed, and more positive-thinking than the researcher had ever known her to be. The family was grateful for a sober, nurturing wife and mother, but they also were watchful and skeptical. After two weeks Molly once again began to get agitated and tense over "little things" such as the disorganized mealtime schedules, Carl's absence in the evenings, her mother's daily calls and probing questions, the dirty dishes that the girls left in the sink after their late night meals, and many other ordinary, but irritating (to her) mechanics of the Andrews' household. After two weeks of abstinence, Molly returned to her former drinking pattern.

CLINICAL DISCUSSION

Seldom does one have the opportunity to see so clearly how social anthropological research could contribute to clinical treatment. The above description provides a plethora of data offering cues for clinical conjecture. The following brief discussion points up some of the issues that could profitably be explored in the treatment process.

A great deal of the material presented about this family was never known or surmised by the therapists of varied sorts who touched their lives. A family whose values, goals, and mores are more internally homogeneous would be difficult to find. What each should achieve, how to achieve, and the specificity of roles in this process are clearly defined. Yet, given the complexity of the dynamics of the family, it is little wonder that the various efforts to treat the alcoholism of a single member were unsuccessful. Separating an individual from this system and attempting to treat in isolation is folly.

If one uses Steinglass' schema of the alcoholic family, the Andrews family falls between the Stable Wet Alcoholic of Mid-Life Plateau and Unstable Wet Alcoholic of Mid-Life Crisis (32). This family is deeply affected by the alcoholism, has made certain adaptations to it, and thus to a considerable extent intoxicated interactional behavior has become habitual for the family. There is internal involvement and investment of every family member in the alcoholism and its impact on the family system.

Major changes occurred in the Andrews family during the reported four years. The largest of these was the move from Centerville, which resulted in an adequate adaptation to the new environment by other members of the family and for Molly just the opposite. Whereas her role in Centerville was broader than the family, here she has no function outside of the family. She is isolated, lonely, depressed, and angry, in contrast to formerly being active in community affairs, knowing everyone in town, and being a warm and nurturing person. Within the family, her desperate drinking results in her being viewed as a "sinner," a disrupting factor in family rituals, and many of her previous roles are sometimes assumed by others. It should be noted, however, that her drinking *does* allow her to continue to be the central focus of the family.

There are some clear signs in this history that indicate that family therapy should have been the treatment of choice. While family therapy was offered to them, it was never really presented as the treatment of choice. Molly at various times demonstrates strong motivation by her willingness to try different intervention modalities, use of Antabuse when she had reason to want to be sober, abstaining when threatened by Carl with loss of her wifely role, or when she was sure the family would be home, and her continuing need to define a role for herself. Carl and the children have a continued commitment to Molly in the face of a chaotic household. Carol remains at home rather than leaving for school in part out of concern for Molly. The achievement orientation of the whole family would probably have lent itself to hard work by all to make the intervention successful for each of them. The issue of Ron becoming Molly's confidant and companion when Carl gives up on her is a strength that could be used, although there are certainly other implications of this for Ron in his establishing his own identity. Other strengths are illustrated by Carl's priority of his family life over employment, and the fact that the family remained intact despite its deterioration and the dramatic dangers to Molly with her combined abuse of alcohol and phenobarbital.

If family therapy were the intervention to be used it would be important from the initial contact that all members gain some understanding of the course of alcoholism and especially its medical implications. Clearly this family would prefer that Molly's problem be anything except alcoholism. The study explicates a belief system that moralistically judges alcohol abuse as a sin and a failing. More education about it might assist them to deal with their cultural beliefs, the stigma they associate with the drinking, and their use of denial. Given this massive denial of the seriousness of their situation, by all home visits by the therapist could not only contribute to obtaining information of the type the researcher has made available, but could no doubt short-cut the period of denial.

Given the failures of other treatment modalities, the use of family therapy would require some evidence of success at an early stage. Contracts between family members about specific problematic issues should be relatively easily established such as: behavior and attendance at the dinner meal could be modified by each member. Morning sexual relations could be changed to evening, depending on sobriety. Carl could modify in part his evening and weekend work schedule, and sometimes take Molly with him when he is showing property. Use of the car for Molly could be earned by abstention. Other issues could be worked out.

One can speculate that a part of the anger and depression experienced by Molly is her impending loss or lack of definition of role once the children leave home. Since this is imminent, it would be important for Carl and Molly to explore each one's expectations of the other, and particularly that they begin to plan a transition to being a couple rather than totally immersed in family life. This would help Molly to define and experience herself in a different way rather than fearing the unknown future. Focused sessions on these subjects would be with Carl and Molly alone.

The study presented above illustrates the richness of data relating to family behavior, structure, and life style that can be made available to inform the therapeutic process. Our previous experiences as researchers and clinician suggest that such data can only be gained through specific and intimate studies of family life as that outlined here.

REFERENCES

1. Ablon, J. Family structure and behavior in alcoholism: A review of the literature. In B. Kissin and H. Begleiter (Eds.), *The Biology of Alcoholism 4*. New York: Plenum, 1976.
2. Ablon, J. The significance of cultural patterning for the "alcoholic family." *Family Process*, 1980, **19**, 127–144.
3. Ames, G. & Ablon, J. Naturalistic studies of alcoholic family life: Practical issues of entree, rapport, reciprocity, and ethics. Presented at the 41st annual meeting, Society for Applied Anthropology, University of Edinburgh, Scotland, April 12–17, 1981.
4. Barker, R. *The stream of behavior*. New York: Appleton-Century-Crofts, 1963.
5. Berenson, D. A family approach to alcoholism. *Psychiatric Opinion*, 1976, **13**, 33–38.
6. Bloch, D. The clinical home visit. In Donald Bloch (Ed.), *Techniques of family psychotherapy*. New York: Grune and Stratton, 1973.
7. Blood, R.O. The use of observational methods in family research. *Marriage and Family Living*, 1958, **20**, 47–52.
8. Bowen, M. Alcoholism as viewed through family systems theory and family psychotherapy. *Annals of the New York Academy of Science*, 1974, **233**, 115.
9. Davis, D.I.; Berenson, D.; Steinglass, P.; & Davis, S. The adaptive consequences of drinking. *Psychiatry*, 1974, **37**, 209.
10. Dreyer, C.A. & Dreyer, A.S. Family dinner time as a unique behavior habitat. *Family Process*, 1974, **12**, 291–302.
11. Ewing, J.A. & Fox, R.E. Family therapy of alcoholism. In J.H. Masserman (Ed.), *Current psychiatric therapies*. New York: Grune & Stratton,, 1968.
12. Fisch, R. Home visits in a private psychiatric practice. *Family Process*, 1964, **3**, 114–126.
13. Friedman, A.S. Family therapy as conducted in the home. *Family Process*, 1962, **1**, 132–140.
14. Hansen, C. An extended home visit with conjoint family therapy. *Family Process*, 1968, **7**, 67–87.

15. Hansen, C. Living with normal families. *Family Process*, 1981, **20**, 53–75.
16. Henry J. *Pathways to madness*. New York: Random House, 1965.
17. Henry, J. My life with the families of psychotic children. In G. Handel (Ed.), *The Psychosocial Interior of the Family*. Chicago: Aldine, 1967.
18. Jackson, J.K. The adjustment of the family to the crisis of alcoholism. *Quarterly Journal of Studies on Alcohol*, 1954, **15** (4), 562–586.
19. Jackson, J.K. Alcoholism and the family. *Annals of the American Academy of Political and Social Sciences*, 1958, **315**, 90.
20. Jackson, J.K. Alcoholism and the family. In D.J. Pittman & C.R. Snyder (Eds.), *Society, Culture and Drinking Patterns*. New York: Wiley & Sons, 1962.
21. Lewis, O. *Five families*. New York: New American Library, 1959.
22. Lewis, O. *The children of Sanchez*. New York: Random House, 1961.
23. Lewis, O. *La vida*. New York: Random House, 1965.
24. Lewis, O. *A death in the Sanchez family*. New York: Random House, 1969.
25. Lytton, H. Observation studies of parent-child interaction: A methodological review. *Child Development*, 1971,**42**, 651–684.
26. O'Rourke, J.F. Field and laboratory: The decision-making behavior of family groups in two experimental conditions. *Sociometry*, 1963, **26**, 422–435.
27. Paolino, T.J. & McCrady, B.S. *Alcoholic marriage: Alternative perspectives*. New York: Grune, Stratton, and Co., 1977.
28. Pattison, E.M. Treatment of alcoholic families with nurse home visits. *Family Process*, 1965, **4**, 75–94.
29. Perry, S.E. Home treatment and the social system of psychiatry. *Psychiatry*, 1963, **26**, 54–64.
30. Steinglass, P. The alcoholic family at home. *Archives of General Psychiatry*, 1981, **38**, 578–584.
31. Steinglass, P. Assessing families in their own homes. *American Journal of Psychiatry*, 1980, **137**, 1,523–1,529.
32. Steinglass, P. Family therapy in alcoholism. In B. Kissin & H. Begleiter (Eds.), *The biology of alcoholism 5*. New York: Plenum, 1977.
33. Steinglass, P. The home observation assessment method (1:00 AM): real-time naturalistic observation of families in their homes. *Family Process*, 1979, **18**, 337–354.
34. Steinglass, P. A life history model of the alcoholic family. *Family Process*, 1980, **19**, 211–226.
35. Steinglass, P., Weiner, S., & Mendelson, J.H. Interactional issues as determinants of alcoholism. *American Journal of Psychiatry*, 1971, **128** (3), 275–280.
36. Steinglass, P., Weiner, S. & Mendelson, J.H. A systems approach to alcoholism: A model and its clinical application. *Archives of General Psychiatry*, 1971, **24**, 401–408.
37. Ward, R.F. & Faillace, G.A. The alcoholic and his helpers. *Quarterly Journal of Studies on Alcohol*, 1953, **14**, 632–641.
38. Wolin, S., Steinglass, P., Sendroff, P.; Davis, D.I.; & Berenson, D. Marital interaction during experimental intoxication and the relationship to family history. In M. Gross (Ed.), *Alcohol intoxication and withdrawal, Experimental studies*, New York: Plenum, 1975.

8

Varied Problems of the Newly Sober Couple:

Strategic Approaches in Couples Group

Stanley A. Terman, Ph.D., M.D.

Alcoholism is widely considered a disease, although confusion may be justified if the usually associated symptoms are the cause or result of the primary disease process. In chronic alcoholism, the distinction between "primary" and "secondary" symptoms is particularly difficult to make. As in any area of medicine, when the list of symptoms is both very long and chronic, clinical experience dictates caution in anticipating favorable therapeutic outcomes.

In the case of chronic alcoholism, the recovery phase marked by "being dry" not only does little in resolving the associated symptoms, it more often makes them appear worse. As the smoke-screen clears, these problems rise to prominence as drinking per se loses its place as the center of attention.

For these reasons, the approach taken by the Alcohol Treatment Clinic at the Long Beach Veterans Administration Medical Center focuses on the associated problems during the first year of neo-sobriety, in the context of weekly couples group therapy as the major vehicle to bring about change.

This case report describes the course of one year in therapy and three years of follow-up for a couple, ages fifty-nine and fifty-eight, married for thirty-three years. They were members of a group consisting of three to nine other couples, of similar socioeconomic background (middle-class, working, white, and Christian). Couples in the group were comprised of male alcoholics and their wives; about half were from World War II, and the other half from both the Korean and Viet Nam Wars.

The patient who will be identified as "B.D." had a primary problem with alcohol that was so chronic, it predated his marriage. Over the past forty years, his longest duration of sobriety was nine months. The secondary symptom/problem list included (his) thirty-five years of insomnia, (his) episodes of over-enthusiasm followed by depression, (her) nagging and criticizing, and their difficulty in closing emotional distance to make positive contact. (Parentheses are used when ascribing a symptom to one or the other member of the couple when actually the symptom is systemic, in order to use ordinary [linear] language.)

The therapeutic style was in general problem oriented in the here and now. No problem was categorically considered inappropriate for the couples group format. The author/therapist used strategic techniques derived from Gestalt, psychodrama, and paradox in dealing directly with couples or individuals, and also facilitated group-related curative factors. The basic motivational theme of therapy was to increase each individual's self-esteem by validation through acceptance of the intimate other in their relationship. In considering a patient's behavior, not only were conscious efforts made not to be judgmental, but the author/therapist did not consider it his professional function to interpret their behavior. Instead, he strived to devise therapeutically effective strategies to heighten patients' awareness as a prerequisite to bring about their potential for change.

BRIEF CLINICAL AND FAMILY BACKGROUND

B.D.'s drinking pattern was inconsistently reactive. At times, he would begin to drink in response to being "too high"; at other times, in response to being "too low." As a solitary binge drinker, he would consume as much as a six-pack of beer and a fifth of whiskey per day, or more. Only rarely did he drink alcohol (such as after-shave lotion) not designed for oral consumption. His binges typically lasted two weeks until he became too ill to drink any more. He then would drink intermittently to drunkenness, until his next binge or a trial of sobriety.

The consequences of drinking for B.D. included family disruption, loss of jobs, and one drinking-while-driving charge. He had experienced blackouts, but no severe withdrawal symptoms. On physical examination, B.D. had spider angiomas, a palmar erythema, and both current bruises and old scars from falling while drunk. In addition to his abuse of alcohol, he also chronically used a variety of sedative hypnotics; currently, he was taking Placidyl, 750 to 1500 mg per night.

With the emphasis on the here and now in this group, information on families of origin reflects what is most important, but cannot pretend to be complete. B.D.'s mother served as an approval figure for his father as well as for B.D., which helped explain how B.D. reacted to his wife, whom he cast in a similar role. B.D.'s relapses to drinking were often out of frustration in proving himself to his wife.

Previous attempts to maintain sobriety included attending Alcoholics Anonymous and taking Antabuse. This time, B.D. was willing to devote a month to inpatient treatment and several nights per week thereafter. His reasons for seeking help at this time included his loss of job, but most importantly, he really believed his wife's ultimatum that if he did not stop drinking, she would definitely leave him. Although she had said as much previously, this time she had secured the emotional support of the rest of the family to carry out this threat.

COURSE OF THERAPY

Before beginning the outpatient couples group, B.D. underwent a twenty-eight-day inpatient stay. Although he seemed willing to participate in therapy and even requested Antabuse himself, staff members gave him a guarded prognosis, noting his expansive and superficial thinking. They considered such statements as "I have grown more in the past 28 days than I have in my whole life. I can approach my problems now without the need of the crutch alcohol" naive. Other staff noted, however, that he was able to talk about intimate things in group for the first time.

The rest of this case report describes the course of therapy by problem area.

DOES SHE CARE?—TRIANGULATION

When a couple is afraid to interact intimately, they may "triangulate" instead, using another object to relate to indirectly. In the case of the drinking alcoholic, the problem chosen can be the bottle.

During the early period of neosobriety, the Antabuse pill often serves as a convenient substitute focus of attention for triangulation. In fact, maximum triangulation is realized by insisting that the wife give the pill to her husband. Patients are "sold" this procedure by using two arguments: the wife's anxiety is lowered when she knows her husband has taken the Antabuse, and she can also serve as an early warning system if for any reason he declines to take the pill.

Both issues of control and dependence are frequently faced using Antabuse administration as the content theme. In B.D.'s case, it brought up the question, "Does my wife really care about my maintaining my sobriety?" B.D. tested how much his wife cared by waiting to see if she remembered to give him the pill.

Months later, the early warning system paid off. She risked exposing his "clever" idea: Why not take Antabuse only every Monday since the drug is effective for two weeks? The usual assumption that any suggestion for change is merely a way of getting back to the possibility of drinking seemed to be valid here. However correct his knowledge of pharmacokinetics—if B.D. missed only one Monday, he obviously would be able to drink the following week. In bringing up this subject, Mrs. D. not only showed she cared, but she may also have prevented a relapse.

DECREASING ENMESHMENT

Clinical experience proves how important the wife's involvement in therapy is, but there is also a potential for resentment as the husband would like to take independent credit for successfully maintaining his sobriety.

For B.D., this issue came out with hostility in several exchanges of bitter words and feelings in group over whether or not she wanted to join him at Alcoholics Anonymous meetings. Even if she did join him, he worried that she might spoil his experience. The global issue was one of enmeshment versus independence.

An intervention was designed to lower their expectations for interacting with each other. Although a stated purpose of the group was to improve communication and foster closeness, the couple was told paradoxically to spend as little time together as possible during "this very difficult period of time of neosobriety." At an implicit level, the opposite message was, of course, that by following this prescription now, they eventually would be able to spend more time interacting with more pleasure (in the future). (Patients usually respond to this type of directive either by feeling more comfortable with their distance, or by proving to the therapist that he is wrong by interacting more pleasantly in spite of his warning.) B.D. and his wife were more comfortable the following week, mostly because of decreased expectations. Subsequent work was needed to allow them to get closer.

MAKING CONTACT

Nonverbal therapeutic techniques can be effectively provocative to bring about change, when words may only continue to sabotage and hurt.

Early in the course of therapy, it was noted that the couple rarely made eye contact. Since their words were distancing them even more, a nonverbal interactive technique was tried. The couple received the following (minimal) instructions: "Stand at the far corners of the group room and then walk toward each other and meet in the middle."

At first, the couple approached each other with their arms crossed in front of their chests, with a great deal of hesitation and awkwardness. After two more attempts, they ended in an embrace. This exercise allowed them both to learn experientially that they each played a role in distancing (with or without words). The "happier ending" also showed, in a small but hopefully representative and predictive way, that working in therapy can help to begin making contact.

THE ISSUE OF APPROVAL

Subsequent verbal interaction yielded an important complaint: Mrs. D. stated she was "unsatisfied with what she was getting from her husband." Again recognizing the potential sabotage of words, a series of exercises was suggested in which only one member of the couple was permitted to speak.

Mrs. D. was directed to make eye contact with her husband and to begin a series of statements with the words, "I want . . ." while her husband remained verbally silent. She thus began to learn both how difficult eye contact was and how difficult it was for her to know and express exactly what she wanted. At this point, it was not clear what B.D. was learning. The exercise was assigned for the couple to continue throughout the week, for twenty minutes each night.

When this assignment was followed up in group the next week, Mr. D. was finally permitted to respond verbally. He began to deny her requests in a patronizing way, which disappointed Mrs. D. Instead of permitting that to go on, the therapist employed the psychodrama technique of role reversal. Now, Mr. D. role-played his wife and asked her for what he thought she wanted. Although he initially laughed at his wife's requests as somewhat ridiculous, one of the statements he spontaneously made also rang true for him: "I want you to take me more seriously." When asked how he related to this theme, B.D. began to own it himself and expressed much affect as he revealed relevant background material. Not only did B.D. need his wife to take him more seriously, but he had long been similarly frustrated in getting his mother to take him more seriously.

Since B.D.'s mother now seemed to be the appropriate object to focus on, the "empty chair" technique of Gestalt therapy was employed. As he talked to his mother in the empty chair, B.D. expressed his old anger and frustration from not getting her approval which he felt he deserved. Experientially, he thus gained some appreciation of his great and longstanding need for approval and the possible confusion with his mother that he may have in the way he reacted toward his wife.

Returning to the more usual format of "talking about the relevant past," B.D. and his wife related a rather significant story. As the first salesman in his region to reach a certain goal, he won a free trip to Europe for himself and his wife. With a burst of enthusiasm, he drove "like a madman across town" to his wife's place of work to announce the news. Instead of getting her approval, he was criticized for a poorly timed and loud interruption. His disappointment at her response was so great that he embarked on a drinking binge. The free tickets were never used. Here was a specific example of how the patient's behavior and mood were directly responsive not only to personal success, but even more importantly, to the subsequent stamp of approval that his wife gave to that success. His wife's (and previously his mother's) approval was given so much importance, that he relapsed to drinking rather than face that disappointment sober.

NAGGING "ZINGERS"

The circular dynamics of the classic case of the "wife nags because her husband drinks because his wife nags because her husband drinks . . ." are understandable during the phase of active drinking. But what can be said of the wife who continues to nag even when the husband sobers up?

In discussing this "problem" with Mrs. D., she admitted that sometimes these things "just popped out." B.D. remarked that his wife's memory even for minor details of long-ago events was surprisingly accurate. She continued to bring up the past in one non-drinking area as well—the business failures which B.D. felt rather guilty about. As he now looked for a new job, the sting was only partially alleviated with this back-handed compliment: "You could do anything in the world *if* you don't drink." This overexpansive statement combined with the drinking qualifier, not surprisingly, did little to boost B.D.'s morale.

As a way of making them more aware of what they were doing in a broader perspective, the paradoxical techniques of positive reframing and prescribing the symptom were used. First, Mrs. D.'s motivation was stated to be constructively motivated: "so that your husband's psychotherapeutic growth could be potentiated." Then more of the "symptom" was prescribed: "Bring up one past experience to your husband on a daily basis as a homework assignment."

Upon initially hearing the assignment, B.D. indicated how difficult it might be for him: "I'll have to double my dose of Antabuse this week." The position on the reframe and prescription was maintained, however. Patients usually have two ways of responding to this type of paradoxical technique. They may continue doing what they are doing and change their attitude about it (accepting the positive reframe) or, despite the apparently authoritative prescription, they may change their behavior and not follow the assignment (as long as the therapist has been skillful enough to metacommunicate that this is somehow okay). In this case, prescribing the symptom of nagging led to its cessation, as the assignment (for this week) was never carried out.

UNEMPLOYED AND DEPRESSED

The patient still felt depressed and inadequate in part because his wife expressed serious doubts about whether he was trying hard enough to find a job. She openly wondered whether he was thorough in reading the newspaper want ads and compulsive enough to follow them up.

The group's sympathies were certainly on the side of the husband who seemed to be trying hard enough, rather than on the side of his "bitchy" wife.

At times, members of the group wished B.D. would tell his wife "to shut up," but his great need for her approval prevented him from doing so. Using the technique of doubling from psychodrama, another husband in the group was recruited as B.D.'s alter ego. Standing beside B.D., he offered him some words to repeat as he talked to his wife. He was thereby able to tell her to "get off my back." B.D. thus experienced for the first time a way of assertively confronting his wife.

B.D. still lacked his own approval, however, and returned the following week depressed, as he was still unemployed. To make him more aware of the connection he was making, the Gestalt technique of "making the rounds" was utilized. He was instructed to stand before each seated member of the group in the circle and to state repetitively, "I am depressed because I am a failure."

As he made the rounds, he could not help using such hedging

words as "right now," "temporary," or "only in my mind." Once, he even reversed the words and said, "I am a failure because I am depressed." When he finished making the rounds, these discrepancies were emphasized. Hearing himself repeat his complaint with these variations and the positive nonverbal feedback he obtained from each person in the group all helped him talk himself out of his hopeless-helpless-worthless depressive position. He remarked that he felt much better from the exercise because he learned that everyone in the room cared enough to listen to him and had accepted him. He thus broadened his base of approval from his wife to the entire group, which gave him a greater degree of security. (The next step he needed to take, of course, was to give himself the approval he needed. In part, that was made possible by obtaining and doing well on a job.)

OVERLY ENTHUSIASTIC

In keeping with his great need for approval, the patient can be characterized as reactively cyclothymic—becoming depressed when he did not obtain approval on the one hand, and becoming overly enthusiastic when things began to work out on the other. At different times, alcohol served either as a self-prescribed antidepressant or as a tranquilizer.

Mrs. D. remarked that she was afraid to give him approval, because he would add fuel to his enthusiasm, and if his bubble then subsequently burst, it would lead to more drinking. Even without bursting bubbles, B.D. admitted the alcohol often served as a tranquilizer to prevent him from becoming too enthusiastic, as well as slowing down "the wheels in his mind so he could go to sleep." In fact, this use of alcohol was even more frequent than its use as an escape from his guilt and depression when he felt he was a failure. Since the sequence leading to drinking usually began with too much enthusiasm and since he might soon be offered "a very exciting job," therapeutic interventions were aimed at trying to help B.D. control his enthusiasm.

The first suggestion to control B.D.'s enthusiasm was a very direct one—a totally restraining prescription. He was told not to share any information—good or bad—about his job hunting with his wife. Fortunately, this assignment was given just in time. After many weeks of looking, he finally found a job early in the week. Had it not been for the assignment, sharing this news with his wife would have most likely led him to sell her and himself so enthusiastically that he would have taken this job. By keeping the news to himself, he was able to keep his options open. Later that week, he found an even better job. His ability to control his enthusiasm was still a great problem, however, for as he related all this in group, he was again becoming overly enthusiastic. It was therefore necessary to try additional therapeutic tactics.

Several attempts to change the system by engaging the wife were not successful. She refused to be the "heavy" when asked to help her husband from becoming too enthusiastic by telling him directly to stop talking. Then, she claimed to be "incapable" when asked to develop a list of questions to fire rapidly at him (as a way of interrupting his spontaneous enthusiasm), even though role modeling by another couple in group showed how this could work. (A systemically oriented dynamic therapist may have wondered whether Mrs. D. had an investment in keeping her husband symptomatic—at least for over-enthusiasm. Nevertheless, attempts continued.)

The therapist turned to B.D. as the other part of the system that might change, and first suggested that he let off his "enthusiastic steam" with his co-workers or his dog. B.D. did not feel this would work. The next intervention was finally accepted: B.D. was to find some minor disappointment each day and magnify it or (if he had to) even make something up that was bad, so that he could have something to tell his wife that he would not be enthusiastic about.

The strategy behind this approach was that it was easier to do something different than to stop what they were already doing. Ironically, the net effect of considering all these alternate plans led B.D. to devise his own plan. Utilizing his motivational energy for approval, he changed from "I'll show you (the wife) that I can get a good job (and not tell you about it)" to "I'll show you (the therapist) that I can control my enthusiasm (without any of your tricks)!" Thus, he simply controlled his symptom of overenthusiasm by becoming tight-lipped to the point of silence.

Over the next several weeks, Mrs. D. became extremely displeased with her husband's method of enthusiasm control, as the silence became his weapon of punishment. When she was encouraged to talk in group she finally gave her husband the approval he had always wanted: she admitted that she had chosen him over one thousand other men available in the service during the war, and one important reason she picked him was because he was so enthusiastic! Now, she missed his enthusiasm. Perhaps because he so rarely had had the upper hand in the past, B.D. remained resistant and continued his silence. Even the pressure of other group members spontaneously leveled at him did not budge him, and he became more rigid defending his position to control his enthusiasm in his own way.

Now that the system had changed, what was needed was an intervention to allow the "pendulum to swing back to midway," that is, for more normal communication in their relationship. The negative effect of his silence needed to be disqualified and reframed positively and the hierarchy of control needed to be restructured. To accomplish all this, the therapist complimented Mrs. B. for her patience with her husband's new behavior of enthusiasm control. Thus, the therapist used his authority to give back to the wife her "one-up" position. Since the effect of silent communication as punishment was now done with her permission, it was no longer to B.D.'s advantage to continue it. (Permission disqualifies punishment.) B.D. then again mobilized his "I'll show you" type of energy, and now showed both the therapist and his wife that he could become more normal in his communication without being overly enthusiastic. Thus, the system changed to a mid-pendulum position—a point which the therapist had stated (paradoxically) he doubted very much was possible.

HELPFUL CRITICISM

B.D. continued to work, and his communication with his wife improved until a few months later, he again complained of her frequent criticisms. Using the paradoxical technique of positive reframing, her criticism was relabeled as good, as it helped her husband to practice his control for receiving criticism on his job. Thus cast in the role of sparring partner, with the goal of helping her husband succeed, Mrs. D. could continue the more positive aspects of her behavior, or B.D. could see it in this new light. Some truth to positive reframes always exists, and obviously there can be more positive aspects of their behavior if the patients choose to emphasize them.

CHRONIC INSOMNIA—ANOTHER DISTANCING MECHANISM

Insomnia was a constant, long standing problem for B.D. He complained bitterly that "it was so bad, he would not want to wish it on his worst enemy." He claimed to be sleeping only two to four hours total in two interrupted shifts, which resulted in his feeling extremely draggy the next day. This prevented him from working at his best. Previously, he had tried a wide range of medications, exercise, and relaxation techniques—all with limited benefit. It is significant to note that the few hours he did sleep usually were mid-evening, a time when intimate interaction with his wife might have otherwise been possible.

Setting the groundwork for a "devil's pact" (in which the patient agrees to the method of cure before he hears what the method is), B.D. was asked if he would really do anything to be relieved of his insomnia. He agreed. Then, a *Cure Worse than the Disease* was prescribed. This strategy was similar to that of Erickson and Haley but the results were somewhat surprising. B.D.'s prescription was to vacuum and to wash dishes and windows during the times he would have been sleeping. If he followed this procedure faithfully, he was told he could expect relief from insomnia within one or two weeks.

The usual effect of the Cure Worse than the Disease–type of intervention is to present the patient with two choices: If he refuses to follow the distasteful prescription, he must accept the label of voluntary insomniac because he refused to take the "cure." Or more likely, he can take a very brief dose of the unpleasant cure and lose his "disease" (insomnia). Interestingly, B.D. thought of a third alternative: He again used his "I'll show you" type of energy and proved to the therapist that he could cure his insomnia his own way.

The following week, he reported five nights during which he slept seven hours without interruption: "The best week of sleeping

I have had in forty years!" How had he done it? B.D. had cured himself by modifying the size and times of his daytime meals. Recognizing the importance of maintaining control over distance with his wife (although at an unconscious level), his cure included a late, large lunch and quick, light evening meal, instead of a light lunch and evening supper (which he had formerly shared with his wife).

Therapists using paradoxical techniques often need to remain skeptical of such rapid and "inexplicable" change, and continue the strategy by predicting an early relapse. When this was done, B.D. responded with more of his "I'll show you" attitude and continued to sleep well. He retained the option of starting his seven hours of uninterrupted sleep during the early evening hours to avoid his wife even more, when it was more comfortable for him to do so. (The dynamics of avoiding intimacy, by the way, were never explicitly discussed with the couple in the context of the problem of insomnia because neither seemed to make this connection nor were they concerned about the loss of potential contact.)

GROUP CURATIVE FACTORS

The interventions described above briefly describe the interaction between the couple and the therapist, but do not adequately portray enough of the curative contribution of group process. Many problems were universal in this homogeneous group. Each couple strove for open, honest, and sensitive communication. Husbands dealt with their guilt and depression, and wives dealt with their anger from the past and their more recent loss of control. Issues of control, dependency, distancing, enmeshment, approval, criticism, frustrations of finding a job, Antabuse administration, and security of maintaining sobriety were common.

Much vicarious learning was possible by listening to other couples work. Seeing their problem across the room was often a less threatening way to begin "to own it." The weekly one and one-half-hour group allowed all couples ample time for giving and receiving feedback as well as for their own work on the same problem. With similar concerns, feelings of altruism and cohesive-

ness were easily fostered. The curiosity of whether unusual assignments would be carried out contributed to the curiosity and
concern for other members of the group in maintaining their sobriety and in improving their relationship. After members of the
group made progress themselves over time, they were able to be
helpful to other newer members, which increased their self-esteem.
While seasoned group members were sometimes able to offer helpful specific information, even more important was their ability to
offer hope for success by setting an example of sobriety with a
good mood and satisfying relationship.

DISCUSSION AND FOLLOW-UP

In one group session, Mr. and Mrs. D. had a significant discussion about the process of therapeutic change. He asked his wife
if she "didn't agree that we have changed more in the last nine
months of therapy than we have in the previous thirty-three years
of marriage. And we owe it all to the doctor." Mrs. D. responded
with a vehement "No! We don't owe it all to him. We did a great
deal of things on our own. In fact, many times we didn't even take
his advice and do what he suggested." B.D. responded by stating,
"It doesn't make too much difference whether we did what he said
or the opposite, it was still in response to what he told us to do."
Thus, B.D. had an intuitive appreciation for the dual responsibility
of therapist and patient to bring about change. The therapist has
the responsibility to provoke the system while the patients have
the ultimate responsibility to decide whether to change, and if so,
in what direction. And Mrs. D. exemplified the ability of patients
who respond to strategic therapy to enjoy a high quality of change,
in that they can take the credit for changing themselves. All that
therapists ever can hope to do is to mobilize whatever inherent
resources the patient has in order to bring about change. It is
fortunate in this case that the couple had the necessary inherent
resources and the motivation to change.

B.D. remained sober for a total of four years as of the writing
of this chapter, including two years after the approved discontin-
uation of Antabuse. His neurotic use of alcohol is rather typical.
His deficit in self-esteem from a lack of self-approval became even

more unbearable when approval was not forthcoming from his wife or his job, and at those times, alcohol was his escape.

Cadogen (1) has provided data indicating that therapy utilizing couples groups, when added to an alcohol rehabilitation program, promoted sobriety. Seagraves (2) reviewed the field of family therapy noting that common transferential problems are dealt with no matter what the specific techniques might be. Haley (3, 4) has written extensively about the strategic psychotherapeutic approaches of Milton Erickson. The success with the variety of problems presented by this couple lies in their willingness to take risks and experiment with new behaviors. These experiences enhanced their self-esteem so that they could give themselves self-approval. With the wider and deeper base of approval from therapist, other group members, spouse and self, there was less of a need for escaping through alcohol. Furthermore, the positive aspects of their communication, the improved quality of their married life together, and their success in business were all now too much to risk for another drink.

REFERENCES

1. Cadogen, D.A., Marital group therapy in the treatment of alcoholism. *Quarterly Journal of Studies on Alcohol*, 1978, **34**, 1187–1194.
2. Seagraves, R.T. Conjoint marital therapy: A cognitive behavioral model. *Archives of General Psychiatry*, 1978, **35**, 450–455.
3. Haley, J., *Strategies of psychotherapy*. New York: Grune & Stratton, 1963.
4. Haley, J. *Uncommon therapy: The psychiatric techniques of Milton H. Erickson, M.D.* New York: Norton, 1973.

9

Breaking Away:

The Use of Strategic and Bowenian Techniques in
Treating An Alcoholic Family Through One Member

M. Duncan Stanton, Ph.D.

Dot called me for an appointment. She explained somewhat
nervously that she had heard me talk on a radio program about
family aspects and patterns of drug and alcohol abuse. Although
she said nothing about substance abuse in her own life, she said
she found the program "very interesting" and would like to meet
me for a "consultation." We set a time. A slight, pert, attractive
thirty-year-old woman appeared the next week looking somewhat
anxious. She was an intelligent person with a responsible job in
public relations.

BACKGROUND

Dot's siblings were Sharon, age 33, and Jack, Jr., age 25. Both
Dot and Jack had completed college and neither had married.
Sharon was divorced and had a fifteen-year-old daughter. The
parents, Jack, Sr. (age 72) and Karen (age 60), had been divorced
for two years and were living two or three hours' driving distance
from each other. The father was a successful professional and the
mother had been very active socially in the community. Except for
Dot, the whole nuclear family resided in the South.

Her paternal grandmother came from an elite Southern family,
many of the members being professional. However, the paternal
great grandmother, the daughter of a university president, had

married a "ne'er-do-well" who drank heavily. Dot's father, a moderate drinker, was third of four siblings, his only brother being the youngest. None of them was alcoholic, but this second oldest sister was overweight, and his oldest sister drank more than he did. Jack Sr.'s brother and second sister were deceased. It was later learned that Dot identified to some extent with her oldest paternal aunt, who lived a rather off-beat, Bohemian existence in New York City and was regarded as a sort of family rebel.

Dot's mother's family was English and all the other members lived in Great Britain. The mother, Karen, had been somewhat cut off from her family for a long time. Karen's mother (still living) rarely drank and had been disowned by the family when she had married a hard-drinking Irishman, described as a dreamer and a Pollyanna, and moved to India for a number of years. Karen had three younger siblings: two married sisters and a brother who had died at age three. Her youngest sister and her husband rarely drank, while the other sister (age 53) had married a man seventeen years her senior and both of them drank heavily.

Among Dot's siblings, her brother and her sister's ex-husband were moderate drinkers, while her sister did not drink. Dot herself took alcohol only occasionally. She was hesitant to drink very much because in the last year or so she had attended a couple of parties and gotten drunk and pregnant on both occasions. Thus she took care to avoid getting into situations that might again lead to pregnancy. (On learning this, I tentatively hypothesized that she might perhaps be getting a message from family members to have a baby.)

COURSE OF THERAPY

First Session

At the first meeting I got some history and I also talked with Dot about her role in the family. She seemed to be functioning as a kind of family peacemaker, or a switchboard for communications for her parents, in that she was always expected to settle intrafamily conflicts. She explained that she had sought therapy because of her mother. Mom was an alcoholic and Dot was feeling that she might have to "throw in the towel" on her. Dot had come to me out of concern for her mother and the way she herself was handling things with Mom. She said that the loss of her "home" hit when her parents separated. She noted, "I really *am* on my own." She expressed a desire for her mother's love, a need to get from Mother what she had missed as a child. She said her mother was presently drinking heavily, was not involved in activities to the extent that she had been in the past, and was slowly deteriorating. I wondered aloud with Dot whether, since her mother's drinking was such a problem, she could be "drunk" to her mother in return. In other words, could she turn the tables and essentially play drunk to her mother (since Dot was always the one who was having to take care of Mom) or, alternatively, could she be more "crazy" than her mother? These thoughts were thrown out in a somewhat round-about way. Another suggestion that I proffered was that she tell her mother all the good things that Mother had done for her, that both she and Mother may have overlooked some of the beneficial features of their particular relationship over the years. These ideas were put forth in an attempt to "loosen up the system." By turning Dot's perceptions upside down, she might be more able to attain a metaview of things and be freed up to attempt something new.

The above technique is usually conducted by asking clients what things they like most about themselves. These are then listed. Next, I ask, "Well, did you get these things (or traits) all by yourself? Did anybody help you with them?" Usually, the client admits that no, they were not obtained by him or herself alone. There is normally an admission that the parents had something to do with it. Consequently, I commonly state something like, "It sounds like your parents aren't really so bad after all, if they could help you to build these strengths. What other things have they done for you that you are thankful for?" It is usually easy by this time for the client to begin composing a list of his or her parents' positive contributions.

It became apparent from the logistics of the situation (i.e., the distance that Dot lived from all members of her family) and Dot's fairly functional adaptation and generally good ego strength, that therapy with this family would, for the most part, have to be done long distance and through Dot. While it is my preference (Stanton, 1981a), in common with Boszormenyi-Nagy and Spark (1973) and Framo (1976), to include parents of an adult client directly, a more Bowenian approach seemed indicated here.

The emotional tone of this session remained at a more or less "reasonable" level throughout. Although Dot mentioned that she often got extremely angry at her mother, her affect was, for the most part, subdued. We arranged to meet the next week.

Second Session

Dot came in appearing far more anxious and shaky than she had been in the first session. She talked rapidly about how badly things were going for her mother. Her concern for this woman seemed to have reached a high pitch. Finally, I asked her, "Would you feel responsible if she committed suicide?" Dot paused for a moment, then burst into tears. It was apparent that she did feel her mother was on a slow but accelerating course of self-destruction and that Dot would indeed feel responsible if it happened. My response was to go completely with the fantasy through use of a "positioning" technique (Rohrbaugh et al., 1981). I proposed that perhaps she needed to do something to try to prevent Mother from killing herself, that certain concrete measures might be necessary. For instance, could she or should she move back down South to her mother's home so that she could watch Mom more closely? Should she have her mother call her very frequently so that she could discern her mother's state on a daily or hourly basis? Or, should she call her mother more often herself? What ways could she use to monitor Mother so that Dot could either rush to her side or mobilize support forces to stop Karen from killing herself? I went on and on with this topic and eventually she came up short, stating, "Well, I really couldn't do *that!*" She was horrified at the prospect of moving back home and it eventually became clear to her, as I continued to talk about ways that she might intervene to save her mother's life, that she herself really could not effect such a rescue. This marked a turning point in the therapy. The strategic intervention had worked.

It should be noted that such a paradoxical tack is quite the opposite of that taken by many therapists. There is a natural tendency to try to dispel the patient's fears by perhaps asserting something like, "Well, you cannot take responsibility for your mother." In most cases such as this one, however, the client would be likely to resist, countering with, "Yes, I know, but that's the way I feel." Consequently, it is often more efficacious to join the system and its resistance to an extreme degree, pushing it "too far" in order to evoke a balk, with the patient asserting, "No, I can't do what you propose. This is too much!"

Once we had determined that Dot could not possibly prevent her mother from committing suicide, she became visibly relieved. I then shifted the emphasis, suggesting that perhaps her mother felt Dot was allied more with her father than with her (Mother), resulting in Mother's feeling left out of the family. Dot revealed that, a year or so earlier, she and her brother had admitted their mother to an inpatient program for alcoholism for a two- or three-week stay. Both Dot and Jack then remained as "co-patients" within the (family-oriented) program, living there for a week or so. Thus, the son and daughter were functioning in the role of parents to their own mother, resulting in a dysfunctional reversal of the natural hierarchy (Haley, 1976). I was therefore not surprised to learn that the effects of the program did not hold up very long. When children are in some way forced or pressured to act as parents to their own parent(s), the parent either will not accept the intervention outright, or any change that occurs will be ephemeral because the parent has to get out from under the children. In other words, the parent initially parentifies his or her children, but eventually rejects the parentification (as do the children). In Dot's family, she and Jack Jr. were essentially serving parental roles and Sharon was cut off from Mother. Several years before, the mother had "disowned" Sharon—a reenactment of her own cutoff.

At the end of this second session, and following some discussion, I gave Dot two directives. The first was for Dot to do something for her mother and not expect thanks. I knew that if she were to expect appreciation she would be back in the old cycle of hurt in which her mother did not come through for her. This task was intended as (a) a true, "benevolent" gift, (b) a means for breaking the pattern (that had apparently existed for a long time) of Dot doing something for her mother and her mother not appreciating it, and (c) a method for Dot to differentiate herself. (As noted above, of course, many of the things that Dot did for her mother were parenting behaviors also and it is not surprising that Mother was ambivalent about them.)

The second task that I set for Dot was for her to read Bowen's (1978) chapter on "Toward the Differentiation of Self in One's Family of Origin." I provided her with a copy and told her that I didn't expect her to be able to understand or absorb it all at once. In fact, if the theory part got boring she could skip to the section where the author talks about how he went back and changed things in his own family of origin. Prior to this task, I had talked to her a little bit about how families seem to get stuck at certain points, getting caught up in repetitive patterns that are almost predictable. We also talked about how Dot appeared to be playing a part in what seemed almost to be a "computer program" that just went on by itself without her being able to stop it.

Second Month

In the next few sessions several issues were dealt with. We met weekly about four more times following the first two sessions. I asked Dot to provide me with a genogram. There were several reasons for this. One was to find out for myself just who was in this family and whether drinking problems were common among them. Secondly, I wanted to find out if Dot was somehow scripted or programmed to follow in the footsteps of some other member of the family; as mentioned before, there was a paternal aunt for whom she seemed to feel a certain affiliation or similarity. Third, I wanted to give her a perspective—an overview—of the family. Sometimes "getting a distance" in which one can see the patterns is helpful so that one can observe how they evolve. This can serve a freeing-up function in which the client can refrain from viewing everything as being caught up in the here and now. A pattern of continuity may emerge and later on this may help him or her to make a conscious decision either to go with the continuity of the script or to challenge it.

The fourth reason for using a genogram and its accompanying information is to explicate the client's role in the family tradition and use it for "noble ascription." The therapist interprets this role positively, saying, "If your family has a tradition of this sort, it doesn't seem that you should want to break it." This is a paradoxical move meant to evoke a negative response on the part of the client, so he or she will say, "It's crazy for me to want to follow that script. Why should I have to be the one who becomes the alcoholic (or the problem person, or whatever)?" In this particular family it appeared that Dot was paradoxically both the peacemaker and the child having problems—the "wounded bird," as she described it.

Jack Jr. was not as upset as she about the family situation. He seemed to be functioning pretty well as an enterprising business-man, while Sharon, although she had not "succeeded" in life (being the least "competent" of the three sibs), did not seem to be under the same kind of pressure as Dot.

Middle Phase

Much of the content during this middle phase revolved around Dot's relationships with the respective members of her nuclear family. Dot complained about her brother. She would often get unsolicited advice from him. If she followed it, Jack would then make unreasonable demands on her. Since he was about to go to Boston where she would meet him, and their father was to join them a day or two later, he did some planning. The general idea was for her to act out of synchrony with the family "program." Taking a positioning stance, I asserted that this would be very difficult for her to accomplish, but if things were going to be a little different, she might have to do something unexpected. Conse-quently, when she met with her brother and they spent some time together, she was able to resist his attempts to get her to act in certain ways that she opposed. He, of course, grew angry and threatened to carry a grudge. She refused to get angry, which had been her previous response. This confused him and eventually, by the end of the evening, they were talking seriously and he seemed more appreciative of her. Nonetheless, the next day he once again became homeostatic and she once again resisted, still remaining calm. She reported later that she was quite pleased at being able to break out of the program.

During this phase of therapy, time was also devoted to Dot's relationship with her father. Of the siblings, she was viewed as the one most closely allied with him (or at least she thought her mother saw it that way). Jack Sr., a somewhat demanding and dictatorial individual, was slowly dying of cancer. Both he and Dot were actively involved in a cancer society. We agreed on the necessity of her spending some time with him in the remaining months or years and the need to talk with him about the things that had been important to her. As with Mother, I encouraged her to tell him the things that she appreciated about him. It is generally true that trying to get people to attack, criticize, or confront their parents in a negative way leads rapidly down the road to failure. The client may engage in it, then feel guilty, resulting in a negative rebound or recurrence of the problem. However, prescribing (unexpectedly) that he or she be concerned only with positives relieves guilt and frees the person up to change. This intervention, of course, requires what Boszormenyi-Nagy terms "multidirectional partiality" and demands that the therapist have a grasp of the total system.

We talked about father and daughter's mutual interest in the cancer society and how she was pleased that this was, in a sense, something that she could carry on after he died. He apparently also saw it that way. In the meeting in Boston (which, incidentally, involved the cancer society) a number of people told her father how highly they regarded Dot. This apparently pleased and also surprised him because he was still seeing her as a young girl and not as someone who was competent in her own right. Dot herself was naturally quite tickled by all this, especially since she wanted to upgrade her father's perception of her.

Finally, we talked a good deal at several points about how she should respond to her mother—what she could do for her, whether she could "save" her, and so forth. She brought in some letters and messages that she had gotten from her mother and we decided that what did seem important was that she, first of all, not do anything that her mother could interpret as negative. Second of all, she ought to be as unpredictable as possible, maybe even a little "crazy." One task was for her to call Mom when she would not expect it. Dot had said that during expected calls her mother would frequently put on a drunk or "unhappy" act as soon as she realized it was Dot calling. Thus, having Dot call unexpectedly and say positive things to her would be "out of program"; it would be breaking the cycle and might help to loosen things up. Dot did this on one or two occasions and it seemed to help her, whether her mother was changed or not. For instance, once when she called, Mother was quite pleased to hear from her and Dot made a point of neither prolonging the conversation nor preaching, which had been her previous habit. We also wondered whether it would be worth trying to tell her mother that things were "not going so well" with her so that, by having her own problems, Dot would be lower than Mother on the family totem pole—that is, in relative contrast, her mother would be higher and therefore more competent. Dot did this once or twice and she seemed to think that it was slightly helpful, although it was not clear that her mother wanted to learn of Dot's troubles. She thought that perhaps her mother was so involved in her own difficulties that she did not want to hear those of her child, as if it were another burden to bear.

A major event during this phase of therapy was Dot's impending Christmas visit to her parents. She wondered beforehand how she should structure it. She had thought of going home on Thanksgiving to stay with her mother and later going only to her father's for Christmas. Her father had remarried a year earlier and Dot had done this kind of shuttling in the past (sometimes without telling her mother that she was visiting Father). We made some preparations for the visit concerning her acting out of synchrony and not lapsing into the family program. Just before the session ended, as she was rising to leave, I hit her with an unexpected suggestion. I inferred that perhaps she should ask her parents if there were anything she could do to bring them back together. My rationale was that she had been serving the function of keeping them somewhat connected anyway, and that this was an opportunity for me to expose the family process and perhaps help her to resist it. Dot was stunned and confused, saying, "What? I don't understand." After a brief pause, she said, "I'm going to have to call you later." She never did call before she left, but the resulting confusion probably helped her to avoid getting "reprogrammed" as she navigated her family system.

Our next appointment was two or three weeks after her visit home. Dot related that she had done some significant things while with her family and felt good about the trip. Although there were both positive and negative times with her mother, and the atmosphere was occasionally strained, she was able to get a little distance from Mom and avoid getting sucked into the old ways of trying to smooth things over, lecture her, etc. Also, when she and Jack Jr. went to visit their father she noticed that she managed to avoid getting caught up in an old pattern in which her father got angry at her because she was about to return to her mother. She said, "I could feel myself in exactly the same position of being torn when my father was angry at me because I was doing something relative to my mother or for my mother. In the past, I would get angry or furious when I was put in that position. This time I didn't act the same way and I was able to at least keep my distance—a sort of observing distance—from it and I felt good about that."

Another item that arose concerned her father's estate. Apparently Jack Sr. was trying to structure the situation so that Jack Jr. would become executor of the estate; he would oversee the monies that would be left to Dot and Sharon. Dot was furious about this because it put her in a role of incompetence and rendered her unable to manage her own funds. I noted that, in order for her to maintain her sense of integrity, she might have to refuse to accept any endowment or bequest, since it came with strings attached. This idea "blew her mind," but she could see that she might have to take such a position in order to differentiate.

Tapering Off

Following the above session, we adjourned for three weeks and then met three weeks in a row. Several issues were dealt with, one of which involved the task of Dot writing Father about her job, since things were going very well for her at work. She had just gotten a promotion and she was to write and tell him how he had contributed to her success. This would, we hoped, allow him to see her as a competent adult. If he got some credit for her accomplishments he might more readily accept her as she was, rather than conveying a subtle, homeostatic message for her to fail (Stanton, 1981b).

Dot also felt that her brother and sister were putting pressure on her to respond in the old ways, to "stay in role." I suggested that during the week she record any thoughts that arose as to how her brother and sister would seemingly want her to behave: What would they like her to be like? At the next session she described, as an example, a letter she had just received from her brother telling her (a) to take care of her teeth—that she needed dental care, and (b) how to manage her banking funds. Dot interpreted these admonitions as manifestations of Jack Jr.'s move toward becoming head of the family. He was assuming the mantle from their father of "taking care" of her and part of that responsibility was to give her advice on monetary and financial matters. We tried to think of ways that she could respond differently. In the past, she might have either ignored these messages or tried to refute them. One idea that we decided was worth putting into effect was that she ask her brother for *more* advice, perhaps even sending him a list of questions that she might have about such matters, even though she privately had no intention of complying with his recommendations. This task of ostensibly "going with the system" (at least until Jack Jr. realized that his suggestions were not being applied and ceased offering them) would be a different way of behaving for Dot. Since she was aware of what she was doing, she was more differentiated, had more control of the process, and would not so readily fall into responding in her usual manner.

Dot also noted that Sharon had a tendency to make suggestions to her about her work, to encourage her to "perk up," to provide her with platitudes on how she should lead her life, etc. Like Jack Jr., Sharon wanted to be her "advisor." Dot saw most of this advice as shallow, especially since Sharon was naive about Dot's experience in an urban context and about life in general. On the other hand, Sharon had developed considerable skill in a particular area—training horses. She had won several awards and it had evolved into her primary area of expertise. Over Christmas, however, when Sharon had mentioned these accomplishments, their father had denigrated them. Dot was angry because she felt that Sharon was being denied an area of growth and competence and it was important that she have one, especially because Sharon was seen as the least successful of the three siblings. Consequently, we discussed what Dot could do to make Sharon a bona fide expert in the eyes of the family. Rather than encourage or directly oppose Sharon's propensity to act as an authority on all matters, Dot decided to reinforce her expertise on horse training. She would ask Sharon about horses in their conversations and letters, become enthusiastic over her achievements, and so on. Dot also planned to note these accomplishments to the other family members at every appropriate opportunity. This move would allow Sharon the limelight on a subject of true expertise, while de-emphasizing those areas where she possessed less acumen. By supporting Sharon in this selective way, Dot could effect a "trade-off" in which both sisters could attain a balance and a level of parity. Each would have her own skills and the systemic rules and structures would have shifted.

Another issue arose concerning the relationships between Sharon, her daughter, Sally, and Dot. When Dot had seen Sharon and Sally at Christmas she had gotten furious with her niece because Sally had acted very disrespectfully toward her. The three of them parted in a strained atmosphere. Dot was not sure what to do because Sally's birthday was coming up soon and Dot did not feel comfortable about sending her a gift. On the other hand, she had traditionally sent something. In response, I recommended that she first send the gift to her niece without any explanations just as she would normally. Then Dot was to send a letter to Sharon and apologize for not writing in so long (even though she was the last one to write and she thought that her sister should be writing her). This was a way of deescalating what could have been an escalating process, i.e., if one sister won't write then the other won't write, and they end up in a standoff. By not writing, Dot was essentially buying into the repetitive, exacerbating pattern. In contrast, by writing and sending a gift, she would be providing Sharon with a face-saver. Dot thought this was a good idea and did go ahead and write her sister, apologizing for being remiss. This normalized the situation and turned things around.

Termination

Following the three consecutive sessions described above, we decided to postpone therapy until Dot saw a need to return. We met for a final interview six weeks later. At that time she felt that she had a pretty good handle on what was happening and on what she could do vis-à-vis her family. Her demeanor was quite positive and she believed she had gone as far as she needed at that time. She was not feeling under any particular pressure. She had some tasks, especially concerning her father, that she wanted to pursue on her own. I was certainly amenable to this because I felt she had made progress, being in pretty good control of what she was doing.

Finally, at the end of the session, she noted that it was not always easy for her to act out of synchrony with the patterns in the family; it took a great deal of effort. I agreed with her that it must be very difficult and I prescribed, in a paradoxical way, that perhaps she should reinstate the old patterns and go back to the old ways once in a while, just to keep in practice. Maybe she should do it for nostalgia's sake. This caught her off guard and she laughed, saying something like, "You've never failed to surprise me!" We terminated on that note and left the door open for her to contact me in the future if she felt the need. The total therapy had involved twelve sessions over six months.

Epilogue

A month later I saw a colleague who had previously been a therapist to Dot and was now a social acquaintance of hers. She complimented me on Dot's transformation. I replied that Dot was a brave young woman and then asked her, specifically, what she meant. She said, "Well, the way she was before she came to you and the way she is now are like night and day." I considered this an indication that treatment had gone successfully, since this therapist saw Dot fairly frequently.

In a follow-up over the phone eight months after treatment had terminated, Dot said that she was doing very well. She had gone to see another therapist for a few months (on a matter unrelated to the content of our sessions) and had subsequently. entered EST training and found it valuable. She had purchased a house and reported no major problems in her family apart from her father's illness. He had been told that he had only three months to live and she was working on this with him. Dot was very pleased with the way her life was going and said that at some point she would like to fill me in on the events that had occurred. I said that I would be glad to meet with her at her convenience.

DISCUSSION

This case demonstrates the use of strategic and Bowenian techniques as applied directly with one family member. A systemic theory and rationale, with clear structural features (Minuchin, 1974) was used throughout. Much emphasis was placed on differentiating the client from her family (Bowen, 1978) and thereby breaking repetitive, homeostatic patterns (Hoffman, 1976). Although alcoholism per se was not the presenting problem, drinking was an integral part of the picture and was dealt with to the extent that it impacted on Dot and Karen's relationship. While the therapeutic thrust was ostensibly one of differentiating an adult member from an "alcoholic system" (Steinglass et al., 1977), both Bowen (1966) and Haley (1962) have contended that if a member of the family system changes, the total system must also change. We do not have data on changes in Karen's drinking pattern subsequent to Dot's therapy, so we can only assume, at best, that it might have improved. Nonetheless, one family member obviously made progress, not only in the area of the presenting problem but with a number of other family-related issues and patterns.

Finally, it should be noted that this therapy is aimed at bringing clients and families to a point of competence, individuation, and structural functionality and then letting them continue on their own. While a provision for return to therapy is built in, the model is designed to avoid sustained, seemingly interminable treatment. The preference is for short-term work, sometimes with concentrated spacing of sessions, and subsequent recontracting as needed.

REFERENCES

Boszormenyi-Nagy, I. & Spark, G. *Invisible loyalties*. New York: Harper & Row, 1973.

Bowen, M. The use of family therapy in clinical practice. *Comprehensive Psychiatry*, 1966, **7**, 345–374.

Bowen, M. *Family therapy in clinical practice*. New York: Jason Aronson, 1978

Framo, J.L. Family of origin as a therapeutic resource for adults in marital and family therapy: You can and should go home again. *Family Process*, 1976, **15**, 193–210.

Haley, J. Whither family therapy. *Family Process*, 1962, **1**, 69–100.

Haley, J. *Problem solving therapy*. San Francisco: Jossey-Bass, 1976.

Hoffman, L. Breaking the homeostatic cycle. In P. Guerin (Ed.), *Family therapy: Theory and practice*. New York: Gardner Press, 1976.

Rohrbaugh, M.; Tennen, H.; Press, L.; & White L. Compliance, defiance and therapeutic paradox: Guidelines for strategic use of paradoxical interventions. *American Journal of Orthopsychiatry*, 1981, **51**, 454–467.

Stanton, M.D. Marital therapy from a structural/strategic viewpoint. In G.P. Sholevar (Ed.), *The handbook of marriage and marital therapy*. Jamaica, N.Y.: S.P. Medical and Scientific Books (division of Spectrum Publications), 1981. (a)

Stanton, M.D. Who should get credit for change which occurs in therapy? In A.S. Gurman (Ed.), *Questions and answers in the practice of family therapy*. New York: Brunner/Mazel, 1981. (b)

Steinglass, P., Davis, D.I., & Berenson, D. Observations of conjointly hospitalized "alcoholic couples" during sobriety and intoxication: Implications for theory and therapy. *Family Process*, 1977, **16**, 1–16.

10

A Likable Couple:

The Use of Interwoven Multiple Family Groups in the Treatment of a Blended Alcoholic Family

Edward Kaufman M.D.
Jane Roschmann, M.A.
Bob Woods, B.A.

Alcoholism is a disease that involves many aspects of the afflicted individual including physical health, family function, job performance, and social interactions. Thus, it follows that a comprehensive treatment approach that deals with all aspects of the problem is necessary. Most private practitioners or even outpatient clinics are not set up to provide the type of total treatment program that is most helpful if not necessary for alcoholics. Thus, treatment is frequently begun in a specialized hospital where the alcoholic's needs can be assessed and met. After hospitalization, there are too few programs that provide comprehensive *family* treatment, particularly a system which involves the total family and network as well as the alcoholic couple.

At the time the Johnsons* entered treatment in July of 1980, we were fortunate in that we were then associated with a comprehensive Family Group Program for Alcoholics. The program included: individual family assessment, a weekly group for alcoholics, a simultaneous group for co-alcoholics (significant other), a bimonthly multifamily group, and a weekly couples group. This program is described in detail in the discussion at the end of this chapter.

*Pseudonyms are used to protect confidentiality.

Kate Trent Johnson called to make the appointment, stating she was in a Master's program and had heard about me (E.K.) from a fellow student. She knew I worked with families of alcoholics and thought I could understand her family because her husband, Dave, was an alcoholic who had been sober for three years. She identified the problem as marital and I accepted this for the first session *only*, as I often do with couples who have not yet identified the problem as family. Kate was very pretty, well, groomed, and youthful looking for her forty years, though a bit overweight. She emphasized her softness and undersold her intelligence and competence. She was also a complex blend of a successful professional person, an attractive sensual woman, and a dependent child. She presented herself in dress and manner with a casual softness and projected a tearful vulnerability. She was employed in a high-level city management position as well as attending graduate school and managing a large family.

Dave's strong physique was striking although he was somewhat overweight. He had a loud voice and forceful manner which contrasted sharply with Kate's meek presentation. He was dressed well, in a tie and jacket. Despite his power, he also exuded warmth and the ability to be a nurturing fatherly type.

I took a brief history from each and constructed a three-generational genogram which was essential in their case because they were a large blended family and at the very least I needed to know the full cast of characters.

Kate was born in a small Midwestern town. She was the middle child in a family of three children. Kate's dad was an accountant who owned his own business with Kate's mom helping to run the business. Kate saw herself as being the "responsible one" of the three children. She recalls feeling that she never got enough recognition for being so responsible.

Neither of Kate's parents was alcoholic. Mom was the dominating force in the family, Dad was openly affectionate. Kate remembers wanting to be like her dad because it seemed to her that he could make people feel good. Mom would nag at Dad and make him feel bad. Kate did not like this. She also thought her mom was selfish. Dad would frequently use money to bribe the children to behave or to follow his directions. Kate learned how to manipulate her dad at an early age. Both of Kate's parents were intelligent and she always admired this quality.

Kate was a good student in school. She went to a local junior college for one year and then transferred to the state university. She met her first husband when she was seventeen. Her parents did not approve of him from the start because of a difference in religion. Kate's first husband was jealous and possessive of her from the onset of their relationship. Kate became pregnant during her second year in college. She quit school and married her boyfriend. Her parents were shocked to get this news; Dad reacted more negatively than Mom.

Kate's first pregnancy produced twin girls. When the girls were two years old, Kate's husband was transferred to a large metropolitan area in another state. Kate's third daughter was born when the twins were fifteen months old. Her fourth child came thirteen months later and was a boy. Her fifth child was born one year after her son. Kate had her "hands full" but she loved living in the suburbs and felt content with her babies. Her husband traveled quite extensively leaving her alone with the children. She enjoyed being with them and read classical literature as her escape. During this period she seldom spent time alone with her husband.

When Kate's youngest child was two years old, Kate felt the need for a change as she was aware her marriage was deteriorating. She suggested to her husband that they move to California in the hopes that this would somehow help. Her husband was able to make a job change and they moved west.

Even though the marriage was still not good, Kate felt that she could "fix it" in time. Her husband's temper had continued to get worse, and when he would get angry, Kate would cry. When he would throw things at her, Kate would leave the house. He began focusing his anger on their only son. Kate had to rescue the boy from his father who had become physically abusive. Among other things, her husband did not like the fact that she was now enrolled in a college program with the intention of completing her degree.

A turning point came when Kate's dad got sick and died suddenly. She went home for the funeral and her husband got angry because she spent money for the plane ticket. When she returned from the funeral her husband began insulting her dad's memory. This was the last straw, and Kate asked for a divorce. They separated on and off for six months. Her husband fought the divorce. Finally after three years the divorce became final. Kate suffered deep guilt over the divorce. She had what she called a "nervous breakdown" shortly after the divorce. She was unable to function in her normal daily routine. She sought medical help and her doctor put her on Valium (diazepam) for depression. She was taking four, 5 mg. pills a day. She was eventually able to cut down to one nightly dose. She felt that the Valium helped her to function again.

Kate sold her house and then moved to another city where she continued college. She was also working to support her family. Her first husband would call her frequently and "harass" her about the children. She began to get depressed again but this time she turned to alcohol to relieve it. She felt under great pressure and finally consented to give her ex-husband custody of their five children as he had remarried by this time. When Kate was about to graduate from college two years later, her husband asked her to take back the twins and Kate agreed. The twins were fourteen years old at that time.

Shortly after starting her first job after graduation, Kate met Dave. She was attracted to him from the start. Dave was drinking at this time, but it did not seem to affect their relationship. They dated for eight months and got married. At the time of their marriage, Kate had custody of the twins and Dave had custody of two of his boys.

Dave was forty-eight years old when he entered treatment. He was born in Portland, Maine, and was the oldest of four children. His parents separated when he was twelve and Dave became the man of the house. He dropped out of school in the eighth grade and started to drink while supporting his family by playing pool. Dave and the family moved to California in 1951. He was drafted into the Army in 1953 and did very well in the service. For the first time he began thinking about his future. He finished high school in the Army and earned some college credits. At this point in his life he described his drinking as "heavy." Upon discharge, he entered college and married his first wife. He carried twenty units, was president of his class, and graduated with a B.S. in Business Management and a minor in Math.

Dave found work as a trainee in industrial management with a major corporation. He climbed the corporate ladder with skill and intelligence. Dave and his wife had seven children in a marriage that lasted seventeen years. He described his first wife as "lacking in intimacy and hard to talk to." Dave had many extramarital affairs and experienced a lot of guilt as a result. They finally divorced because of these problems.

Dave met Kate when she came to work for his company. When they entered treatment, they had been married six years. Dave described their early relationship as being based on their being good drinking partners. After two years, their drinking became a major problem. They were "screaming and fighting" and were both "emotional wrecks." Soon, Dave was drinking around the clock and was very concerned about the blackouts and the amount of alcohol he was consuming. Kate at this point was staying away from Dave out of fear.

Finally, Dave knew he must stop drinking, but he was aware he couldn't quit by himself. He entered a hospital alcohol program for a four-week stay but left after one week. He entered AA and submerged himself in the program—once a day for sixty days, and then at least four times a week for about a year. He had maintained once-weekly contact with AA for three years prior to entering treatment and was committed to sobriety.

At the time they entered treatment, three children from each of their prior marriages were living in the household and several of their mates were constantly in the house. Five of the six children fell between ages sixteen and nineteen and in addition, there was Dave's thirteen-year-old son.

After the history was given (though some of this historical information was obtained later), we shifted to giving each of them a chance to present the family's problems. They focused on two problems: their children and Kate's drinking. They had attempted to establish a contract that all of the children belonged to both of them, which they were unable to enforce. Kate's children came to her for controversial requests, and she gave in as did Dave with his children. This consistently caused problems with the other parent and his or her children. Their last power struggle over the children involved Kate's seventeen-year-old daughter, Kate Jr. Dave found Kate Jr. hugging her boyfriend, Ralph, in a bedroom, thereby breaking a ground rule about keeping the door open when they were in the room alone. Dave was furious about this and verbally attacked Kate Jr. for it and then Kate herself when she told Dave he was overreacting.

Kate admitted to drinking one to four glasses of wine a night, five nights a week, a pattern which she had resumed two years before entering treatment. Dave didn't quibble about the quantity of wine, but focused on her behavior when she drinks. He stated that her speech slurred and her personality changed after one drink, and that she responded to his confronting her about her drinking by drinking more, which in turn led to an argument. He admitted that he had been driving her to the store to buy wine, but had stopped because her drinking was worsening. I ended the session by asking Kate to deal with her drinking problem by re-suming attendance at AA meetings at least twice a week (because she was not ready to attend more frequently) and Dave to leave Kate's drinking to me. Kate was a bit shocked that I focused on her drinking rather than Dave's alcoholic history, and we joked about the switch as well as her own recognition of a drinking problem. Fortunately, I had joined with her sufficiently that she agreed to work on her drinking and they both agreed to come back with all the members of their household in four days.

They arrived for their family session with all six of the children who were living in the household. They were all handsome, bright, athletic, and articulate. After a brief social interchange with each of them, we heard their versions of the problems in the family. Several of the older children had been asked to leave because of substance abuse. Tim, the youngest at thirteen, stated that there were too many arguments and that his two oldest brothers (one Johnson and one Trent) assumed too much responsibility for him. Each child supported the idea that there were too many arguments and that a clear problem was the parents' taking sides against the children of the other. The children all supported the idea that Kate's drinking was a problem and that arguments were much worse when she drank. I assigned Dave to spend fifteen minutes three times a week with each of his two older sons from whom he'd been distanced. He agreed to this and to the idea that if Kate didn't drink, he'd feel more supported in the family and could control his excessive shouting. The family all agreed to participate in the system of family groups discussed previously and they began that program the following week.

The Early Phase of Group Treatment

Kate and Dave made a great first impression in the group with their intelligence, sophistication, and attractiveness. Dave imme-diately emerged as a powerful figure, contrasted with Kate's pas-sivity and pliability. They were both extremely well liked by the group from the first meeting and this feeling continued throughout their treatment.

Dave was prone to lecturing and when he lectured her, Kate would cry. This appeared to be an old game. This lecturing/crying behavior added drama to the group at first, but as time progressed, the group began to see the predictability in their interaction. We used a directive approach to deal with this problem. We made each of them aware of their behavior. We instructed Dave to stop his parental lecturing and Kate to find a more effective rejoinder than tears. We were guessing that behind Kate's tears was anger, and behind Dave's lecturing was frustration and sadness. This proved to be true.

The first half of the evening the group was divided into two segments: the alcoholic and the co-alcoholic group. We placed Kate in the alcoholic section and Dave joined the co-alcoholics. When separated from Dave, Kate's anger surfaced. She was also able to recognize and verbalize her fears. In the weeks that followed, Kate began to realize that she had been running away all of her life. Kate's fear of rejection was rooted in her own sense of inadequacy and weakness. It was her own omnipresent dread that one day she would become too weak to function and Dave would leave her. She saw no way out of her passivity and fear except to drink. A major treatment goal was to find alternative solutions to deal with this dilemma.

In his group Dave seemed uncomfortable being the only male. He was ill at ease discussing emotions in front of women. It appeared that Dave felt that expressing feelings was weak. He attempted to stay on an intellectual level. He knew he both provoked and supported her drinking, yet had difficulty changing these behaviors.

The groundwork for their growth started in their separate groups. Kate discovered her fear of rejection, and Dave began to discover the power of emotions. When they were together in the combined group, Kate began to take risks by confronting and challenging Dave's authority. On the surface, Dave seemed to be supportive of this more assertive Kate, and verbalized that this was one of his goals for her. As Kate approached these goals, however, Dave became confused and uncertain of his role. Kate's risk taking was forcing the relationship off balance. Dave seemed to be scrambling to get it back on the track. At this point, Dave's conflict was that while he "loved" having his wife sober and strong, he didn't know how to handle the changes. In Dave's three years of sobriety prior to family therapy, he kept his image as a success but had experienced little personal growth.

The multifamily sessions emphasized the split between Kate and her children versus Dave and his. However, another important coalition appeared in this group: a coalition by gender. Thus, Kate and all the female children were on one side, and Dave and the male children were on the other side. This appeared to be generated by Kate, who subtly encouraged this rivalry as an acting out of her hostility toward men.

The children from both sides of this blended family became closer in the group. They asked for and received support from each other and gave a lot of support to the children of other families. The youngest child, Tim, seemed lost in this busy and capable family. He was given individual recognition for his intelligence and likable qualities. Family members from other families came to look up to and respect Tim by the second session. We encouraged Tim to begin speaking directly to his father and step-mother, using his feelings about chore allocations to actualize his assertiveness. Since Dave was such a "model client," he quickly picked up on our cues and began to give Tim the attention he craved. Dave and Tim began to report that they were spending more time together. The older brothers and step-siblings also began to give Tim some positive feedback in the group. Tim's self-esteem rose in a matter of a few sessions.

We also worked on the general problem of chore allocation, which was a very prominent issue with every family with teenage children in the group. The families all chipped in to decide what level of chores was fair for each child in the Johnson family and then applied these principles to their own family. As a result of these groups, the family developed their own regular family meetings at home for problem resolution.

Middle Phase

Kate continued to act more assertively and told the alcoholic group of a dream that confirmed her struggle and her growth: "I'm being chased by a few people with pointed objects. I'm scared and

I run and run until I come to a house. I run in and make sure all the doors are tightly locked. The people poke the pointed objects through the door. I feel scared but somehow I get hold of a knife and begin fighting back. I still feel vulnerable but I feel I'm fighting back and that feels better."

Although she could assert herself with Dave in group, she was just beginning to be able to assert herself with him at home. We see in the dream that self-assertion is so difficult for her because it has such frightening life-threatening connotations.

Dave's insecurity and sense of inadequacy surfaced one night when he cautiously began to discuss some employment problems. It was obvious to the group that he was a badly shaken man, but he insisted on walking "around" the central issue without becoming specific about what had occurred. The group therapists applied heavy pressure on Dave to give exact details. It became apparent that he felt something awful had happened, but he did not want to risk the loss of his image by admitting what it was. He was in an emotional bind. On one hand, his fear of group rejection was very high, and on the other hand his need to share his pain was almost overwhelming. As close to tears as he had ever come, he told the group of making an error in judgment that had left him in a precarious position in his management role and that he feared he might get fired. To give this admission of less than perfect behavior seemed to be like pulling the pin on a handgrenade. However, it made him less perfect and more human to the group. The group was instantly supportive and Dave received the emotional nurturance that he needed. Later Dave was to say that this was the first time he ever trusted his emotions enough to share them with a group of people. The sudden knowledge that he could do this safely changed Dave's life. This job crisis gave Dave permission to show us and Kate his vulnerability. This initiated real growth in Dave. The group was able to give Dave the message that he was okay and that to feel vulnerable is not to be weak. We worked hard to get Dave to put his feelings into words. We encouraged him to use different words to describe different feelings and thus to distinguish between his emotions. He learned that what he had thought was anger was anguish, what felt like fear could be excitement, and what was guilt could be sadness and regret about the past.

Kate was able to let Dave lean on her and be supported by her.

This gave her what appeared to be a new identity in relation to him. She utilized this role of the supporter quite well. This was the first time we became aware of an important pattern in their relationship. If Dave felt strong, Kate had to feel weak. If Dave felt weak, then Kate could begin to feel strong by caring for him. She was also attending AA about once a week at this time. We had encouraged her to attend AA on a more regular and frequent basis, but she was still very resistant to this because AA meant giving in to what Dave wanted her to do, which in turn deprived her of a source of inner strength independent from Dave.

Along with bringing Dave and Kate closer together, the job crisis motivated Dave to investigate the possibilities of moving to another company. He was amazed to find out that he received excellent job offers almost immediately from several highly rated firms. Dave began to understand his own worth. He began to believe that he really was good at his job. This knowledge, plus the group's unconditional acceptance and Kate's total support, gave birth to a congruent self-image. For the first time in his life, Dave was beginning to feel like a complete human being.

During this time the relationship between Dave and Bob, the male co-therapist, began to grow. Dave began to admire and respect Bob for a variety of reasons. Dave admired his professional skills and yet was comfortable with Bob's casual, easygoing style. Dave was to say later that Bob was one of the first men he had ever met who could freely admit being flawed. Compared to himself, he saw Bob as a more balanced human being. Dave was in need of a role model and Bob fit his needs. He began to reach out to him and share more of himself. He was less rigid and more relaxed, dressed more casually and exhibited less need to dominate the group. As Dave became more relaxed, Kate became able to discuss sensitive issues more easily, and finally began to enjoy the group.

As Dave became more confident with his new self, he again became too strong for Kate and she started to feel weak and helpless. She drank for the first time in three months and Dave became furious at her and exaggerated her hangover symptoms. Kate responded seriously with, "I guess I should just do as he says." She continued to drink during the ensuing Christmas holidays, becoming intoxicated on two occasions. Dave worked on reacting with loving detachment, stating, "I am not going to say she's an alcoholic. She will have to find out for herself. I love Kate sober. I don't like the person she becomes after a few drinks." At this time, it became quite clear that when Dave was feeling strong, then drinking was the only way Kate felt she could separate from him and maintain any sense of her own autonomy. However, this backfired and made her feel more weak and dependent. This was pointed out to Kate and she responded by drinking in a controlled manner for several months. Dave did not overreact to her continued drinking but communicated his firm disapproval. Dave continued to be too strong for her, which Kate dealt with by manipulating him into agreeing to terminate treatment. This move surprised the group, who disagreed with their decision but they were adamant. They said that their plan was to conduct meetings of their own family based on what they had learned in group.

We felt good about Dave's growth but were not sure where Kate was with her drinking. She had never even admitted that she was a problem drinker, let alone an alcoholic, and had therefore never committed herself toward sobriety. We were convinced at this time that Kate had a real drinking problem with a potential for alcoholism. It was in this climate that they left family group treatment. Shortly after they left, the group terminated, motivated in part by the loss of the Johnsons as a stabilizing force.

Post-Family-Group Treatment Phase

Shortly after they terminated from family group, Dave approached Bob about the possibility of working as a volunteer in Bob's clinic. Dave also enrolled in a local university and pursued a Certificate in Alcoholism Studies. He joined one of Bob's ongoing groups as a volunteer co-counselor and was well accepted. He displayed a new warmth and candor, and was beginning to find solutions to his own problems in solving the problems of others. This was a good time for Dave. Kate, however, was threatened by the confidence Dave experienced as a result of his new role of helping other recovering alcoholics. Once again, the delicate balance of the relationship was upset.

At this time a friendship emerged between Dave and Kate and Bob. Bob and Dave began to discover that they had many mutual interests. Kate also joined them in dinners, movies, and picnics. Bob, being an avid outdoorsman, introduced Dave and Kate to backpacking and camping. This friendship seemed to be appropriate and offered no conflict to Bob since the therapeutic relationship appeared to be over. This was a pleasant period for Dave and Kate and Bob, but because of the friendship, Bob was unable to deal with emerging difficulties between Kate and Dave. They began to discuss their marital problems separately with Bob, which led him to feel triangulated by them and further ineffective. Kate began to drink again, and appeared to resent Dave's role as a paraprofessional therapist. Dave then made the critical mistake of trying to be Kate's therapist, which was an extension of their prior problematic relationship. A real crisis soon developed. Dave informed Bob that Kate wanted a divorce because she had met a man at work to whom she had been attracted. Dave had met the man and described him as being good looking but weak, and another "drinking partner" for Kate. It was apparent that Dave was absolutely crushed by this turn of events. This blow was a total surprise and hit him at a time when everything seemed to be going so well for him. Suddenly Bob found himself drawn back into the role of therapist.

Dave's pain slowly turned to anger. The anger had to be defused and Dave had to be grounded before he made any irrevocable, rash moves. There were two examples in Dave's behavior that showed us the real strength and depth of his personal growth: (1) he did not drink, and (2) he was willing to take advice. Bob advised Dave to avoid overt action and to stay with the situation long enough to see where it was headed. Still speaking from a therapist's point of view, Bob explained to Dave that in past marital problems he had been the "actor" and Kate the "reactor." He suggested that Dave put the ball back into Kate's court and let her make the next move. Bob felt that Kate would be uncomfortable with this role reversal. Deprived of Dave as a scapegoat, she would now be forced to take responsibility for her own actions.

At this time the multifamily group program had ended and Kate called E.K. for an individual session to which he agreed after touching base with Bob about what had transpired after they dropped out of the group. Kate appeared for an individual session one year after I had first met her. She focused on her affair. She stated that she and this man had been friends at work until he told her he loved her. The idea of being loved by another man enhanced her feeling of self-esteem. She described him as an old-fashioned type who was nineteen years older than she. He didn't want to have sex outside of marriage. She was attracted to him because he loved her and he was not as successful or powerful as Dave, and this let her be herself. She described her improved golfing as a metaphor of her present relationship with Dave. She had won several tournaments, yet he scored twenty strokes lower than she did, and she let this destroy her own satisfaction from golf. With her new man she felt needed again, as she had with Dave when he had job-related problems.

Kate returned a week later stating she had made a decision to live by herself for a while and that making the decision helped her feel powerful again with Dave—so powerful in fact, that she was considering remaining with him. I confronted her with the paradox of her statement and her need to face what would happen with Dave when she lost her present leverage. I also pointed out to Kate that she drank a little to prove to Dave she could defy him, and she drank a lot when she felt obliterated by him. She stated she had again promised him she wouldn't drink, which she could fulfill as long as she felt she had some power with him. I closed the session with enforcing the importance of Dave's joining us, to which she agreed.

Despite their complaints of recent poor communication, Dave and Kate were quite open in their joint session. Kate, perhaps using me to give her permission to do so, confronted Dave, "You've been withdrawing from me. You dominate me by withdrawing from me passively just as you do with your power." Dave asked Kate if she expected a perfect relationship. Kate admitted that she'd been passive-aggressive by getting involved with another man, rationalizing that she just wanted someone to love her. Dave owned that he had been withdrawing. They were beginning to draw close at this point until Dave asked Kate if she still saw her lover. She replied that she saw him at work but had stopped the relationship. This caused Dave to get angry about her still seeing him and Kate to get defensive as she stated, "I don't care about being with you when you don't talk to me." Dave replied, "Can I ever love you enough?" At this point, they were so distant that I prescribed further distance, suggesting that they spend the weekend apart, to which they both agreed.

Kate returned without Dave the following week, stating that he said, "Kaufman is your doctor" and that he didn't like the anger that emerged in the session (or Kate's assertiveness). I suggested that a lot of feelings they'd both been denying for a long time came out and had perhaps been attributed to the therapy. I stated that family therapy was necessary at this time and that either Dave and I could meet to work through his feelings about me, or they could see a family therapist whom they both felt comfortable with, like Jane or another colleague of mine. She agreed that she and Dave would reenter family therapy after their vacation. However, they did not, but both continued a combined therapeutic and friendly relationship with Bob.

Kate and Dave separated in December of 1981. Dave continued as a co-therapist in one of Bob's groups, and in early 1982, became primary therapist for a group of his own at the same clinic. Kate was arrested for driving while intoxicated and joined another of Bob's groups as a client. After four months in this group, Kate announced she felt she was strong enough to leave group as she had done in the family group. The rest of the members did not agree with her decision, but were willing to let her follow her own inclinations. Bob confronted her with anger. In a strong voice, he pointed out that she was fighting back tears and that her lip was trembling. He stated her new-found strength was only "between her ears" and that she was speaking from her intellect and denying her emotion. Kate agreed that she really wasn't strong enough to leave group, but that she wanted to feel that strong. She continued in group and again worked on her problems for several months in a meaningful way.

By June of 1982, Bob, realizing the complications of his friendship with the Johnsons, withdrew as their friend though he continued his co-therapy relationship with Dave. Kate left Bob's group for several weeks to study for finals and received her Master's degree in Psychology. Upon her return, she focused on being physically tired and minimized her depression. She was confronted about the latter by Bob's co-therapist in the group for the past year, Dr. Tom Backus.

Bob, Jane and Ed met to discuss the Johnsons' treatment in August 1982 for the first time in a year. They agreed that a major problem for Kate had been her unwillingness to accept her alcoholism and that Ed had supported this by his own ambivalence about whether she was truly alcoholic or not. They agreed that Kate had either to accept this or be asked to leave treatment. Dave called Ed for an appointment with himself and Kate which was scheduled for August 31. Dave arrived looking thinner, confident, and calm. Kate wore dark glasses, looked puffy about the face, and stated she had sinusitis and had recently recovered from pneumonia. They described their two attempts to get back together over their six-month separation. Kate focused on not wanting to deal with the stresses caused by struggles between their respective children and Tim's attacking her for drinking at one of their attempts at a family reconciliation session. Dave minimized the struggles and the attack, stating that whenever they got close to getting together, Kate would find an excuse as to why they could not do so. He also stated that she fails to manage conflicts and that this invites him to resolve it, which in turn causes her to feel badly. He then confronted her about her drinking as a refuge. Ed asked Kate if she considered her present level of drinking a problem. She admitted that drinking was a problem when she first entered treatment, then denied that it was a problem now. At that point Dave moved over close to Kate because, "It looks like we're ganging up on you," yet confronting her with, "I want to get together with you but I can't when you drink." Kate felt that Dave's moving closer was not supportive, but that he was "attacking closer." Ed acknowledged her feeling moved in on but then he asked for the specifics of her present drinking. Kate described that she had recently drunk as much as eight glasses of wine at several parties to celebrate her graduation. She then quickly countered with, "But since then I hardly drank at all." When asked what "hardly at all" meant, she stated, "a few glasses of wine a day, for four days in the last three weeks." Ed confronted further and asked what happened after she drank the eight glasses of wine. She stated that one night she was drunk at her own home, so she just went to bed. However, the other night she drove home intoxicated, and readily admitted how self-destructive she was. At this point, Ed gently confronted Kate. "For two years now, you've been fooling yourself by controlling your drinking for weeks at a time, but always returning to problem drinking. Our new psychiatric classification [DSM-III] has a term for that, *Binge Alcoholism*." She nodded in agreement during my confrontation and stated that she drank because it made have her a kind of macho power. Dave said, "I don't need to be stronger than you anymore, but I can't work on our problems alone." Ed asked Kate what her plan was to deal with the drinking. Kate said that she knew if she wanted this

relationship she would have to stop implying that part of the problem was Dave's AA-biased view of her drinking. Ed stated that it
wasn't Dave and if she wanted any relationship she would have
to stop drinking and that she needed a system to stop. Kate agreed
to make a full commitment to AA, including a woman's step-study
group. Ed said to Kate and Dave that it was up to them to follow
through on the program at this time. They agreed to come back
to see me again if Kate still had difficulty in finding power in the
relationship, after a consistent pattern of not drinking was established. We all hugged one another firmly and said goodbye. Three
weeks after that session they informed Bob that they had moved
back together. Dave told Bob that the session had helped him to
confirm his own needs to control and win power struggles. Since
he has quit doing this, Kate and the kids have been much happier
and Kate's problems with Dave's kids have lessened. Kate has
started a step-study group and will also be a group therapist at
Bob's clinic. Both of these activities should help Kate to feel she
is on the same level as Dave.

DISCUSSION

The case history of the Johnson family and their treatment raises
many important issues that are worthy of examination. These include: the need for comprehensive treatment, multifamily and couples groups, alcoholic and significant others groups, the handling
of alcoholism and alcohol intake, the recovering alcoholic as co-
therapist, and collegial and friendly relationships with former patients.

COMPREHENSIVE TREATMENT

The need for a comprehensive treatment program was described
in the introduction. There are certainly times when family therapy
with a single nuclear family is by itself sufficient to change the
family's problems and underlying pathologic relationships. This
is not the case when drinking has been severe enough to cause

medical problems or chaotic family functioning. One advantage of an interwoven system of family-oriented groups with other treatment approaches such as AA is that this system impacts the alcoholic and his or her family in a multitude of ways as well as on a daily basis. Thus, in addition to up to three hours of family groups twice a week, the alcoholic attends AA two to seven times weekly. We emphasize the inclusion of step-study groups as a valuable and often crucial part of AA work that can lead to intrapsychic change and enhanced ego strength. Family members regularly attend AlAnon and AlAteen groups in addition to family therapy. Thus, we achieve a multiple-impact approach to therapy which is sufficiently comprehensive to shift these difficult families.

MULTIFAMILY GROUPS

Couples groups are a widely used modality in the treatment of alcoholism. Too many programs overlook the importance of children as well as the parents and other significant relatives of the alcoholic. The multifamily group permits the integration of other family members who have a role in perpetuating the alcoholic family system as well as the power to change that system.

There may be as many as ten to fifteen families and forty to fifty individuals in a multifamily group. A more intensive experience may be achieved by limiting such groups to only three or four families, though three families is a minimum.

Families should be oriented and interviewed prior to entry in the group. The group includes identified patients and their immediate families as well as any relatives with significant impact on the family (1).

The total group frequently functions as adjunctive family therapists. Usually family members take their cues from primary therapists and will be appropriately confronting, reassuring, and supportive. At times the family's own needs prevent this and their anger at their family alcoholic will spill over onto other identified patients in the group. At other times the family's protective and possessive qualities may be inappropriately directed toward group members. Families also share experiences and offer help by acting as extended families to each other outside of the actual therapy hours. Many family members easily recognize problems in other families that they can readily apply to themselves after they have seen them in others.

In meetings, the group is seated in a large circle with co-therapists distributed at equal distances to provide observation of the total group. Families sit together and their seating arrangements are carefully observed as they usually follow structural patterns. They may be asked to separate if there is a great deal of whispering or disruption. The group begins with everyone introducing themselves by name and role. A group member will describe the purpose of the group, generally stressing the need for families to communicate honestly and openly. At times, the description of purpose emphasizes the importance of understanding and changing the familial forces that have led to alcoholism. Usually, one family at a time is worked with intensively. The first family frequently is worked with for about an hour. The conflicts they focus on set the emotional tone and influence the topics discussed in the entire group. Many other families will identify with these conflicts, express feelings, offer support and work on similar conflicts. Generally, three or four families are worked with intensively in a night, almost all families participate verbally, and usually all families are emotionally involved. The group Kate and Dave attended generally ended with the Serenity Prayer* with each member placing an arm around the shoulders of the person next to them in a tightly knit circle. This was a tradition the group had begun when it was initially a part of the outpatient program at Care Manor Hospital.

The informal contacts that take place before and after group are crucial. Therapists should mingle and interact during these pre- and postgroup sessions. Many presession contacts are excellent grist for the therapeutic mill. Postgroup interaction may confirm insights and validate feelings or undermine therapeutic work if not monitored (1). Families of alcoholics who leave treatment should continue to attend group to maintain their personal growth and new-found roles and to encourage the identified patient to return to treatment.

The therapeutic team must include a primary therapist who is experienced in group and family therapy and comfortable in large

---

*"God grant me the serenity to accept the things I cannot change, the courage to change the things I can, and the wisdom to know the difference."

groups. There should also be at least one co-therapist including a recovering alcoholic; a male-female balance in the co-therapy team is also preferred. The multifamily group is an excellent modality to train therapists in the dynamics of families and the techniques of group and family therapy.

The multifamily group is a stimulating and rejuvenating experience for therapist, treatment program, and family. The therapists become the paternal/maternal figures for a host of families who become a single family network and, in ways, a single family. The therapists assume temporary parental control of all of these families and at the same time are children in each family. Thus, the therapists give and take in a multitude of parental and childlike roles. At the same time, the therapist must step away from emotional entanglement and be objective. The therapist must always keep in mind that a critical function is to be a supportive ally to every member of the group. Co-therapists permit a division of joining functions when it is impossible for the primary therapist to ally with everyone in the group. The therapist must also be in control of the group and feel the right to interrupt any communication that is destructive or disruptive (1).

COUPLES GROUPS

Many of the basic principles of multifamily groups apply to couples groups. Couples groups solidify the boundary around the marital dyad and permit couples the opportunity to work on their problems without interference from other members of their family and network (2). Frequently issues can be worked on by a couple and their position solidified in the couples group and tested subsequently in the multifamily group. The support of other couples who attend both groups helps the spouses follow through with their contracts and alliances and better deal with other family members. The discussion of alcohol intake is minimized in these groups and the focus is on six major issues: control, money, sex, intimacy, communication, and children.

Couples are taught how to fight creatively and how to resolve conflicts involving these key issues. The group helps the couple "exhume" tender feelings that have previously existed and been buried in the family strife. Sex is much easier to deal with in a couples group than in multifamily groups. For many couples, sex had become an abortive experience and a source of manipulation and pain rather than pleasure (2).

In addition, alcohol use and dependence physiologically diminish the sex drive. Sexual communication must be slowly redeveloped. Difficulties also arise because the recovering abuser has given up the most precious thing in his life (alcohol) and expects immediate awards. The spouse has been "burned" too many times and is unwilling to continue to provide rewards. We encourage spouses to begin to trust and reward at the same time as we ask dry alcoholics to reevaluate their expectations.

As the couples get pleasure from their own relationship, the use of the children as a battlefield diminishes. The generational distance between them and their children becomes appropriate and realistic. They also begin to separate themselves from their own families of origin (2).

In the couples group, the pronoun "we" begins to be used more and more, especially when couples deal with their problems with their children. They are often amazed at how easy it is to manage the children when parents are in agreement. From this they develop constructive ways to talk to each other about the children and, consequently, their general communication improves.

Members of couples groups are alert to covert alliances between parents and children and readily point these out to each other. The members of the couples group become increasingly aware that parents are the center around which the family revolves. As long as these two feel good about themselves and each other, problems with the children are minimal (2).

Many traditional family therapy techniques are used with couples. Some techniques, such as examining and shifting triangulation, are particularly suited to a couples group. The therapist must be aware that couples will suck him or her into a triangle, replacing issues such as children, money, power, drugs, alcohol, and affairs with their relationship to the therapist. The therapist must not become the subject of the couple's triangulation. Nor should he or she take sides lest he become a part of the problem rather than the solution. If carefully planned, co-therapists may each take the side of one marital partner as long as the therapists do not become a foil for expressing the spouse's disagreements and each therapist is ultimately joined with both spouses.

In the therapy of the Johnsons, there were many periods where Bob's alliance with Dave or Kate's with Ed prevented structural changes or total family participation in therapy.

ALCOHOLIC AND SIGNIFICANT OTHER GROUPS

Many family therapists who do not specifically work with alcoholics might question the need for separate groups for the alcoholic and co-alcoholic. It is our experience that such groups are quite important on their own in addition to being part of the multiple impact on the alcoholic family. Long before the advent of family therapy, group therapy had emerged as a highly successful modality for the treatment of alcoholics. Fox (3) noted in a 1962 publication that the emphasis on group treatment of alcoholics may have evolved from the "spectacular success of the group approach of Alcoholics Anonymous."

Since all alcoholics are encouraged to attend AA, the group and family therapist should be aware that at times the principles of reconstructive group therapy and AA may be antithetical. The "high support, low conflict, inspirational style" (4) of AA may inhibit attempts at the uncovering of underlying affects and conflict, yet the support of AA may be necessary to maintain abstinence. The beginning group with alcoholics should be educational, directive, and supportive, and impart knowledge of alcohol as well as coping skills to deal with the anxiety and depression inherent in stopping drinking. In the middle phases of group therapy, alcoholics work through feelings, responsibility for behavior, understand interpersonal interactions, and recognize the functions and secondary gain of alcohol behavior. They become able to analyze defenses, resistance, and transference (3). The multiple transferences that develop in the group should be recognized as "old tapes" that are not relevant to the present.

The success of the middle phase of group with alcoholics depends on the therapist's ability to relieve anxiety instead of relief through alcohol. In this vein, it is important not to end a session with members in a state of unresolved conflict (5). This can be avoided by bringing closure when troubling issues are raised. This closure can be achieved by the group's concrete suggestions for problem resolution. When this is not possible, group support, including extragroup contact by members, can be offered. By the closing phase the alcoholic has accepted sobriety without resentment and is continuing to free her or himself from underlying neurotic and characterological problems (3).

In free-standing group therapy, alcoholics tend to become quite dependent on the group despite apparent intrapsychic gains. When the therapy is integrated with family therapy, termination is much easier as the dependency needs are gratified by spouse and family with mutual giving on the part of the alcoholic.

Co-alcoholic and significant others groups are also necessary to deal with the special problems of living with an alcoholic as well as to facilitate personal growth in the individual. AlAnon and AlAteen are also encouraged which facilitate an attitude of loving, detached acceptance. Ablon (6) stated that the chief dynamic of the group process of AlAnon "is learning experience resulting from a candid exchange and sharing of reactions and strategies for behavior related to living in a household with a problem drinker." The experience of others provides a basis for a comparison and a stimulation of self-examination leading to new insight in all areas of life experiences. However, AlAnon is frequently not enough for the spouse, perhaps because their approach is not sufficiently individualized to deal with the unique problems of the spouses or the different types of problems presented by alcoholics. A specific example of this is finding an appropriate AlAnon group for a male spouse like Dave, many of whose problems are different from those of the wife of a male alcoholic. In addition, his dominance would bring out strong transferences in submissive spouses which are not generally dealt with in AlAnon groups. Spouses married to an alcoholic who continues to drink and/or drop out of treatment are encouraged to continue in their own group. Frequently, when they have gained sufficient personal strength to diminish their reactivity to alcoholism, the alcoholic will return to treatment with a full commitment.

THE HANDLING OF ALCOHOLISM AND ALCOHOL INTAKE

We generally require that alcoholics make a contract with the therapists and group that specifies their system for controlling their alcoholism. The alcoholic is given a choice of a twenty-eight-day inpatient alcohol treatment program and/or a full commitment to AA and/or Antabuse. A crucial problem in Kate's treatment was that she never made a total commitment to a program that would achieve abstinence. The therapists' problem was that we never insisted on abstinence and a method of achieving it as a precondition for entering or remaining in treatment. This was in part because Kate was not dependent on alcohol at the time she entered treatment though she was clearly a problem drinker. The major difficulty with her lack of acceptance of her drinking problem was that she was not able to avail herself of the benefits she could obtain from AA. A commitment to AA would have controlled her drinking and enhanced her self-confidence. We hope that she has now made that commitment.

THE CO-THERAPY TEAM

The senior author has been committed to the concept of a co-therapy team approach for the past twenty years. He prefers a male-female team but more importantly the team of a professional and a recovering substance abuser (7, 8), although the latter may also be a professional. Jane offered the women in the group a strong but nurturing figure to identify with, particularly in the co-alcoholic group which was predominantly women. The recovering alcoholic (Bob has ten years of sobriety) is essential because he has a deep understanding and empathy with the subtle nuances of alcoholic thinking and behavior. He can join with the alcoholic at each stage of the struggle toward sobriety, including "slips" back to alcoholic behavior. He can also confront the alcoholic with love and concern at the same time as he can facilitate the alcoholic's expression of rage. He is a person with whom the alcoholic can identify as someone who has been through it all and has "made it." Many of the alcoholic's gains will come from direct identification with the strength of the recovering alcoholic therapist, particularly early in therapy. The professional therapist may be respected early but not identified with until much later in the therapeutic process.

RELATIONSHIPS WITH FORMER PATIENTS

Bob found Kate and Dave as likable as everyone else in the group, including the other therapists, found them. They became crucial to the group and the group's ending was certainly related to their withdrawal. However, Bob continued his relationship with Kate and Dave as a teacher and friend and at times still as a therapist. His friendship and co-counselor relationship with Dave reinforced Dave's power with Kate, and Bob's role as Kate's group therapist reinforced her passive role with Bob, and by association, with Dave. On the other hand, his continuing relationship with them after they left group enabled him to continue to serve as a change-agent for the Johnson family. Bob's problem with Kate was sorting out three different types of relationships: therapist, husband's colleague, and friend. As he realized the impossibility of maintaining all three types and as her need for a therapist grew, he was able to reverse their relationship and be therapist rather than friend.

Every therapist is aware of the taboo against developing extratherapy relationships with patients and that the taboo continues after therapy terminates. This is because transferences continue long after the end of therapy and developing a friendship all but eliminates any future possibility of resuming therapy with a friend should a return to therapy be necessary. This relationship split may be difficult in the alcoholism field where one's patient may be one's colleague at a host of AA meetings and activities. In the case of Bob and Dave, this collegial state extended to a co-therapy relationship as well. However, it did reinforce Kate's passivity, as described above.

The success of the therapy with Kate and Dave and their family cannot be evaluated until many years have passed. Dave is certainly more confident, in touch with his feelings, and better able to give Kate up if he cannot tolerate her drinking and behavior. Kate has much more self-knowledge, a successful career, and good relationships with her own children. However, she has been neither successfully assertive with Dave (when he has been strong) nor content with her passivity, particularly in relation to him. We couldn't help but be pleased to learn that their attempts at becoming reunited have been successful just as we were finishing this chapter.

There is still no guarantee, however, that they will live "happily ever after," though it makes for a nice ending. Still, we wonder which way the see-saw will go or if it will be stuck or perfectly balanced somewhere in the middle in the years to come.

REFERENCES

1. Kaufman, E. & Kaufmann, P. Multiple family therapy: A new direction in the treatment of drug abusers. *American Journal of Drug and Alcohol Abuse*, 1977, **4** (4), 467–478.
2. Kaufmann, P. & Kaufman, E. From multiple family therapy to couples therapy. In E. Kaufman, & P. Kaufmann, (Eds.), *Family therapy of drug and alcohol abuse*. New York: Gardner Press, 1979.
3. Fox, R. Group psychotherapy with alcoholics. *International Journal of Group Psychotherapy*, 1962, **12**, 50–63.
4. Brown, S. & Yalom, I.D. Interactional group therapy with alcoholics. *Journal of Studies on Alcohol*, 1977, **38** (3), 426–456.
5. Blume, S.B. Group psychotherapy in the treatment of alcoholism. In S. Zimberg, J. Wallace, & S.B. Blume (Eds.), *Practical approaches to alcoholism psychotherapy*. New York and London: Plenum, 1978.
6. Ablon, J. Al-Anon family groups. *American Journal of Psychotherapy*, 1974, **28** (1), 30–45.
7. Kaufman, E. Group therapy techniques used by the ex-addict therapist. *Group Process*, 1972, **5** (1), 3–19.
8. Kaufman, E. A psychiatrist views an addict self-help program. *American Journal of Psychiatry*, 1972, **128**, 841–851.

11

The Family Who Wouldn't Give Up:

Structural-Dynamic Family Therapy with a Dry
System

Edward Kaufman, M.D.

Paul and Sandy Martin* entered treatment in October of 1981.
They were referred by their former family therapist on the East
Coast whom they called for a referral after being out of treatment
for about two years. Paul was an alcoholic at the time he entered
treatment with that therapist, but had been sober for the past three
years as a result of both the therapy and an active commitment to
Alcoholics Anonymous (AA). Sandy had been in a woman's group
with that therapist in addition to couples therapy, and had made
many steps to personal growth. She was employed full-time at a
middle-management level and attended college at night as well as
mothering three children. Paul was quite husky, looking like an
ex-football player who no longer exercised. He dressed very in-
formally, belying his executive status in a technical field. Sandy
was thin, attractive, lively, and well dressed. They were both depressed under their facades, though Paul's was more overt that
day and attributed by him to being physically ill. Both spoke with
East Coast accents that were immediately recognizable to me because they had grown up in the same city where I had spent my
first twenty-four years. I shared the commonality of our back-
grounds and that I had been a member of my high school debating

*Pseudonyms used and specific life situations altered slightly to preserve confiden-
tiality.

293

team which had successfully defeated his school's team although they eventually won the city championship that year. Paul and I teased each other about this and joining with him through teasing helped establish and maintain our relationship throughout the therapy. Sandy and I joined through discussing her former therapist with whom we both felt close. Their interests, politics, hobbies, and jobs were as different from one another as were their physical appearances. I then took a brief genogram from them which is shown in Figure 11-1. Both Paul and Sandy had strong family histories of alcoholism. Sandy's father had died four months prior to their entering treatment with me though his death was not directly attributable to alcoholism. Sandy had been married to a heroin addict for two years who overdosed and died three years after their separation. John, now sixteen, was the product of that marriage and he presently lives in the Martin household. Carl and Steve complete the home and none of the children has serious problems. The boys, however, are described as provocative and Paul as overreactive, frequently in ways that are counterproductive. Each partner was given the opportunity to specify the problems in the marriage. Sandy began by stating, "We're at the end of our rope. There is no intimacy or sharing. I can't give to him. I can't make the move to leave." I asked Sandy if her agenda for the therapy was to be able to leave. She responded, "If I can salvage it, I'd like to try one more time." Paul agreed about the problems but not the prognosis: "I flash back to the nicer moments and feel we could still get along, but the polarization is uncomfortable." Sandy said that a turning point for her had been the recent death of her father and her mother's hospitalization in a critical condition. "I feel very mortal now. If I'm going to be happy, I better find out now. If we continue to make each other miserable, I will not stay out of duty and loyalty. Paul gets wrapped up in everything else but me no matter how trivial and is very insensitive to me."

In the first session, we also dealt with the effects on their relationship of Paul's AA involvement and the move to California. Paul had been drinking heavily for three years prior to beginning AA. He finds AA very important to him because it helps him keep his ego from going out of control and is generally a centering experience for him, in other words, it provides a lacking sense of inner homeostasis. Back East he attended meetings daily, but at the time of entering treatment he was only going once or twice

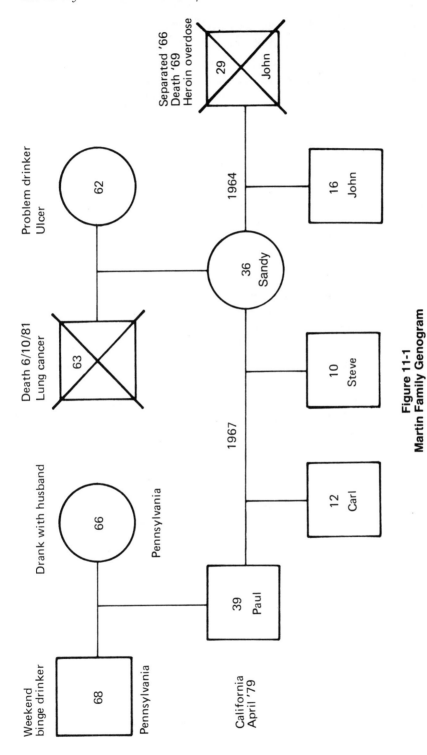

Figure 11-1
Martin Family Genogram

weekly. He stated he was less involved in AA because he was busier, traveled a lot and didn't like the people and the meetings in California as much. He had also phased out of his working the twelve steps and step-study groups. Sandy said she had felt abandoned when Paul went to a lot of meetings but lately she liked the space when he was away. Sandy had attended AlAnon for two years as a precondition of her psychotherapy in Pennsylvania but had not connected to AlAnon in California.

Sandy was angry that Paul had made the decision to move to California without adequately consulting her. She was also angry because she felt he had ordered her to get a job to make $75.00 a week for food. Now she enjoys working and her work creates problems for him because he feels she is not sufficiently available to him and the children.

The session closed with a verbal contract that included the cost of therapy, length of sessions, behavioral tasks, and the involvement of all three children. I did not offer a ten-session duration with renegotiation as I usually do because it would obviously take much longer than a few months to resolve the incredible distance between them. I included three tasks in the contract. Paul was to resume his active involvement with AA and two specific step-study meetings were chosen to facilitate that work. Sandy was asked to resume attendance at AlAnon. In order to probe their capacity to shift their disengaged stance, they were both asked to plan a pleasant surprise for each other and not to talk about it till the following session.

The following session they reported that Paul had resumed more active AA involvement but Sandy had not gone to AlAnon. Sandy had taken him out to dinner and Paul had taken her to Laguna Beach for an afternoon. Both surprises had gone well. Paul was looking happier and had lost weight because there was a contest at work for who could lose the most. They further discussed their disengagement. Sandy is very social and Paul prefers to stay home with the entire family. He gets anxious whenever people visit the house. Sandy stated that the only things they ever shared with each other were their genitals. Although the act of intercourse is generally satisfying, they both had problems with each other around sex. Sandy felt guilty when she turned him down and so she frequently just had sex to get it over with. She also felt that if she turned him down, he would "pounce on her" when she was asleep or in the morning. I asked Paul to talk to Sandy in the sessions about his wanting more closeness. He said it was hard to do this for fear she'd leave him. He also felt that each time he did something nice for her she'd get in a "bitchy mood." We planned for the children to join us for the next session and to deal with Paul's problems in being with the two younger boys at that time. I repeated the AA and AlAnon tasks as well as the mutual pleasant surprise.

The children appeared for the next session. All three were verbal, expressive, and well behaved. Paul and Sandy agreed that they were not together when it came to dealing with the kids. Carl stated that if one parent turned him down for something, he could frequently go to the other and get a yes answer. Steve said he knew which parent would agree to certain requests and he would go to that parent to get what he wanted. Sandy felt Paul frequently overruled her with the kids. Paul said he didn't discuss these issues with her because he had difficulty when she disagreed. However, their problems with Carl and Steve were minimal compared to their issues with John. Sandy states that Paul gives John no privileges in the house but loads of responsibilities like babysitting and working on Paul's car for hours. Paul felt anxious whenever Sandy and John interacted,. Sandy said that was because Paul was very jealous of John. "If I'm with John, Paul sends him upstairs." Paul had wanted to adopt John at the time of the marriage but initially couldn't because John's father refused. When John Sr. died, Paul was too angry about the initial rejection to reimplement adoption proceedings. Paul refused to let John drive the family car or be insured under their family policy. He stated that John was the son of a drug addict and raised by an alcoholic father so he couldn't be trusted to drive a car. Paul also stated that his own father had never spoken to him or taught him anything and therefore there was no need for him to give anything to John, who could make it on his own as he himself had done. With fifteen minutes remaining in the session I asked John to take the younger boys out to eat, underlining his adult competence and providing the parents a separate space from the children to discuss an important spousal issue. I told Sandy that her closeness with John had undermined and excluded Paul. I then confronted Paul with a lot of feeling on my part. I said that his mistreatment of John had deeply affected his relationship with Sandy. His observations about John's driving had no genetic basis and it was time that he at least considered insuring John on their family policy, particularly if he bought his own car as he had planned. Paul agreed to discuss the facts with his insurance agent.

Paul procrastinated doing anything about John's insurance for several weeks. He ended up, however, not only arranging for the insurance at a reduced family rate but also participating in helping him buy his own car. Sandy was in ecstasy over Paul's giving attitude to John and their relationship rapidly improved. However, they had a long established pattern that whenever closeness developed they would both get threatened and push the other away. I used the metaphor of a brick wall to describe the phenomenon, stating that when they were close to each other it was like they had each taken a few bricks out of their protective wall. They then both feared that if another brick were taken away, their entire wall would crumble. I paradoxically suggested that they build up the wall before it all falls in. During this phase of therapy they were also able to establish the mutually set limits on their boys, including appropriate limits on television and telephone.

Sandy had an individual session when Paul couldn't attend because of a business trip. She revealed that John had a sizable savings account as a result of his social security insurance checks from his deceased father. This income was used exclusively for John and almost never utilized for other family expenses. I pointed out to Sandy how these monies solidified a wall around her and John and further alienated the rest of the family. When Paul returned with Sandy for the next session, we began to focus on their problems about money. Paul knew about John's money but not the extent of his savings. It seemed that its existence was generally denied by him. They are the only married couple I have ever treated who always pay with two separate (equal) checks. Sandy feels that Paul controls not only his money but hers as well. Paul rationalized his control by stating that she had managed the money in the past and it had been her fault that they had gone into debt. One measure he used as part of his overcontrol was that all the bills were sent to a post office box so that he paid them away from home. They constantly bickered over who was responsible for paying for minor items and over Sandy's exclusion from major financial decisions. Sandy suggested that they work toward the distribution of their total income with mutual consideration as to where it should go.

Paul said that wouldn't work because he couldn't trust her. I told Paul that he treated her like a slave about money and that, like a slave, she was constantly rebelling and undermining him. We then talked for several months on mutual decision making in financial areas. Paul, in his usual fashion, would object and refuse to compromise but ultimately came around and included Sandy in a major decision about a tax write-off.

In January of 1982 I again met with their entire family with a focus on Paul's relationship with the younger boys. In this session, his love for them was obvious, but so was his hostile teasing. In the following couple session, I shared with him that it made me sad that he loved them so much but kept pushing them away. I then gave Paul the most tasks, by far, I have ever given anyone in session. There were twelve in all and most of them were ways for him to change so that he could relate better to his younger sons. These were called "The Twelve Steps to Paul's Happiness." They were:

1. Check his teasing them.
2. Do not bully them.
3. Do not get down to their level unless it's fun for them.
4. Express his love in a more direct way so that they feel his love.
5. Be tender with Steve at bedtime in the same way he had learned to be tender with Carl.
6. Remember that Steve is not you, even though he's as stubborn as you.
7. Put yourself in a position so that you can be affectionate with Steve.
8. Ask Sandy for help if you are on the verge of blowing up at the boys.
9. In decisions about discipline or limits, both Paul and Sandy should discuss them, both should present them, and both should implement them.

The last three tasks dealt with Paul's relationship with Sandy.

10. Diminish teasing Sandy and work on communicating directly with her.
11. Help with the dishes when you do not have an AA meeting.

12. He is forbidden to suggest to Sandy that she quit her job at all, but most particularly that he should not focus on her not working as the major solution to the boys' problems in school and obeying limits. To highlight that this topic should not be mentioned at all as well as to introject the type of humor that Paul responds to so well, this was called "number three." This task was restated as Paul should never again say "number three." This task came down rather tough on Paul but was necessary because his repeated mentioning of "number three" made Sandy defensive and hostile and a nonproductive argument always ensued.

Sandy was given four tasks.

1. To talk to Steve's teacher about a program for his school difficulties.

2. To serve dinner by no later than 6:15, but preferably by 5:45 (to prove she could take care of the house even while working).

3. Not to side with John in a way that alienates Paul.

4. If Paul does six of his twelve tasks he is to get a sexual surprise.

In addition, if she does all four of her tasks she is also to get a sexual surprise. At the next session they reported that they had done many of the tasks and felt so close together that they both feared their walls were crumbling. Sandy had given Paul a sexual surprise and they both grinned contentedly as they did not share the content with me. Sandy was late with dinner several times, once because she went out with friends after work, which angered Paul. However, their major problem was permitting John to get in-between them. Paul was furious when Sandy and John both interfered with his helping Carl with English. It appeared to me that John's relationship with Sandy would continue to keep her and Paul apart as long as he lived in the house. He was old enough to leave, and for a number of reasons, wanted to. I stated that it would be best for John and for the other four family members if John went away to school for his senior year to a place where he could learn the auto repair trade in which he was very interested. Sandy responded tearfully, "You mean get rid of the kid."

The next session was three weeks later and Sandy reported an important insight based on the above intervention. She began with,

"What a manipulative jerk I've been. I married Paul to have a father for John, I had Carl so Paul could learn to be a father for John. I've hung on to the idea that I could make the relationship better between Paul and John. This was jerky because I can't control Paul's reactions. After the last session, I gave up on that." I confirmed how important her insight was, stating, "You can't make Paul be his father. He may become his father, but not the one you want him to be." Paul emphasized her inability to change in regard to John, stating that she brought up his birthday in the middle of Steve's party. Sandy was given the task of helping John look into the possibilities of schooling. The school would have to be out of town for there was no local school that taught the trade John wanted to pursue. Paul was also coached further about complimenting the younger boys and Sandy about not setting Paul up to be the bad guy with the boys.

Sandy had received a promotion at work, but her car broke down, requiring a month to be repaired. This made her dependent on her friends and Paul and quite angry at him. She was unable to ask him for help because she felt too vulnerable. She also felt that in order to have time with Paul she had to beg and plead and she no longer wanted to make the effort. They were feeling particularly distant and I related this to the stress of Sandy's not having her car. I pointed out that at times of external stress they attacked rather than supported each other. I stated that they could not expect to build closeness again until the car problem was solved, which relieved the pressure they were then feeling. Indeed, they did begin to build closeness again once Sandy got her car back in working order.

In late April they reported that John had moved out of the house and was living with the family of a friend. The immediate move did not help their relationship but stressed it still further. I stated that this was a very stressful time but his moving out could be very helpful to them if they did not let his ghost get in the way. We jointly worked out the initial steps necessary to facilitate this process. These tasks were:

1. Paul would look into the legal aspects of John's becoming an emancipated minor.
2. Both Paul and Sandy would work on "releasing" John emotionally. Emancipation was necessary for Paul to do this because

he feared continued financial responsibility for John if he could not control his behavior.

3. Sandy and John would have dinner together one night a week outside of the house.

4. John would not be permitted back in the house for one month (to help him break away).

5. Sandy and John would work out how often John should visit Carl and Steve and:

6. How they would utilize John's room.

7. Sandy would become aware of and control her hostility to Paul about John's leaving, particularly after having just spent time with John.

The following session Sandy reported that she had made John's SSI money available to him so that he could be financially independent. She then made her first slip in therapy, calling John an "exterminated minor." I don't frequently use slips in family therapy but this one was very powerful. I pointed out that not only was she mourning John's loss but she was guilty about her own role in the "extermination" and projecting the blame to Paul and then attacking him for it. At this point, Paul was chasing Sandy for closeness. He was given the task to stop chasing her and she the task to let him in from time to time.

John began to get into difficulties that were new for him. He received a traffic ticket, necessitating that Sandy come to court, and also began cutting classes. Sandy felt he was asking her to become reinvolved with him by setting limits and she decided to do so. I supported that her limit setting was appropriate but that she should also be open to discussing their mutual feelings of loss and pain. Paul and Sandy had been getting along in a loving way for several weeks until Paul suffered acute back pain. Paul agreed to see an orthopedist and they both agreed to use the spa together in an attempt to be closer while Paul had this physical problem. In retrospect, this may have been in error because it went against their cyclical need to disengage. In the following session, they were distant again and Paul had taken a strong stand that his car was his castle and Sandy was to have no input into what kind of car he bought even though they had no car suitable for the entire family to travel in.

The following week Sandy retaliated by making a date with a

woman friend to see a play in Los Angeles on a Saturday night without first consulting Paul. He was furious and stated that if she didn't want to be with him on a Saturday night, then she didn't ever want to be with him and they should separate. I confronted them both, stating, "You have got to learn to compromise or you will have a terrible divorce." I gave them the tasks that each should make one compromise a week without concern about the other's compromise.

I then left for the East Coast for several weeks and saw their former therapist at a meeting. I shared with her that I was disappointed because they had done so much good work together, but now seemed at an impasse. She was surprised that they'd stayed together while Sandy continued to grow stronger and become her own person.

When I saw them again for the first time in a month, Paul looked tanned, thinner, and relaxed. I complimented him about this and he attributed looking good to taking off work in the afternoons. This was unusual for him, since he is a workaholic. They announced that they had traded in Sandy's old car and purchased a Vanagon which the entire family could use for trips. They had already taken a trip with it as a family and stated it was the best trip they had ever had. Paul had agreed to help pay for the car and Sandy felt he had given her a great deal of helpful input in buying it. The car was something Sandy had wanted for a long time. Paul was pleased at how warm and uncritical Sandy had become but was concerned about her maintaining this attitude stating, "I can't buy that many Vanagons." I underlined their progress, stating that they had learned to gratify each other's needs without feeling they were jeopardizing their sense of self. Sandy said that she worried about the change because she had not worked for it and that Paul had made it all happen. I asked Paul what gave him the strength to do it and he replied, "I'm stubborn," Sandy didn't understand his answer until I reframed it. "He's so stubborn, he'll even prove he can be wonderful to you." I closed the session with a reminder that the bricks were falling down rapidly and they'd better be cautious.

Two rather good months followed this turning point even though they were not in therapy for most of this time. One reason why this period was so good was that Sandy went East with the boys for several weeks and Paul became aware of how much he missed all of them. The boys stayed away for an extra month, giving Sandy and Paul a lot of time alone together which they handled rather well, taking several trips in their Vanagon. Although the childfree month of August had helped their relationship the past few summers, Sandy felt this time was better. "I felt close to Paul and didn't have to demand that he come closer. In the past I could feel independent until it was necessary that we both agree. Now I feel more like we're a couple and that I can agree and still feel independent." This marked the end of eleven months of therapy. Although they no longer require weekly sessions, their therapy should continue for at least six months in order to solidify and work through their gains. They need to learn to continue to tolerate closeness without creating an explosion to drive them apart. They need to tolerate distance without an anger that drives them further away. They need to be supportive in times of external stress and to be able to deal with the intrusion on their closeness of others and of a multitude of activities. They also need to realize how different from each other their personality styles and interests are, how neither will ever change these, and that they must accept these differences if they are to stay together. Nevertheless, they have already made significant strides in all these areas.

DISCUSSION

Therapy with a family in as much conflict and so close to dissolution as the Martins is always very difficult and demanding on a family therapist. However, there is a sense of exhilaration when things go well because they and you have worked so hard. When I begin therapy with a family like this, who are ready to give up but unwilling to separate, I am aware that I will have to commit a tremendous amount of energy and effort regardless of whether they choose to remain together or to separate. Paul's three years of sobriety were a necessary building block to a good relationship with Sandy. Yet at the time they entered therapy with me, there was a three-year period during which there had been little change in their basic patterns of relating. If anything, Sandy's independence had driven them apart and caused more conflict. Despite his sobriety, Paul, like many sober alcoholics, had not learned to overcome his fears of intimacy or to share his wife with his family or his family with others. I would have preferred to have begun therapy with them when they were still a drinking (wet) system. The initial impetus for achieving "sobriety" is frequently a powerful thrust toward restructuring the family and achieving individual change. In addition, it is very difficult to overcome the rigid distancing patterns that develop over three years in a dry system.

The techniques I used with the Martins have been described in detail in earlier writings (1, 2). Several of these techniques will be described in detail as they were used in this therapy, including joining, marking boundaries, tasks, enactment, reframing, the paradox, interpretation and creating intensity, balancing and unbalancing. It is rare that a single family therapy technique can be utilized without combining several techniques and principles. However, for didactic purposes, each technique will be discussed separately. Each therapist must learn what techniques he or she is able to use best as well as what techniques work best in different types of families and individuals. It is only when the specific techniques are individually mastered and when the therapist has a system of assessing the family and change that the therapist can spontaneously interact with each family (3).

JOINING [3, 4]

The therapist must join the family as a prerequisite for changing it. In joining, the therapist accommodates to the family by changing him or herself and also becomes a part of the family (4). Joining begins with the social stage of the first session in which the therapist makes the family comfortable through providing social amenities. I shared the commonality of my background with theirs, including my knowledge of Paul's high school and my friendship with their previous therapist. I was also able to join with them as an expert because I had been recommended based on my national reputation with alcoholic families. I adopted Paul's teasing mode and used it to help him change. I tapped into my own "macho" to continuously relate closely to Paul. At the same time, I utilized my commonality of interests with Sandy and my "feminine" sensitivities to join with her. I found things to like in both of them, which helped me to join and feel closer to them. My frequent use of complementarity helped me to join their spousal system. However, the deepest joining with the Martins, as with any family, came from my communicating my understanding of their problems and my providing them with systems to help them change.

MARKING BOUNDARIES [3, 4]

A most important boundary that was repeatedly reinforced in this therapy was the one surrounding Sandy and Paul and separating them from John. Several restructuring maneuvers were used to accomplish this. Building Paul's positive relationship with John was helpful because it lessened Sandy's need to join with John to protect him from Paul. Solidifying Sandy's ties to Paul lessened her need to stay enmeshed with John, breaking the cycle of distance from Paul—closeness to John—increased distance from Paul. Sandy was unwilling to give John the transitional space he needed to pass from adolescent to young adult. Permitting John to become an autonomous young adult provided him with that space, albeit after a protest on John's part in which he acted out to keep Sandy involved with him.

The tie between Sandy and John, however, was so enmeshed that a physical separation was required before it could be sufficiently disengaged to facilitate Sandy's bonding with Paul. The boundary around Sandy and Paul also needs to be solidified vis-à-vis Sandy's friends or to become more semipermeable so that Sandy can be with her friends and be accepted when she returns home. The boundary between the parents and the two younger boys has been easier to maintain but many of the "Twelve Steps to Paul's Happiness" have been necessary to keep Sandy from rescuing the boys from Paul and from forming a coalition with them against him.

TASKS [5]

Giving tasks is the cornerstone for getting families to change. Tasks intensify the family's relationship with the therapist and continue that intense relationship between sessions (5). I give tasks in almost every session with every family and the Martins were no exception. I usually give one to three tasks. I evolve them during the session but they are always summarized and restated at the end of the session. The sixteen tasks I gave them in one session in January 1982 were far more than I have ever given in a session. The first eight of these were behavioral suggestions for modifications for Paul's overreactivity with his younger sons. However, I think I gave such a multitude of tasks because I felt the therapy was at a plateau and wanted to create intensity. Tasks should be specific and not general, stated clearly and firmly and not suggested (5). Everyone in the family should be involved in this and they should generally be given with complementary balance. I frequently give tasks in the session and tasks I know will be successful before I incrementally build to more difficult tasks. Tasks that fail are excellent opportunities to observe clearly maladaptive family coping mechanisms. Tasks that are forgotten or avoided should be restated until they are at least attempted. The therapist should do whatever is necessary so that he or she remembers every task, and generally tasks are rediscussed at the beginning of the following session.

ENACTMENT [3, 4]

Enactment, like other therapy techniques, probes more deeply as therapy evolves. In the initial phases of therapy, the therapist observes the spontaneous interactions that occur between family members (3). These spontaneous enactments should occur throughout the therapy and permit the therapist to assess the current state of the family and their responsiveness to prior treatment techniques. John's role in keeping Sandy and Paul apart was clearly demonstrated in the spontaneous interactions that took place early in the first session with their entire nuclear family.

The second type of enactment consists of scenarios organized by the therapist (3). These may even be used near the end of the first session, but are used throughout the therapy to demonstrate the reality of the family's growth. Sandy and Paul, like most alcoholic couples, are constantly involved in power struggles. They have a natural proclivity to want to repeat their personal versions of the struggle and to have the therapist judge who started it and who was right. The therapist should avoid being triangulated in this way but should ask them to choose an unresolved aspect of the argument and resolve it in the session. Then, the therapist can observe their arguing styles and teach them how to resolve conflicts appropriately—e.g., don't fight about the past, don't anticipate or mind read, resolve one issue before you are arguing about affect and not issues. These rules for fighting fairly are one example of the third type of enactment. Here the therapist suggests alternative methods of relating and creates a scenario in which the family can utilize them such as, "Discuss this without bringing up your old grievances." Asking Paul and Sandy to discuss their parenting differences only after the children have left the room is another example of a scenario that develops alternative problem solving.

REFRAMING [3, 4]

This technique is used from the onset of therapy in the problem-statement phase of the first session. The therapist gathers the information in a manner that communicates that the problems brought in by the family can be resolved (3). He or she reframes the reality that the family presents as one that can be modified or expanded (3). Reframing includes providing the family with alternate transactions for coping with problems and selecting elements relevant for change that can be easily changed. Then the therapist can organize the data around a shifted theme that has a new and more modifiable meaning (3). An example of this is interpreting Sandy's closeness with John as providing her with needed distance from Paul. On the other hand, I repeatedly pointed out to Sandy and Paul that much of their fighting was because they had an intense need for each other, rather than an innate enmity. This continuously helped them to strive for closeness. I reframed Paul's provocative teasing as a major way of expressing love that helped him to be more direct in his loving and the family to recognize his underlying warmth.

THE PARADOX (3, 4, 5)

This is a technique that I, through my own idiosyncrasy, tend to use less often than other structural interventions. The Martins are good candidates for paradox because of their longstanding, rigid, repetitive patterns of interaction (6). The other major criterion for using the paradox is the lack of response to direct interventions such as logical explanations, suggestions, and tasks (6).

The Martins responded to my directiveness as often as they resisted. Rather than paradoxing them when they resisted, I generally chose to become more emphatic and intense in my directives, to which they ultimately responded, often after several weeks of inactivity or resistance. I was able to achieve this because we were joined so well and continued to trust each other. I felt that the use of too much paradox would have broken this trust. When I utilized the paradox, as in asking them not to get too close too fast because they needed the distance, I prescribed the reason why each person should continue their behavior in the symptom-producing cycle (6).

INTERPRETATION AND OTHER PSYCHODYNAMIC TECHNIQUES

Interpretation is the heart of the dynamic aspects of structural-dynamic family therapy. This technique should be used without dwelling on the hopelessness of longstanding fixed patterns or permitting past experiences as a rationalization for continuing present behavior that is disruptive to the family. Repetitive patterns and their earlier derivatives are pointed out to individual family members. Their maladaptive aspects to themselves and the family are pointed out and they are given tasks to help them change patterns in the here and now. Thus, when it was identified that Paul wouldn't help John with his automobile insurance because his own father never helped him with anything, he was asked to change his inappropriate behavior based on his father's cruelty about which he was very ambivalent. Many of Sandy's overreactive behaviors to Paul were based on feelings toward her own authoritarian, alcoholic father that she had never worked through. This was also pointed out and she was asked to change her reactivity in the here and now. I feel that at least a brief family history of each individual in family therapy is very helpful in providing information that can be used to achieve change in the present. This family history should also include recognition of the repetition of triangulating patterns from one generation to the next, which can then be changed by restructuring the nuclear family. Other psychodynamic techniques that can be used in family therapy include dreams and slips of the tongue. Sandy's slip of the "exterminated minor" helped her to understand her ambivalance about permitting John to individuate and helped her to detach from him. Kate Johnson's dream in Chapter 10 is an example of the use of dreams to achieve change in a family member. It must be emphasized that the family therapist cannot be psychoanalytic in terms of participation in therapy but is a real individual who interacts, shares from his or her own family experiences, and becomes a member of every family with whom he or she works.

CREATING INTENSITY [3]

The therapist must frequently create intensity so that his or her message can be heard. This may be done by cognitive construction, increasing the affective component of the message, and competing for power in the family (3). In order to create intensity, the therapist not only frequently repeats his or her message but reemphasizes it in a number of different transactions directed to the same pathological relationships and their restructuring. Thus, the many tasks assigned to mark the boundary around Sandy and Paul and to separate her from John are examples of creating intensity through many different ways of achieving the same goal. Many times with this family I created intensity by using my own affective responses, particularly my involved concern and my righteous indignation.

BALANCING AND UNBALANCING

Every family member has a role in producing and perpetuating maladaptive behavior. When suggesting ways to change this behavior, it is critical that the therapist present ways for each family member to change his or her contribution. This is called complementarity (3) or balancing. I generally make a great effort to point out the balance of responsibility for problems and to provide a balance of mutual participation in problem resolution. With the Martins I found myself instinctively favoring Sandy and so I consistently worked at balancing my change maneuvers so that she carried her share of the burden of change.

Unbalancing is also necessary at times. In using this technique the therapist affiliates for a time with one individual or subsystem in the family (3). I consistently allied myself with the parental system, strengthening it over the child system. Yet, at times I allied with John, recognizing his Cinderella role with his step-father and helping him get part of what he deserved, as well as later to individuate. Thus I unbalanced, but later balanced. I confronted Paul about his treatment of John and Sandy about the inappropriateness of her making a date with a friend for a Saturday night without discussing it with him. Minuchin (3) calls this alternating affiliations and warns against the therapist who holds justice in dispensing alliances as a more important goal than restructuring the family.

In closing, working with the Martin family was a very stimulating and exciting adventure for me as I hope reading about them has been for the reader. In my years as a therapist, I have learned many techniques that have influenced my work regardless of the type of client or the problem of the identified patient. The three most predominant theoretical influences that have shaped my conceptualization and utilization of structural-dynamic family therapy have been psychoanalysis, the techniques of ex-addict and recovering alcoholic therapists (7), and structural family therapy, (3, 4). Like every therapist, I am also an individual who came from a family. Having been raised in an enmeshed, three-generational family and married for twenty-two years has certainly greatly influenced who I am as a therapist, which techniques I utilize, which I use well, what kind of families I work with best, and what goals I covertly impose on them. The reader as well is an individual with his or her own personality style, family, and intellectual background. It is hoped that this chapter has presented strategies and techniques from which the reader can pick and choose and incorporate in his or her own therapeutic work.

REFERENCES

1. Kaufman, E. The application of the basic principles of family therapy to the treatment of drug and alcohol abusers. In E. Kaufman & P. Kaufmann (Eds.), *Family therapy of drug and alcohol abuse*. New York: Gardner Press, 1979.
2. Kaufman, E. & Pattison, E.M. Differential approaches to family therapy in the treatment of alcoholism. *Journal of Studies on Alcohol*, 1981, **42** (11), 951–971.
3. Minuchin, S. & Fishman, H.C. *Family therapy techniques*. Cambridge, Mass.: Harvard University Press, 1981.
4. Minuchin, S. *Families and family therapy*. Cambridge, Mass.: Harvard University Press, 1974.
5. Haley, J. *Problem solving therapy*. San Francisco: Jossey-Bass, 1977.
6. Papp, P. Paradoxical strategies and counter-transference. In A. Gurman (Ed.) *Questions and answers in the practice of family therapy*. New York: Brunner/Mazel, 1981.
7. Kaufman, E. Group therapy techniques used by the ex-addict therapist. *Group Process*, 1972, **5** (1), 3–19.

INDEX

Abstinence, 4, 19, 40, 133
  maintenance of, 68-69
Acting out, 134, 183-84, 200, 274
Adaptability, 102-105, 107, 110-12
Addictive cycle, 106
Adjunctive family therapists, 283
Adler, Alfred, 159
Adlerian theory, 172
Affective disorder, 25
AlAnon, 2, 14, 21, 25, 283, 288, 296
  steps, 124
AlAteen, 2, 13, 14, 21, 283, 288
Alcohol Treatment Clinic, 237
Alcoholics Anonymous (AA), 2, 12, 21, 25, 88, 171, 220, 228, 229, 239, 287, 294, 296
  commitment to, 289, 293
  model, 123
  spirituality of, 136
  sponsors, 69
  steps, 120, 122, 124, 147
  step-study groups, 282, 283, 296
  vs. reconstructive group therapy, 287
Alliances, 81, 90, 286
  pathological, 91
Anchoring, 15, 18
Antabuse, 3, 8, 15, 19, 217, 232, 239, 240
Anxiety, 31, 96
Areas of Change Questionnaire, 32
Autonomy, individual, 102

Balancing and unbalancing, 305, 310-11
Bandler, Richard, 2
Behavior chains, 41, 42-43, 46-47, 48
Behavior therapy, 23, 24
Behavioral intervention, 20
Binge alcoholism, 281
Blackouts, 34, 79, 88, 96, 97, 239

Blended family, 274
Bowenian approaches, 2, 255, 265
Brainstorming, 51
Butler Hospital (Providence, RI), 39

Ceiling effect, 72
Chaotic flippers, 112
Charting, 81
Circular causality, 100
Circumplex Model, 102-105, 107, 128. *See also* Adaptability; Cohesion
Clinical Rating Scale (CRS), 107
Coalitions. *See* Alliances
Cocaine, 80, 139
Cognitive restructuring, 25, 59
Cohesion, 102-105, 107, 108-109
Communication, 7, 12, 14
  in the Circumplex Model, 102
Complementarity. *See* Balancing and unbalancing
Conditioned responses, negative, 11
Conditioned stimuli, 9, 10, 30. *See also* Triggers
Consequences of drinking, 28, 239
  adaptive, 202
  negative, 25, 29, 30-31, 34, 41, 55, 56
  positive, 29, 41
Contracts, 155, 285, 289, 296
Control, loss of, 89
Co-therapy team. *See* Therapeutic team
Countertransference, 180, 189
Couples issues, 10, 11
Couples therapy
  conjoint, 10, 25, 26
  group, 239, 267, 283
  preparation for, 9
Covert reinforcement, 56, 57
Creating intensity, 305, 310
Cues for drinking. *See*